10286/1

H

a+R

12/

G000140926

DATE DUE

AY-1999

HAWTHORN SECONDARY COLLEGE
BURGESS STREET
EAST HAWTHORN, 3123

ULURU

LOOKING AFTER ULURU~KATA TJUTA ~ THE ANANGU WAY

919.4291
508. 94291
BRE

ULURU

LOOKING AFTER ULURU~KATA TJUTA ~ THE ANANGU WAY

STANLEY BREEDEN

SIMON & SCHUSTER

ULURU: LOOKING AFTER ULURU-KATA TJUTA THE ANANGU WAY

First published in Australasia in 1994 by
Simon & Schuster Australia
20 Barcoo Street, East Roseville NSW 2069

A Paramount Communications Company
Sydney New York London Toronto Tokyo Singapore

© Stanley Breeden and members of the Mutitjulu community 1994

All rights reserved. No part of this publication may be reproduced, stored in a retrieval system, or transmitted, in any form or by any means,
electronic, mechanical, photocopying, recording or otherwise, without the prior permission of the publisher in writing.

National Library of Australia
Cataloguing in Publication data

Breeden, Stanley, 1938–
Uluru: Looking after Uluru-Kata Tjuta the Anangu way

Includes index.
ISBN 0 7318 0359 0.

1. Uluru National Park (NT). [2] Aborigines, Australian —
Northern Territory — Uluru National Park. 3. Natural
history — Northern Territory — Uluru National Park. I. Title.

919.4291

Designed by Jack Jagtenberg
Map design by Design To Print P/L
Typeset by Asset Typesetting Pty Ltd, Sydney
Produced by Mandarin Offset in Hong Kong
Printed in China

Title Page: A light evening shower over Uluru.

Contents Page: Honey ants, or tjala, *are a much sought after delicacy for Anangu.*

FOREWORD

The story that this book tells is an important one, and the book tells that story with truth and clarity. By reading this book, and thinking about the ideas inside it, you will learn things of real and lasting value.

I am very happy to be able to write this foreword, because seeing these important ideas on paper really pleases me. These are our ideas, our stories from the past, that Stanley has put down on paper here. By drawing them together and putting them down on paper, I hope that Stanley will help people to understand us and our history and Law. I hope that understanding will draw all of us together as one people.

Putting stories down on paper is new for us Anangu. We have always kept our history and Law in our heads and in our hearts; we can never drop our story in the dirt and lose it. Books seem strange and ephemeral to us, but we know that other people use books to record important things. By putting our Law and history in this book, we are hoping that other people can learn that Law and history, and take it into their heads and hearts. We hope that they will honour and treasure this book, and use it to remind themselves of our important truths. We hope they also will keep our Law from dropping to the ground.

We are sure that it is right to commit our ideas to paper, and that the way we worked with Stanley was a good way. We worked together to share and to avoid untruths and misunderstandings.

This book began as blank paper. Stanley pulled our words together to put them down on paper. We explained these words to him, and clarified with him what they meant. Our purpose, like his, is to explain and clarify our understanding of our world so that others can understand. We are delighted with the results. This is fine work, and we believe it will foster understanding towards a better world.

We commend this book to you, and affirm its accuracy and value. We Anangu are strongly committed to our culture, and we believe that this book shares in our commitment.

Tony Tjamiwa
Traditional Owner,
Uluru-Kata Tjuta National Park
(Translated from the Pitjantjatjara by Jon Willis)

Following the decision of the federal government to hand ownership of Uluru-Kata Tjuta National Park to its traditional owners in 1985, the Australian Nature Conservation Agency joined with Aboriginal people in the challenging task of managing one of the country's most prominent tourist landmarks. Often we have grappled with the problem of encouraging visitors to see beyond the striking scenery and the simple urge to climb the Rock. It is so difficult because most people go there only once in their lives and then only for a day or two. *Uluru* provides a wonderful reference work to enrich the experience of every visitor. It explains not only what they see and feel but also what lies behind — the people, the environment and the bold novelty of joint management.

Many journalists, film makers, writers and artists are drawn to Uluru-Kata Tjuta National Park to try to capture, and convey to their audiences, something of the grandeur, complexity and wonder of this place. So often their efforts are poor because their brief visits are more like information raids than genuine attempts to learn. Stanley Breeden has succeeded because he has done it the proper way — with patience, respect and a spirit of generosity.

He began more than two years ago; visiting the Park, meeting those who work and live there and offering to share the profits of his work with the Aboriginal people from whom he hoped to learn. His infinite patience, deep respect for others and willingness to share fitted well with the principle of working together, which underpins the management of this national park.

Because he lived in the Park for many weeks at a time he was able to see and photograph the shy wild animals and the periodic flush of wildflowers. He was able to go bush with Anangu, he chatted with tourists and shared working days with Park rangers. The author has come to know the Park and its people, as no visitor has before, and he has the rare skill of being able to convey his comprehensive insight to other visitors.

This beautifully presented book with its effortless, personal writing — like a long letter from a good friend — is a milestone in teaching Australians and visitors from around the world about one of the most important places in our land.

Peter Bridgewater
Chief Executive Officer,
Australian Nature Conservation Agency

ACKNOWLEDGMENTS

For a total of eight months I was privileged to live within sight of Uluru and to be able to roam over most of the National Park. I am deeply grateful to the Mutitjulu community for permission to do this and also for making me feel welcome in their midst. It was a time of extraordinary insights and discoveries for me. I especially wish to thank Tony Tjamiwa, Barbara Tjikatu, Peter Kanari, Maureen Natjuna, Kata Kura, Elsie Malpangka, Billy Wara, Kunbry Pei Pei and Edith Imantura Richards, who spoke freely about their lives and shared their knowledge.

I am indebted to the Australian Nature Conservation Agency for providing the means for me to work full time on the writing of the text and finding room for me to stay at Uluru.

ANCA staff also made me feel at home and helped in so many ways in making my stay fruitful and very enjoyable. Julian Barry and the Anangu trainee rangers gave me much support throughout, and Julian's help with translations was invaluable. Lynn Baker gave me much background information on the early days of the National Park and she, Pip Masters and Geoff Lundie-Jenkins helped me to track down and photograph many elusive animals. While any mistakes and inconsistencies remain entirely mine, Steve Morton, Ian Sweet and Graham Griffin were kind enough to read certain chapters and correct errors. Geoff Monteith identified the insects I photographed, and Peter Fannin gave generously of his knowledge of the plants. Andrew Dennis and especially Cliff and Dawn Frith looked after the home front while I was away and gave encouragement during the writing of this book. Marian Hill, Bob Seaborne, Marcus Sandford and Prue Adamson gave much assistance. Elva Castino was most efficient in transforming my handwritten scribbles into neatly typed pages. To all these people, and many others, I owe a debt of gratitude that I can only inadequately express.

I would like to single out three people for particular thanks for their help and above all encouragement throughout. David and Margrit Carter always welcomed me in their home and I value their friendship. The long discussions we had about the book, particularly in the early stages, helped in shaping my ideas.

Jon Willis also became a good friend and with his incisive and sympathetic assessments gave me great encouragement. He has a deep knowledge of Anangu and Uluru-Kata Tjuta, which he shared generously to give me many insights that would otherwise have eluded me. I am also greatly indebted to him for the many hours he spent translating what Anangu told me.

Belinda Wright made it possible for me to resume still photography after many years. Without her intervention the pictures on these pages would not have been possible.

CONTENTS

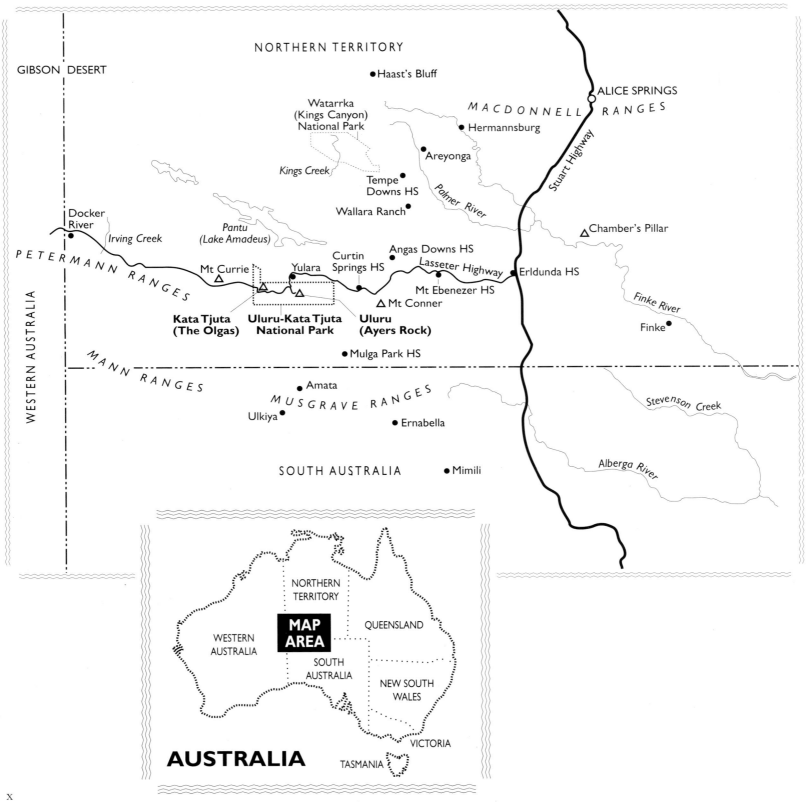

NORTHERN TERRITORY

GIBSON DESERT

●Haast's Bluff

ALICE SPRINGS

MACDONNELL RANGES

Watarrka
(Kings Canyon)
National Park

●Hermannsburg

●Areyonga

Kings Creek

Stuart Highway

Tempe●
Downs HS

Palmer River

Docker
River

Wallara Ranch●

△Chamber's Pillar

*Pantu
(Lake Amadeus)*

Irving Creek

Angas Downs HS●

PETERMANN RANGES

Mt Currie
△

Yulara

Curtin
Springs HS

Lasseter Highway

Erldunda HS●

WESTERN AUSTRALIA

Kata Tjuta
(The Olgas)

Uluru-Kata Tjuta
National Park

△Uluru
(Ayers Rock)

Mt Ebenezer HS●

△Mt Conner

Finke River

Finke ●

MANN RANGES

●Mulga Park HS

●Amata

MUSGRAVE RANGES

Ulkiya●

●Ernabella

Stevenson Creek

SOUTH AUSTRALIA

●Mimili

Alberga River

NORTHERN
TERRITORY

MAP
AREA

QUEENSLAND

WESTERN
AUSTRALIA

SOUTH
AUSTRALIA

NEW SOUTH
WALES

AUSTRALIA

VICTORIA

TASMANIA

ULURU NATIONAL PARK

Recently Burnt Area

KATA-TJUTA

ULURU

Satellite image provided by Australian Nature Conservation Agency and
Mapping & Monitoring Technology Pty Ltd.

INTRODUCTION

Was I looking for Australia's heart and soul, its very spirit, on that first visit to Uluru-Kata Tjuta in July 1991? In the cold light of day it seems a grandiose, overly dramatic notion, but then the monoliths in their austere setting engender those kinds of feelings. I certainly was on a journey that I hoped would reveal something of that perhaps mythical place — variously called the outback, the centre, the never-never, the back of beyond — that permeates the psyche of most Australians. Was there, somewhere in the continent's interior, a location that stood as a symbol for this legendary place as a whole? If there were, I suspected Uluru-Kata Tjuta to be it.

For half a lifetime travelling Australia I had skirted around the interior. The time had come to go deeply into Australia's heart, into the arid zone, to discover if it was anything like my imagined region full of the romance of inspiring rock formations, of hidden secret pools, of endless plains — sometimes desolate, sometimes ablaze with flowers — of brilliant birds and lizards, of delicate small mammals, of red sandhills and of hardy trees.

Could all this be found in one place and, if so, would its reality match my romantic imaginings? Uluru-Kata Tjuta exceeded my wildest expectations on many levels. I discovered that this national park, a mere 1325 square kilometres in size, is indeed the dramatic centre point of Australia's arid zone, which takes up more than 70 per cent of the continent. It is the outback in microcosm and as such has become its symbol. For non-Aboriginal Australians, and a great many visitors from overseas, to go to Uluru is to go on a pilgrimage. I have seen on the faces of many visitors to the Rock the same expression of almost euphoric fulfilment as I have on the faces of Hindus visiting a shrine in the Himalayas or Buddhists at the birthplace of their founder. To the region's original inhabitants, the power of Uluru is a vital part of their culture and central to their beings.

The plant and animal life too, I came to realise, is remarkably representative of the arid zone as a whole. The species diversity is as rich here as in any area studied and in the case of reptiles supports the greatest diversity so far known. Many of the upheavals and much of the turbulence that over millions and millions of years shaped Australia, created its climate and cradled the evolution of its plants and animals can be read in Uluru-Kata Tjuta's rocks and in its sands.

Traditional Aboriginal people have a sagacious and detailed grasp of natural history, of how plants and animals live. Being primarily a natural historian, I was drawn to the people and their special knowledge of the wildlife. This deep knowledge of the Aboriginal people, who call themselves Anangu, has only recently been recognised by Piranpa scientists, an acknowledgment that had its origins largely at Uluru-Kata Tjuta.*

Uluru-Kata Tjuta National Park is owned by Anangu. The day-to-day running of the place is entrusted to the Australian Nature Conservation Agency and is overseen by a board of management on which Anangu have a majority. By working together to run the Park and for the two cultures to reach a mutual understanding, Anangu and Piranpa have created a human aspect to rival the natural one in fascination and symbolism. I was soon as absorbed by the people as I was by the region's natural forces. Looking over their shoulders as they went about their tasks, I came to know and respect Tony Tjamiwa, the eloquent elder statesman; Jon Willis, uniquely capable in reconciling the two cultures; Barbara Tjikatu, wise and humorous; Bob Seaborne, the calm but deeply involved park manager; Peter Kanari, a kindly man who lived to adulthood as an arid zone nomad; Lynn Baker, ecologist and indefatigable champion of Anangu natural history; Edith Imantura Richards, extraordinary naturalist and tracker; David Carter, steady and amusing with a scientist's detachment; Fiona Peek, committed ranger; Julian Barry, a Piranpa fluent in Pitjantjatjara who trains Anangu to become rangers; and many others.

Through the determination and goodwill of these people, Uluru-Kata Tjuta has become yet another symbol — a shining example of a national park owned and run by indigenous people. It works so well here, despite inevitable problems and frictions, not because of enlightened government policy and legislation, though these help, but because of the special quality of the people involved. It is a quality you cannot legislate for.

Uluru-Kata Tjuta, an isolated tiny patch in Australia's vast arid zone at the very centre of the continent, is the symbol for a special, almost intangible quality of the continent's interior but also for the co-operative human spirit. It is one of the most remarkable places on earth. From the start I was determined to find out as much as I could about it.

Anangu means 'people' or 'person' in the Pitjantjatjara language. *Piranpa* is the word for 'pale' or 'white' and has come into common usage for white people. Both 'Anangu' and 'Piranpa', meaning Aboriginal and white people, are used throughout this volume.

FROM A SAND DUNE

The sandhill is not very tall, about 10 metres, yet it gives me a comprehensive view of the infinite, flat landscape. The sand, its redness intensified by the late afternoon sun, lies exposed in patches. Strong winds have shaped it into ripples on the dune's crest. Standing on this ridge of sand, feelings of spaciousness, of being overwhelmed by the immensity of the land are inescapable. This is arid country and can be harsh, hot and inhospitable. But the seasons have been kind, as they often are. On this afternoon in spring it is warm with a light cooling breeze. I am enveloped by birdsong and flowers. It is a benevolent and peaceful place.

Unlike a dune in a true desert, this one is lightly clothed in a rich variety of plants. At the base grow desert oaks, robust tall trees with pendulous foliage that whispers in the wind. Smaller mulga trees with dense grey-green 'leaves' grow in thickets in the swales between the dunes. The sandhills themselves are hosts to shrubs, grasses and annuals, many of which are in flower: desert grevilleas are covered in nectar-rich orange brushes, rattlepods have white sweet-scented flowers in the shape of candles, and the smaller heath myrtle bushes carry countless small flowers, faintly tinged with pink and with a smell of honey. Wattles of several kinds, from soft-leafed bushes to prickly shrubs, add splashes of yellow. There are ground-hugging plants with deep purple flowers, the wild tomato, a kind of nightshade. Between the shrubs grow circular clumps of a dry zone grass, the prickly spinifex. Among these perennials crowd the ephemerals, stimulated into growth and flowering by rain that fell about a month ago — yellow and white daisies, blue brunonias, purple peas. An almost lush sweep of vegetation as far as the eye can see.

Yet these are unmistakably the plants of an arid climate and infertile soils. The plants' leaves are often small, sometimes spiky. They have a grey-blue tinge. Trees are gnarled, testimony to slow and tortured growth as the result of frequent droughts. Their bark is thick and fibrous, their wood hard and close-grained. Those that have died lie almost indestructible in the sand, bleached by the sun and polished by the wind. Long dry spells have bred a hard and brittle suite of plants. Throughout there are patches of exposed red soil and red sand, another pointer that this is the arid zone; there is only enough rain to partially clothe the landscape, not to cover it in a dense tapestry of plants.

A wedge-tailed eagle soars overhead. The smaller birds pause, silent, watchful, in their foraging. But the large eagle lacks the finesse and speed of falcons and goshawks and poses no real threat to them. It is after larger, less agile prey. Soon spiny-cheeked honeyeaters change their calls from the 'toc' of alarm to the bubbly liquid notes of their wistful songs. A male pied honeyeater resumes his courtship flights, rising steeply into the air then descending almost vertically, calling 'tee-titee, tee-titee'. Dodging between spinifex clumps a pair of crimson chats, the female muted brown, the male flamboyantly red, chases insects. From a mulga thicket below the dune drift the haunting notes, 'pan-pan-palala', of the crested bellbird.

On top of the sandhill masked and black-faced woodswallows, neat trim birds, perch on the dead branches of a rattlepod bush, just a few metres from me, between sorties after flying insects. A small flock of green budgerigars flies by, low and fast. On this warm day of light wind insects are out in force. Painted lady butterflies, mostly orange, sip from the flowers of silvertail bushes. Ants of all shapes and sizes scurry across patches of open sand. Reptiles, too, have awakened from their winter torpor. A sand goanna sits at the entrance to its burrow. Strikingly coloured and patterned skinks dart from one spinifex clump to another. The orange, yellow and brown thorny devil, another lizard, plods up the dune's slope, rocking back and forth at every step, short tail arched over its back. It briefly stops to examine my boot before trudging on. Birds, reptiles and beetles, all write their passage in the sand, adding to those left by the geckoes, marsupials and rodents during the night.

This particular dune in most respects is like a million others in central Australia's arid, featureless vastness. But in one way it is like no other for it lies midway between two of the world's best-known and most wondrous and dramatic rock formations. To the east, about 12 kilometres away, stands a gigantic monolith, a rounded prominence, 348 metres tall. As the sun nears the horizon, the rock, scored by vertical lines of erosion, glows a warm red-brown. Uluru is all the more imposing because of its isolation. Nothing else appears on the eastern horizon. But to the west, at about an equal distance stand the numerous, taller and more mysterious domes of Kata Tjuta. Mount Olga, the tallest, is 546 metres high. These outcrops appear a deep purple-blue as the sun descends behind them. *Kata Tjuta* means 'many heads' in the Pitjantjatjara language.

For an hour or more the clouds have been building up in the south; pure white towers with blue-black undersides. Some trail dark skirts of rain over spinifex- and mulga-covered dunes and plains. Lightning sparks to the ground and from cloud to cloud. Thunder rolls towards the dune. Three of the largest storm clouds coalesce and speed towards Uluru. Large cold drops of rain fall, pockmarking the sand and erasing all tracks.

Previous pages: A shower of rain has intensified the colour of the sand. Kata Tjuta is about 11 km away. Above: Parrot peas on a sandhill.

Above left: Painted lady butterflies on silvertail flowers. Above: A wedge-tailed eagle. Left: A thorny devil trudges up a sandhill.

CHAPTER TWO
RAIN OVER ULURU

From about half a kilometre's distance Uluru is an overpowering colossus. There are no intervening dunes; it rises sheer from a sandy plain, dwarfing everything around it. What at first I take to be tall grass stems turn out to be trees and what appears as a small bird, a slow-moving swallow perhaps, on closer inspection is a wedge-tailed eagle. The light of the setting sun slanting under the storm cloud suffuses the monolith with an ever-deepening red flush.

Soon the massive black cloud rolls over Uluru, its underside brushing the summit. Lightning flashes down to the plain and one bolt strikes the Rock itself. Thunder hisses and crackles and bounces off it in waves. Rain pours down, darkening the Rock to a glistening brick-red and extinguishing its glow, even though it remains in the sun. A spicy tang of wet earth and spinifex resin pervades the air. Within minutes Uluru's grooves and channels fill with water that rushes down in a series of waterfalls. Some are strong-flowing streams leaping from one plunge pool to the next. Others race down before cascading over the edge in sheer drops. Briefly a rainbow arches over the Rock, then the sun sets and all colour drains away. Sky, plain, spinifex, rain, Uluru — all are grey. The runnels and rivulets streaming down look like white chalk marks on the dark surface. Some are bold broad stripes while others form fine, spidery traceries describing elegant bends and curves.

At the base of the Rock the sound of the raging elements is deafening. The storm has brought a fierce wind that tears at trees and shrubs and howls around rock faces and through caverns. A crow flying out from the lee of a large rock is catapulted far out into the plain, its calls of protest lost in the general tumult. Thunder echoes and reverberates around walls and in enclosed canyons. Windblown raindrops hiss on the vegetation. Waterfalls boil, roar or whisper depending on their size. In hidden corners streams that drain large areas of the dome plunge into secluded, tree-lined pools. These overflow into creeks that run out into the plain where they soon dissipate, absorbed by the sand. So strong is the wind that my umbrella is turned inside out and my plastic raincoat is torn to ribbons.

One waterfall rushes into Mutitjulu waterhole. In the twilight I can just see white water gushing in one end of the roughly circular pool and flowing out the other along a bed of pale sand. Soon it is dark. The storm passes. A few last clouds

Previous pages: Waterfalls on Uluru's western face. Kantju Gorge is on the extreme left. Above: Water rushes from one water-sculptured plunge pool to the next. Above right: A pair of shoe-maker frogs in amplexus, ready to spawn. Plant seeds float around them.

speed past a half-moon directly over the pool. The wind drops. Except for the one running into Mutitjulu the streams soon cease to flow.

Yet it is not quiet. The pool and the rain attract a multitude of frogs that had been buried in the sand during the cold of winter. Many are calling. On the water's edge I catch scores of small frogs, boldly patterned in black and yellow, in the beam of my torch. Their huge gold-flecked eyes are prominent, even for a frog. Nearly all are males calling in short explosive notes, 'toc, toc, toc', endlessly repeated. At every 'explosion' the frog's throat is distended, so amplifying the sound. The chorus is like a gathering of shoe-makers tapping at their craft, and as a consequence these have been called shoe-maker frogs. A few females have also made their way to the pool and are accosted by the ardent males hopping and swimming towards them. Still calling, a single male eventually clasps a female in amplexus. In time each pair will spawn.

The males of a somewhat larger, allied species, the trilling frog, call while floating. I have to wade out into a flooded depression to take a closer look. They inflate their whole bodies, not just their throats, as resonators for their voices. In the moonlight they look like tiny, floating balloons finely marked in black and yellow. From patches of half-submerged grasses and herbs come the strange bleating calls of a kind of water-holding frog known only by its scientific name of *Cyclorana maini*. Tapping, trilling, bleating, the frog chorus echoes off the rocks and carries out over the plain, where more frogs erupt from the ground and make their way to the water.

Another storm sweeps up from the south. The wind lashes the trees and grasses again and the moon is obscured. Large raindrops pelt down in a heavy shower, and soon the air is filled with the sounds of water rushing down Uluru once more. Lightning illuminates the streaks of white water.

On one side of Mutitjulu are rock overhangs sheltered from the elements. Running through the cold rain I reach a cavern before I am completely soaked. A barn owl has also taken refuge here. Lightning flashes light up the cavern, revealing not just a white bird perched on a rock, but circles, footprints and other designs painted on the walls in white clay and red ochre.

The violence of the storm soon abates but a gentle rain persists. The frogs continue to sing. Shortly before dawn the sky clears. The half-moon has long since set but the sky is so clear that Uluru's domed bulk is outlined against the stars' faint light.

At dawn the air is still heavy with humidity. The largest waterfalls are reduced to pencil-thin trickles but the Rock still glistens with moisture. I make my way to a nearby dune to the south-east of Uluru. The view is of a gigantic, dark, humped form crouching on the plain. To the east are mulga thickets and tall desert oaks. A low mist rolls slowly over the trees, rises at Uluru and envelops it in a halo of cloud. The air is fresh with scents of wet vegetation. Birds sing exuberantly as the sun rises. Purple and red emu bushes, pink fringe myrtles, faintly mauve daisies, yellow and orange grevilleas are sprinkled with large drops of dew. The patches of wet sand are a deep red. It is cool. For a moment the arid zone's face is as lush, as tender, as that of any spring day in a moist climate. It is a good day to circumnavigate Uluru.

At Mutitjulu waterhole most frogs have fallen silent. The early sun does not reach into these folds in the Rock. The main stream into the waterhole is only a trickle emerging from between gigantic boulders about a third of the way up the Rock. Other streams no longer run but their places are marked by glistening black lines of lichens and algae. Standing at the pool's edge I am enclosed by rock walls 100 metres high on three sides. Though still wet and dark the Rock's almost vertical strata are visible as stripes of faintly different colours. Around the pool's edge grows bright green grass. Bluebells and wallflower poison bushes flower under bloodwood trees.

One of the rock walls, after rising 20 metres or so, curves outwards, creating a protective overhang for a small cavern. The rain did not reach there and the dry reddish rock, stained with yellow ochre, is a warm contrast to the dark wet

Mist lingers around Uluru after rain.

Above: Desert fringe myrtle
flowers covered with dew.
Above right: Uluru at dawn after
rain. In the foreground are desert
fringe myrtles.

surroundings. A nankeen kestrel, its brown colours complementing those of the dry rock, circles inside the canyon, calling 'keek, keek, keek', a long-tailed lizard clutched in its talons. After a few circuits it flies into the cavern where it is greeted by its three hungry chicks.

Moving out of Mutitjulu canyon's shade, I head in an easterly direction. The plain and Uluru are flooded with brilliant light, almost blinding by contrast. Soon it is warm. Hugging the Rock is a fringe of tall bloodwoods, a narrow strip of closely spaced trees. Only here is there enough soil moisture to sustain true forest. Some trees have died, during a past drought perhaps or from a lightning strike, and stand as stark, leafless but sturdy skeletons. Some of their main branches have been hollowed out by termites. In one such hollow, in an especially large hulk, a pair of pink cockatoos has made its nest. The birds have half-grown young. The female, distinguishable by her reddish eyes, sits at the nest entrance. The male, whose eyes are brown, calling 'quee-air, quee-air', flies in and lands not far from his mate. Both raise their large crests, white, orange and red, and flick their heads at each other in greeting.

The increasing warmth draws a black-faced goanna from its hiding place between some boulders at the foot of Uluru. Slowly the medium-sized lizard with

an enormously long tail walks up the side of the Rock to a sunny patch. The cockatoos have spotted the movement. Screeching loudly in alarm they fly out to the sunbathing goanna and land about a metre from it, clinging precariously to the steep rock. With crests raised, wings spread, revealing their pastel pink undersides, the pair continues its ear-splitting screams. Slowly the goanna scuttles down the slope again and, escorted by the cockatoos, returns to his retreat. For some minutes the birds continue to screech at it.

I continue eastward. Uluru's face here is not quite sheer but follows a steep even curve. At its base the Rock has been undercut, giving it the shape of a wave about to break onto shore. At a place where the screen of trees is narrow Uluru meets the plain in a field of small yellow daisies called billy buttons, the dark harsh rock seeming to plunge into a pool of fragile flowers. This promontory is surrounded by gigantic boulders tumbled from the slope. About 30 metres above it, carved out of the sheer face, is an elongated cavern shaped like a smiling mouth. It is Ikari, the laughing cave. I climb up by following a line of boulders that leads from the base to the cave's entrance. The sun is still low enough to flood it with light. Only in the furthest recesses is it dark. A barn owl, possibly the same one that sheltered in the cavern last night, roosts here in the daytime. Its favourite

Above left: A pink cockatoo at the entrance to its nest in a hollow bloodwood. Above: A black-faced goanna sunning itself on Uluru's rock.

Fruit of the rock fig.

dark chamber is littered with pellets, the oval packages of its prey's indigestible bones and fur that the bird regurgitates. The floor of the whole cavern is strewn with the tiny bones of small mammals and lizards — testimony of perhaps a century of owl hunting skills. Some of these bones, as we shall see in Chapter Nine, are of great significance.

Ikari cave acts as a trap and amplifier of sounds from the pocket of bloodwood forest below. The songs of honeyeaters, butcherbirds, magpies, rufous whistlers, brown songlarks and others combine into an impassioned chorus of enhanced clarity and volume as though the birds were singing in a concert hall. No wonder Tjintirtjintirpa, the willie wagtail woman, laughed when she heard this effect. Intermixed with the songs are the twitterings of fairy martins, small swallow-like birds. Many bring beakfuls of mud and begin to cement their nests to the cave's ceiling. They will have to work fast, for soon the patches of mud and areas of surface water will dry up. The martins' old, red-coloured, bottle-shaped nests hang in rows and clusters from the rock.

The early sun slants across the plain, emphasising its flatness and featurelessness, and Uluru's isolation. From this distance the sandhills are barely perceptible ripples. On the horizon are a few low blue ranges of hills.

From Uluru's easternmost corner, jutting out like an enormous toe, a sheer wall runs to the north-west. Rock is close beneath the surface here and as a consequence plant growth is sparse. Adding to this sense of barrenness is the labyrinth of fallen boulders of all sizes. The full force of the sun is out. It is hot among the rocks.

This sheer face of Uluru is not smooth with soft curves but pockmarked with caverns, some large some small, in outlandish and grotesque honeycomb patterns. Shallow caves with high ceilings run along the base for much of its length. Their floors are covered by boulders. About 150 metres away from Uluru is a miniature outcrop called Taputji. Taputji's long and narrow sheets of rock bulge out of the ground to a height of about 10 metres. Grooves made by Kuniya, the mythical python, run lengthways along the rock, seeming to separate it into several layers. The top layer is fractured along its full length and also sliced across. To me these deeply eroded rocks look like a large dismembered dinosaur. To Anangu these are the Mala women made widows by the monster dingo Kurpany.

About halfway along its north wall Uluru's sheerness is softened by more gentle slopes that drain a high catchment. A thin trickle of water still runs down this gully and into Ininti waterhole, a deep circular pool hidden among boulders and folds in the rocks. Tongue lolling from its mouth and giving me a quick sidelong glance, a dingo trots up to drink, scattering a blizzard of hundreds of butterflies that had been sipping water from the wet sand. Blue and red dragonflies skim over the water. Huge tadpoles rise to the surface to gulp air. A water scorpion, also known as a toe-biter, scuttles across the sandy bottom of the pool's edge.

It superficially resembles a scorpion but really is a large aquatic bug. Leaning close to the water is a bushy tree with leathery deep-green leaves. Its branches are laden with yellow and purple fruit, and its roots are tightly wedged into a deep crevice. Black-faced cuckoo-shrikes and white-winged trillers eat the fruit of this rock fig.

Having slaked its thirst the dingo trots off again, following Uluru's contour. I soon lose sight of it among the tall grass and shrubs as it turns the north-west corner. Its passage is marked by the alarm of other animals. A small cobalt-blue bird with white wings rises like a butterfly from the undergrowth and perches on the topmost branch of a shrub. 'Trrit, trrit', the male blue and white wren scolds the dingo. Further along three euros leap from their resting place beneath a clump of shady wattles and bound towards the rock. Jumping onto a large flat boulder, ears forward, noses twitching, they follow the predator's passage.

These earthbound dramas are of no interest to two birds of prey circling low over Uluru's topmost ramparts. They focus their attention entirely on each other. The smaller of the two, the male, clutches a small bird in its talons and rises steeply into the air. The larger, more robust female chases him at breathtaking speed. Finally the pair of peregrine falcons alights at the entrance to a small cave where the male surrenders his catch to the female. No doubt the pair will soon nest there.

The north-west corner is a mysterious place. Deep caves are half-concealed by gigantic boulders, their entrances flanked by pillars of stone. Waterworn grooves carry powerful streams down the Rock when it rains. The outflow of water has encouraged pockets of forest and tall grass. These are sacred places to Anangu and can only be visited by initiated men. But just around the corner is Uluru's deepest canyon with sheer walls cradling another waterhole and the densest, most extensive patch of forest. The bloodwoods of Kantju Gorge stand in an understorey of tall shrubs, hop bushes, emu bushes and wattles. Bluebells flower around the water's edge. Giant nephila spiders have built webs of golden silk in gaps between the trees. It is cool and shaded. Variegated wrens and grey-headed honeyeaters flit through the brush in pursuit of insects. Tiny mistletoebirds, the males shiny blue-black with red throats, eat the fruits of the plants whose name they bear.

The sun has passed its zenith and shines on the gorge's perpendicular walls, which radiate warm colours and warm air. The Rock's surface is textured in a pattern of large angular flakes, giving it the appearance of the scaly skin of some gigantic reptile.

High in the tallest bloodwood a pair of Torresian crows has built its nest. The birds' white eyes miss very little and they bring a constant supply of caterpillars, beetles and occasionally the nestlings of other birds to feed to their own four young. Few birds can raise their broods in the crows' territory — their eggs and young are nearly always stolen. Yet a pair of tawny frogmouths has successfully

A black-faced cuckoo-shrike on its nest.

raised two chicks in the shadow of the crows' nest tree. Perhaps the frogmouths' camouflage has saved their young. When in repose, with eyes closed, they look exactly like a brown and grey rough-barked bloodwood branch. Mostly active at night, the frogmouths sit immobile and probably unnoticed on the nest during the day while the crows go about their business.

Strong, bold and assertive as they are, crows do not feel entirely secure about their nest. They perceive the giant 1.5 metre long goanna, a perentie, striding along the forest edge as a danger. The pair is soon on the attack. One faces the lizard and scolds it in harsh notes. Its partner pulls the goanna's tail again and again. The perentie hisses and lashes its long tail but otherwise continues unhurriedly on its way. While the perentie does occasionally climb a tree, it would probably not go to the small upper branches where the crows have built their nest. If, however, the young fledged and found themselves on the ground as yet unable to take off quickly, it is unlikely their parents could save them.

Uluru's western scarp is more rugged and sculptured than any other with more canyons, caverns, plunge pools, boulders and scree slopes. Rocky waterholes and giant fig trees hide damp recesses where ferns grow and small wildflowers hide their colours, where birds come to drink and lizards hunt insects. For Anangu this is the realm of the mythical Mala, the rufous hare-wallaby, and the ceremonies associated with it. This area stretches along most of the northern face and from Kantju Gorge to the place where Piranpa park their cars and buses and climb to Uluru's summit.

For reasons I will go into later, I do not climb Uluru. But I have been told its summit is not the barren rocky place it at first appears to be. In hanging ravines, cut deeply into the rock, there is permanent water. Mount Olga wattles grow larger than usual there for fire, which kills them, never reaches the summit. Shield shrimps and other invertebrates live in the water. Cracks in the rock trap enough soil and moisture for small tufts of grass and other plants to grow, providing sufficient food for a small colony of rabbits.

Around the other side of the climb's spur the afternoon sun washes Uluru's south-western face with a warm reddish colour. It is a benign face, mostly smooth with gentle curves. At the base are rows of fractured rocks beneath shallow caves with honeycombed walls. Other smaller caves rise in tiers to Uluru's summit. In the middle reaches a red-backed kingfisher sits at such a cave and calls incessantly, mournfully 'peel, peel, peel'. Perhaps he sees the hollow as a possible nest site, though usually these birds excavate their nest tunnels in earthern banks.

In a clump of trees directly below him a black-faced cuckoo-shrike builds its nest by attaching pieces of straw and flakes of bark to a horizontal bloodwood branch with spiderweb. Lower still a zebra finch sits on eggs in its domed grass nest among the prickly foliage of a wattle called dead finish. Honeyeaters of several

Flowers of the wallflower poison bush, which grows in thickets among the bloodwood trees.

species probe the flowers of emu bushes for nectar and white-backed swallows skim low, scooping up insects hovering over yellow daisies. Spring burgeons at Uluru.

Skirting more caves and boulders and winding among fig trees, the path turns Uluru's south-west corner and once more I am back at Mutitjulu. The late sun slants over the southernmost ridge and illuminates fractured and rounded rocks and the topmost branches of the trees. Already it is cooler. A pied butcherbird, clinging to one of the scales of Uluru's skin, sings and its pure flutelike notes carry far down the gorge. Little woodswallows, dark-brown birds on graceful pointed wings, zip back and forth across the rock face and catch flying insects. A few are perched in a small high cavern. At dusk, fifty or more will cluster together for the night, clinging to the Rock and to each other.

I pause a while before completing the circuit at Mutitjulu. I climb onto a large boulder and sit in the late sun, facing the ever-fascinating fractured outcrops that shelter the waterhole.

Walking around Uluru has given me two great surprises. One is the sheer size and bulk of the Rock, the constant feeling of being dwarfed, of being around a colossus where everything is on a much grander scale. Nothing prepared me for this; I had to see it, to feel it. Secondly, I had always thought of Uluru as a smooth monolith standing naked and unadorned on the plain. In fact, it is elaborately ornamented with caves and hollows. All around its base there are arrangements of boulders, some as large as a two-storey house, and rock pavements run through by long and jagged cracks. These rocks have fallen from or split off Uluru and are a haphazard collection of debris. Yet as I look around at the large boulders and at the gentle slope beyond, where a perfect arrangement of stones, large and small, round and square, are poised as if to slide down, it seems as if these had been carefully placed for maximum dramatic effect, to take advantage of every shift of light — ever changing, ever stimulating. Anangu recognise a purposeful placement. For them many rocks are life turned to stone and dramas literally petrified. They see these rocks not as a chance scattering but a vital part of the force that binds life and the land together.

The sun sets in a cloudless sky. The half-moon stands out brilliantly, planets and stars appear gradually as daylight drains away. The kestrel flies back to his young, clutching one last lizard. The female pink cockatoo returns to her nest hollow. Goannas, other lizards and snakes escape the cold of night in burrows and rocky shelters. A boobook owl emerges from a tree hollow and calls its far-carrying double note. The barn owl leaves Ikari cave and resumes its hunt for rodents, which are already gnawing the seeds and stems of grasses. Uluru's black humped presence, silhouetted against the moon, is as powerful at night as it is during the day.

CHAPTER THREE

ORIGINS: ANANGU AND *TJUKURPA*

How did these isolated rocks, Uluru and Kata Tjuta, with their mystical auras, come into being and how did they attain their final shape? Anangu say it happened during the time of *Tjukurpa*, the time of creation. The earth existed before that, for it always had, but it was flat, it was dark, it was silent and it was cold. Not a living thing was abroad, no river flowed and neither mountains nor hills raised their heads.

At the beginning of *Tjukurpa* the sun, the moon and the stars came out and brought light and warmth to the land. Creator beings, the Anangu's heroic ancestors, arose from the earth. Some came as humans, others had animal forms and others again changed from one to the other. These creator beings travelled all over central Australia, building up mountains, gouging out rivers and digging waterholes. Many paused at Uluru and Kata Tjuta in their immortal journeys. Battles were fought here, quarrels settled, lessons taught. Evidence of these mighty deeds remain carved in the rocks. Most of the spirit ancestors then moved on again, creating more landforms as they travelled and so established *Tjukurpa* paths across the country. A few came to rest here where they remain in the rocks. The spirit of all of them and of the *Tjukurpa* pervades the monoliths.

The great creator beings made weapons and implements, and hunted and gathered food, which was distributed among them according to strict rules. They camped, travelled and performed ceremonies — painting their bodies, and dancing to the music of epic poems being sung. They did all the things that Anangu do today. They also gave the people their languages, their kinship connections, their codes of behaviour and their sense of right and wrong. This is how the spirit ancestors brought the Law, the *Tjukurpa*, which is as timeless and immutable as the sun and stars. By being humans, animals and plants, and residing in the very landforms themselves, the ancestral creative beings demonstrated that all life is connected into a single force, *Tjukurpa*. Anangu constantly pass this knowledge, and the understanding of humanity's place in nature, on to their children and grandchildren. They do this by example, but above all through ceremony — that is, story telling, singing and dancing — constantly distilling and dramatising their knowledge. This knowledge is a vast, complex web of insights that, Anangu say,

Previous pages: Rainbow over Uluru. Above: A mala, or rufous hare-wallaby. Much of Anangu ceremonial life at Uluru centres around Mala men and women.

exists only in the heads of the fully initiated men and women and takes a lifetime to acquire. None of it exists on paper and to Anangu that is how it should be. *Tjukurpa* and all its subtleties and complexities should reside only in the people.

However, some of the stories about the ancestral beings and how their activities shaped Uluru can be told to the uninitiated.

The main creator beings were Mala, the rufous hare-wallaby; Kuniya, the woma python; and the Liru, the poisonous snakes. Lesser beings also participated: Lungkata, the blue-tongued lizard; Panpanpalala, the crested bellbird; Itjaritjari, the marsupial mole; Luunpa, the red-backed kingfisher; and Tjintirtjintirpa, the willie wagtail. All have left indelible marks on Uluru.

At the creative time of *Tjukurpa* the Mala people came to Uluru from Warlpiri country to the north. They travelled via what Piranpa call Haast's Bluff. They had come for important ceremonies centred mostly around the northern and north-western sides of Uluru. The men carried something between them, taking it in turn. It was a ceremonial pole, the *Ngaltawata*. It is still at the Rock's north-western corner as an almost detached curved pillar of stone. It will always be there. More and more Mala people came, until a large number were camped beside the *Ngaltawata*.

When all the people had arrived a group of senior men climbed to the top of Uluru and planted the pole at its highest point. The ceremonies had now begun. The women in the meantime had gathered enough food for everybody. They prepared it and stored it in caves at Taputji, a small separate outcrop at Uluru's north-eastern side. Not long after the men had begun the chants and dances of their secret ceremony, an invitation to attend *their* ceremonies came from the Wintalyka men, the Mulga Seed men, far away to the west beyond Kata Tjuta. But once a ceremony has begun it must be completed without interruption. The Mala men had no choice but to turn down the invitation.

Gravely insulted, the Wintalyka men decided to wreak vengeance for this breach of courtesy. They created a *manu*, a malevolent spirit, in the shape of a large dingo-like animal, and sent it racing to Uluru in a swirling storm whipped up by their powerful magic. The Mala women, camped at their ceremonial cave called Tjukatjapi, did not hear his approach, but Luunpa, the kingfisher woman who lives at Ininti waterhole, saw the approaching storm and recognised Kurpany, the monster dingo. She yelled out a warning just in time and the women fled, right into Malawati, the place where the men were in the midst of their ceremony. The ceremony was ruined and Kurpany fell on the men, killing and devouring a great many. Some Mala men escaped and, with great fear in their hearts, ran helter-skelter to the south for many hundreds of kilometres with Kurpany still hunting and killing them. The story down there belongs to the *Tjukurpa* of Anangu of different places.

The widows of the slain Mala at Uluru sat huddled together at Taputji, where they are to this day as rows of weathered boulders. At Ininti waterhole Luunpa, the kingfisher woman, still keeps watch but she is now a large rock. Just above her Kurpany's footprints are deeply impressed into the rock and stride towards the east and south. Malawati, where the Mala men were ambushed, remains as a honeycomb of horizontal shallow caverns.

Taputji, where the Mala widows rest, also shows the signs of another mystical being, Kuniya, the woma python. She came from far away to the east. She arrived carrying her eggs on her head in a shallow wooden bowl called a *piti* and then placed them in the cave at Uluru's north-east corner, a place called Kuniya Piti. She left her eggs on the ground, and they are still there now as a circle of stones. Parting the rocks she then plunged into the earth.

In this way Kuniya camped at Taputji and hunted in the nearby sandhills. Her enormously powerful coils pushed deep grooves into the Rock as she left and entered her camp. These grooves are still there.

One day Kuniya had to draw on all her physical and magical powers to avenge the tragic death of her nephew and to redeem her honour. Her nephew, a still-young Kuniya, had somehow roused the ire of a party of travelling Liru warriors. The Liru, which are venemous snakes, came from the south-west and surprised the young Kuniya at the base of Uluru, at a sheer rock face. On his own the Kuniya had no chance. The Liru moved in on him and speared him to death. Many spears hit the Rock with such force that they pierced it, leaving a series of round holes. When news of the young python's death reached his aunt at Kuniya Piti on the other side of Uluru, she was overcome with grief but she was also seized with fury. She plunged into the ground and burst out of the rocks at Mutitjulu waterhole, where she confronted one of the Liru warriors. The smaller, more agile poisonous snake at first did not fear the slower, more cumbersome python. He mocked and taunted her. At this the large Kuniya began a dance of immense power and magic. She scooped up sand in her coils and saturated it with poison. The sand scattered close to the rock where it showered down on fig trees and spearbushes, forever spoiling them, so Anangu can never eat their fruits nor use their stems. Still in a fearsome dance, she grasped her *wana*, her digging stick, and struck the Liru on the head, just hard enough to draw blood in a 'sorry cut', of the kind that Anangu use on themselves in times of mourning and grief. But Kuniya's rage was now beyond restraint. She hit the Liru again, with such force that he fell dead, dropping his shield. Signs of this terrible conflict are still on the rocks around Mutitjulu waterhjole. Kuniya herself remains as a sinuous black line on the east wall. The blows she struck are two deep cracks on the western wall and the Liru's shield lies where it fell, now a large boulder.

Top: These holes in Uluru's south-western face were made by the spears of the Liru, the poisonous snakes, that killed the young nephew of Kuniya, the woma python. Above: These cracks in the rock to the west of Mutitjulu waterhole were made by Kuniya when she struck and killed a Liru with her digging stick.

Above: Kuniya, the woma, which is a kind of python, lived in the rocks at Uluru where she fought the Liru, the poisonous snakes.
Right: Just east of Mutitjulu, Kuniya appears as a sinuous black line across Uluru's rock.

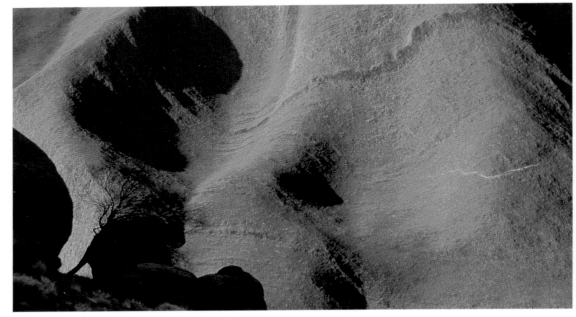

Mutitjulu is the permanent home of yet another snake, the dangerous water serpent, Wanampi, who can control the rockhole's water supply. When water is very low, Anangu will climb on the rocks above and recite certain special phrases. This may persuade Wanampi to regurgitate more water and refill Mutitjulu.

The story of Lungkata's dishonour and the revenge of the Panpanpalala brothers has also left its mark around Mutitjulu. The crested bellbirds, the Panpanpalala, had speared and wounded a Kalaya, an emu. The giant bird ran off towards Mutitjulu. Lungkata, the blue-tongued lizard, lived in a cave high on Uluru to the west of Mutitjulu. He had come from country to the north, burning the land on the way, showing Anangu how fire is necessary to maintain the country properly.

This day Lungkata was hunting near Mutitjulu. Suddenly he saw Kalaya, still moving but with a spear through its body. So Lungkata knew full well that the wounded bird belonged to other hunters and it would be most dishonourable for someone else to kill it off and eat it. Yet this was exactly what Lungkata proceeded to do. He killed the emu, cut it into pieces and began to cook it over a fire he had quickly lit. The Panpanpalala brothers had lost the Kalaya's tracks but they saw the smoke of Lungkata's fire. They hurried over and asked Lungkata if he had seen their wounded quarry. Lungkata, hiding the dismembered emu, said he'd seen nothing. The brothers moved on. Moments later they found Kalaya's tracks and immediately worked out what had really happened. Lungkata, guiltily aware of his treachery, ran towards his camp, carrying as many emu pieces as he could. In his agitation, he dropped most of them, leaving a conspicuous trail of lumps of meat. At Kalaya Tjunta, literally 'emu's thigh', he dropped a huge drumstick, which remains there in stone. He dropped other pieces west of Mutitjulu, forming a maze of large rocks.

The Panpanpalala hunters caught up with Lungkata as he started to climb Uluru towards his camp. The brothers built a great fire beneath the slow, fat lizard as he struggled upwards. Lungkata choked on the smoke and was burnt by the flames. He fell down and his body shattered in many pieces. It is what befalls the greedy and dishonest. The smoke and ash from the fire still coat Uluru's steep slopes above where the broken rocks, representing Lungkata's body, lie.

In his haste to hide the emu he had 'stolen' from the Panpanpalala brothers, Lungkata hid pieces of emu meat around Mutitjulu waterhole. These are still part of Uluru today. The drumstick was dropped at Kalaya Tjunta (meaning 'emu's thigh').

These were the major events that gave Uluru its shape. Creator beings came, had their adventures, then moved on again to other events, making Uluru a node in a great web of *Tjukurpa* paths. Not all the creator beings travelled or were angry and bent on revenge. Itjaritjari, the marsupial mole woman, for example, has always lived at Uluru and was on very good terms with the Mala. She built herself a *yuu*, a small windbreak, which still stands as a wedge-shaped stone just north of the climb. In sheer exuberance she tunnelled in and out of a huge rock above

Above: The Panpanpalala brothers set fire to the bush beneath Lungkata's lair and so caused him to fall down and die. His broken body remains as this pile of rocks at the base of Uluru and the fire's smoke is represented by lichen growing on the slope. Above right: Ikari cave with its fringe of bloodwood trees. Right: Itjaritjari, the marsupial mole.

her shelter as she would do through sand when after prey. The tunnels are still there.

Tjintirtjintirpa, the willie wagtail woman, was also of a cheerful disposition. She was in Ikari cave, east of Mutitjulu, the day when she heard the sounds of a ceremony far away magnified by the cave's acoustics. It made her laugh, a laugh that remains carved out of Uluru in the shape of a laughing mouth. *Ikari* is the Anangu word for 'laugh'.

These stories, some with deeper meanings than others, are reflected in ceremonies. As one Anangu says:

These are important ceremonies and teach young people to keep the Law properly in their hearts and minds.

Another adds:

We want to keep this *Tjukurpa* strong. For us the past and the present are one. These stories from the creative time of *Tjukurpa*, we bring them alive today in our ceremony. It is our duty to look after the *Tjukurpa*, it provides us with our reason for living. Our Law is how it should be.

Kata Tjuta is also intimately and powerfully bound up with creative beings. But the activity of these spirit ancestors are central to secret rituals. Only the fully initiated men are allowed to know anything about them. The sacredness and secrecy are absolute, and casual visitors are excluded from this knowledge. It only adds to Kata Tjuta's mystery.

Itjaritjari's yuu, *or shelter, where she dug holes through the rock for the sheer pleasure of it.*

CHAPTER FOUR
INTO KATA TJUTA'S INTERIOR

Spring has given way to summer. I stand on a tall sandhill on the edge of a plain. The eastern sky is a fiery red at this hour before sunrise but the land is still dark. To the west, across the narrow plain, the high domes and ridges of Kata Tjuta absorb some of the light and glow a deep red. There is no wind, yet it is refreshingly cool. Gradually the sky brightens, revealing the landscape in a flat, shadowless light. Colour momentarily drains away, reducing the rocks and the plain to a muted monochrome. On the eastern skyline Uluru, backlit and looking small, has more colour — a dark purple.

Suddenly, just to the south of Uluru, the sun bursts over the horizon. Monochrome is dispelled and the land takes on its colours suffused with the orange of the early sun. Long dark shadows give shape to grass, rocks, sandhills, trees. The desert oaks are grey-green, the sand red, the spinifex bleached a golden-yellow. Kata Tjuta's walls and turrets, intercut with black valleys, are a dark red ochre. Some of its walls are streaked with bands of black and grey. The sun is warm on my face immediately. It liberates the insects, especially the flies and ants.

There has been no significant rain since early spring, four months ago. Flowers have matured into seed pods, most of which have opened and broadcast their contents. A few everlasting daisies, still bright yellow but dry and withered, sway and rustle in the gathering breeze. No pied honeyeaters rise in display flights, no budgerigars twitter at their nests. There are no kingfishers or swallows. Crimson chats are scarce and few woodswallows, and only the black-faced species, hawk after flying insects. A lone spiny-cheeked honeyeater sings its casual song. A foraging party of variegated wrens is silent. A pair of yellow-throated miners scolds and chases a crow, which caws in seeming derision.

To enter the trail into the Valley of the Winds, I have to make my way to the other side of Kata Tjuta and pass close beneath its western aspect. The sun has not yet reached here and the high broad ridges, like gigantic headless sphinxes leaning towards each other, are dark, almost black, and overpowering. The tallest, ending in a raised dome, is Mount Olga. The sun is just high enough for its light to stream through the valley.

Previous pages: Kata Tjuta from the air at sunrise revealing the many domes and ravines. Top: A flower spike and seed capsules of a desert corkwood tree. Above right: An earless dragon, having the same colour and texture as the rock, is difficult to detect. Above: Fallen cones and needles of the desert oak.

The trail strikes out towards Kata Tjuta's largest massif, presenting an unclimbable, indomitable wall several hundred metres high. Deep cracks run in spidery lines across its rounded summit. Enough soil and moisture is trapped there for spinifex and a few Mount Olga wattle trees to grow precariously. On the other side of the trail is a low rounded hill of only modest proportions. The trail rises and meanders across gravelly soil supporting a few small trees. The compact black gidgee with dense foliage of large, straplike greyish 'leaves' looks quite luxuriant. Mulla mulla plants, still with a few flowers, and dry grass grow at the gidgees' bases. Several score of zebra finches are feeding on the grass seeds and fly up almost from under my feet. Calling in soft nasal voices, 'nyii, nyii', which is also the Anangu name for these small birds, they fly to a small wattle bush. On the skyline, where there are no plants, only broken rocks, stands the silhouette of a tall erect euro. The sun will soon be hot and the rock kangaroo bounds down the slope to seek refuge in the coolness of a cave.

At the massif's north-western corner the trail reaches the saddle between it and the low hill. All at once there is sun, and the pleasant breeze is funnelled into a fierce wind that tears at my shirt. Also, for the first time, the rock wall is within touching distance. Already it feels warm. The sun is still low and backlights the rocky slope ahead. Boulders scattered over the ground and steep slopes have been polished to a satiny sheen. The sheer cliff, though made up of boulders of many sizes, some more than a metre across, is nevertheless reasonably smooth.

On the opposite side of the trail, where the rock rises gently in a series of steps, there seems to have been a recent upheaval. The conglomerate here is of a rough uneven surface with the component pebbles, many waterworn and rounded, sticking out at all angles.

One of the smaller pebbles moves and runs a small distance before settling again. The earless dragon chases a small grasshopper and snaps it up. The tiny lizard is the same rusty colour as the rock and of a similar texture. Even its rounded shape imitates the rocks. When it remains still it is almost impossible to find. Sometimes the glint in one of its small bright eyes, as it scans the sky for predatory birds, gives it away. At my approach, a boldly striped Burton's snake-lizard glides deep into a clump of spinifex. It moves quickly and smoothly among the plant's hard spiky blades, where it is quite safe, never puncturing its soft sleek body.

Capsules of the rattlepod grevillea.

The descent from the saddle follows the base of the towering cliff. It is a long way down a steep slope to a point much lower than the trail's entrance. With each step the rock wall takes on an increased grandeur. The great massif, the rubble underfoot, the low gentle hill opposite, the gigantic detached fragments of conglomerate littering the valley — all of them slowly seep into my consciousness. They infiltrate my mind just as they dominate the landscape. The rocks' colours, textures and shapes, their majestic dimensions become part of my perceptions of the place as a whole, the windows through which I see all the land and all its natural inhabitants. Walking along a dune or in a mulga thicket I become absorbed in the way a falcon hunts, a bellbird calls, ants excavate their nest, or just by the sheer beauty of a jewel-like skink. But always Uluru and Kata Tjuta are there at the edge of my mind, just as they are visible on the horizon whenever I look up from my preoccupation, a benevolent force that enhances my appreciation. It makes Uluru-Kata Tjuta National Park like no other, and never do I feel this more keenly than when descending into the Valley of the Winds.

At the lower levels sand mingles with the rocks. There is enough moisture and soil to support large trees. At first these are the same bloodwoods as at Uluru's fringing forest, though more widely spaced. Lower still, another kind of eucalypt grows. It has a smooth white trunk with here and there a light wash of green or pale yellow-gold. Like the rocks, the bark of these river red gums has a satiny gloss. The largest gums grow at the very bottom of a slope where a major stream, now dry, drains Kata Tjuta's interior. Massive trunks lean low over empty rockpools and the luxuriant green foliage is speckled with the red of mistletoe flowers. Singing and grey-headed honeyeaters, which are mostly yellow, come to gather their nectar.

The trail turns sharply south. Invitingly the path leads on to a narrow opening and winds on among a receding series of domes. Some are in the sun and an almost yellow-brown at this time of mid-morning. Others are dark and shaded. A tumble of jagged blocks of conglomerate at first conceals the entrance. These

River red gums flourish at Kata Tjuta, unlike at Uluru where only one or two grow.

squat pillars have fallen in recent times and have not yet rusted. The constituent pieces of granite are of a pale-pinkish colour, while the basalt is a greyish-green. Here and there are patches of a bright-green mineral called epidote, which is associated with basalt.

A kestrel is perched in the top of a small dead tree as if guarding the entrance, and watches me intently. Pied butcherbirds and magpies sing briefly, their clear carolling voices echoing and re-echoing down the canyons.

After negotiating the maze of stone blocks the trail enters a narrow valley between sheer walls hundreds of metres high. A stream rushes through here in times of rain. Higher up there is a low waterfall and black lines show where water sometimes cascades down the rocks, from one suspended, sculptured pool to another. Beyond the dry waterfall shaded by a large river red gum, the valley opens out just a little to form a courtyard. It is dark here and cool in the green enclosed forest. Water may trickle from beneath a giant boulder here somewhere and certainly it is not far under the surface. Some of the tall bushes beneath the red gums still have a few flowers. The striped mint bush has white flowers veined with fine purple lines. Most of the others are yellow: the guinea flower, butterfly bush and the desert lantern allied to the hibiscus. Bright butterflies, orange lesser wanderers and blue lycaenids flit through the dark underbrush. From deep within a thicket come the rasping voices of western bowerbirds. Small flocks of zebra finches and budgerigars fly in and out of the narrow passage into the forest, a sure sign there is water here somewhere. Right in the centre of the courtyard grows a patch of coarse green grass. A female euro grazes here while her young at heel leaps playfully around her, unperturbed by my presence. Above me in a red gum a pair of ring-necked parrots whistle at each other while swishing their tails vigorously from side to side. Their green and yellow colours are so vivid that the birds seem alien in this landscape of muted colour. They appear to belong more to some lush tropical forest.

This is the very heart of Kata Tjuta, where the canyons are narrowest, the towers of rock pressed closest together. It is the place of greatest mystery — an oasis of green, of trees, flowers and birds seemingly immune from the heat and harshness of the outside world.

The trail turns east again, up a narrow passage where the sun and the heat come streaming in. It rises to a saddle. I look back towards the secluded and inviting forest cradled among tall sheer cliffs. To the east stretch more of Kata Tjuta's formations, smaller domes, spaced further apart. Heat shimmers around them and across the limitless plains beyond.

Mount Olga Gorge, between two of the tallest ridges, faces west. By late afternoon the sun pours into the valley's wide entrance. The southernmost wall rises to a

Above left: A gibber grasshopper mimics the pebbles of the gravelly soil around Kata Tjuta. Above: Flowers of the striped mint bush. Left: Olga Gorge, Kata Tjuta's most austere face.

BURGESS STREET
EAST HAWTHORN, 3123

high broad dome, Mount Olga, the highest point in the National Park. Tall pieces of detached conglomerate, crashed down or otherwise coming adrift during some cataclysm in the distant past, stand throughout the rocky pavement of the valley floor. They appear like ranks of monumental statuary. The hot sun reflects off the walls and pavement. The feeling of heat is intensified by the rocks' warm red and deep-orange colours enhanced by the late sun. I feel like I am walking into a furnace. A strong breeze brings a little relief and keeps the flies out of my eyes. A stony creek runs the entire length of the gorge and though like all the others it is not flowing, it provides enough moisture beneath the surface for shrubs and some trees to grow along its course; a line of green running the length of an otherwise austere, ochre-coloured chasm.

The northern wall is dark, covered in streaks and patches of black lichens and algae that mask, but do not completely hide, the rust-brown underneath. Shallow caves and narrow slits have been gouged out of its rocks. Mount Olga's wall is smoother, redder, as is the stony valley floor. If the Valley of the Winds is Kata Tjuta's green heart, Olga Gorge is its most austere, most severely stony face.

Eventually the gorge ends in a steep-sided V at the base of which is an impenetrable thicket of spearwood bushes. Anangu call these plants *urtjan* and make their long kangaroo spears out of their bent and crooked stems. But these are easily straightened over fire.

As I look west along the length of the gorge, the sun touches the horizon in almost the centre of the valley. The small waterhole catches the last-remaining light. A flock of budgerigars, tiny points of bright yellow-green speeding against the dark rock, flies to the water and lands beside it. Quietly the birds drink, making the throng of tadpoles hide in the green murk of the pool's bottom. Half a dozen white-plumed honeyeaters, small yellow birds with white ear tufts, gather nectar from the pink tubular flowers of an emu bush. A pied butcherbird gives a few bars of song. The sun sinks beneath the horizon, the wind drops and the flies descend in a seething, buzzing multitude, trying to enter my eyes, ears, mouth and nose. A spotted nightjar, exposing the white patches on its long silent wings, flies on to a large boulder. Soon it is dark. Kata Tjuta's domes, for a few moments, reflect the sky's orange glow, then they are black, mysterious shapes against the deep indigo of the night.

Far left: Kata Tjuta from the north. The Valley of the Winds is behind the tall dome. Above: Scented emu bush; the plant was used as a medicine by Anangu.

CHAPTER FIVE

ORIGINS: PIRANPA AND GEOLOGY

The rust-red domes of Uluru and Kata Tjuta have an air of permanence about them, as though they have cast their shadows over sand dunes and spinifex since time began. But the present landscape, on the scale that geological events are measured, is of recent origin. The turbulent and occasionally violent events that eventually shaped these rocks, however, began at a time so long ago that there was no life on land, and life in the sea had not advanced beyond such simple and often microscopic organisms as algae, bacteria, protozoa, sponges and jellyfish.

According to the Piranpa science of geology it all began 900 million years ago with the formation of the Amadeus Basin, a vast depression occupying the area that is now bounded by the MacDonnell Ranges in the north, the Gibson Desert in the west, the Petermann and Musgrave ranges in the south and the Simpson Desert in the east. The basin was an arm of a shallow sea that covered most of central Australia.

Sediments that had been eroded from the surrounding lands were washed into the depression. Over the hundreds of millions of years that these deposits were laid down the basin rarely rose above sea level, even though between 3000 and 4000 metres of sediments, mostly sand and fine mud, accumulated. These were compressed and cemented into rock. The sea bottom, therefore, must have subsided at roughly the same rate as the sediments were deposited. The deposition took place at an infinitesimal rate, measured perhaps at no more than a few millimetres per year.

Changes began about 550 million years ago. The south-western shores of the Amadeus Basin, the region that contained the rocks that were to become Uluru and Kata Tjuta, slowly rose above the sea. Great upheavals within the earth's crust thrust up mountain ranges. During this era of mountain building, called the Petermann Ranges Orogeny, the rocks laid down during the previous 350 million years cracked along fault lines. Along these faults one block of rock rose against another. Strata laid down as horizontal beds were buckled, compressed and folded, causing further rises in the mountain ranges.

Previous pages: Lines of dunes around Uluru. Sandridges are the National Park's most recent landforms, having been shaped by strong southerly winds about 30,000 years ago. Above: The Petermann Ranges — lines of hills eroded out of the surrounding plain.

As soon as the rocks began to rise, erosion set in and deposition of sediments began all over again. Just how tall the mountains became is difficult to gauge now, but it is not inconceivable they were 2500 or even 3000 metres high, and that their summits were covered in snow and ice.

There still was no life on land. There was no greenness — no ferns, mosses or other plants impeded the force of streams and waterfalls of an at times very wet climate. Erosion was rapid. It must have been noisy and turbulent on occasions. When sunny days were succeeded by clear nights, the alternating heat and cold cracked the rocks, sending jagged boulders down mountain slopes. During heavy rain the accumulated debris was swept along steep-sided valleys with such force that even boulders a metre or more in diameter bounced down the slopes and rolled out over the plain for as far as 5 kilometres.

As well as large fragments of rock the streams carried vast quantities of sand

and mud. All were mixed up in a slurry that once issued from the mountain valleys lost momentum and spread out in a wide deposit. These deposits are known as alluvial fans. The alluvium furthest from the mountains was made up of the finest particles, sand and mud, and was carried some tens of kilometres away from the valley mouth. Closer to the mountain the deposits contained all size classes from mud, through sand to large boulders a tonne or more in weight.

Two of these ancient fans along the shores of the Amadeus Basin are of particular interest. One was made up of mostly coarse sand to a thickness of 2500 metres. It was out of those deposits, over time compressed into sandstone, that Uluru was carved. The other fan, about 25 kilometres away and one that must have been much closer to the ancestral mountains, is 6000 metres thick and of a very different composition. Among the sand and mud were boulders up to 1.5 metres across. Most were granite and basalt but pieces of other rock were also among them. These too were compressed, the boulders being set in a mixture of sand and mud, to become a sedimentary rock called conglomerate. In these bouldery deposits lie Kata Tjuta's origins.

By 500 million years ago the mountains thrust up by the Petermann Ranges Orogeny were eroded away to virtually a level plain. The present-day hills known as the Petermann Ranges, about 80 kilometres west of Kata Tjuta, are not the remains of the original mountains. They have been re-etched out of the plains in more recent times. The ancestral mountains were much closer to Kata Tjuta — nothing remains of them on the surface.

The alluvial fans and the eroded plain once again subsided and sank beneath the sea. Slowly they were buried beneath sand, mud and limestone. To the north enormous quantities of loose sand were laid down along the sea's edge.

Seventy million years later (about 430 millions years ago) the sea receded from the entire Amadeus Basin, never to return. Primitive spore-bearing plants, the forebears of mosses and ferns, appeared on land. In the seas the first animals with backbones, fish, had evolved. But there was not yet sufficient plant growth on land to sustain animal life. There was little impediment for the wind-driven sand, which was blown in great swirls across the whole of central Australia.

Over about 100 million years, beginning about 400 million years ago, the whole of central Australia, not just the Amadeus Basin, rose permanently above sea level. This was part of a large-scale and protracted era of mountain building known as the Alice Springs Orogeny. The conglomerate of the Kata Tjuta alluvial fan and the sandstone of Uluru's fan, buried deep beneath perhaps thousands of metres of sediments, were now themselves subjected to the great stresses of mountain-building forces. Their rocks were folded, compressed and twisted. Uluru's original horizontal layers were tilted 90 degrees to become almost vertical. At Kata Tjuta several gigantic cracks ran through the rock. A great block of conglomerate, possibly

Kata Tjuta's rocks are conglomerate, a kind of sedimentary rock in which pebbles and boulders are set in what was originally a mud and sand matrix.

Kata Tjuta itself, was thrust up along one such fault line. Its beds were tilted only slightly, about 15 degrees.

The mountain-building forces lifted Kata Tjuta's and Uluru's alluvial fans well above their present height, and wherever uplift occurs erosion follows. In time the covering sedimentary rocks that had imprisoned the conglomerate and sandstone were stripped away, exposing parts of the ancient alluvial fans.

Sediments filled the area between the alluvial fans that had now become Kata Tjuta and Uluru, but these were eroded away, and a wide valley several hundred metres deep was carved out between the two. Seventy million years ago the drainage of this valley became impeded. Marshes formed. By this time plants and animals flourished on land. The valley was covered in dense forests, which filled the marshes with their remains. In time, under the weight of subsequent deposits, these became compressed into thin layers of brown coal. The pollen grains of some plants growing there between 70 and 40 million years ago have been preserved in this coal as fossils. The preservation was good enough to identify some of the plants to which they belonged. Among them were many rainforest species, clear evidence that at that time central Australia, like most of the continent, had a warm, moist climate. Among the plants were species belonging to the families Myrtaceae and Proteaceae, the progenitors of such typical Australian plants as the eucalypts, paperbarks, bottlebrushes, grevilleas, banksias and hakeas. These plants, over time, evolved and adapted to the continent's gradual drying until most now grow in arid places, including present-day Uluru. They are thought to have become established and diversified during the last 2 million years. Rainforest now exists only in small isolated patches of high rainfall along Australia's east coast. Some plant species not all that different from those of Uluru's rainforests still grow there.

The aridity that slowly overtook central Australia began about 20 million years ago. About half a million years ago the conditions had become much as they are today. By that time the whole of what was the Amadeus Basin and other vast areas of the inland had been eroded to a virtually flat plain. Only the more unyielding outcrops and mountain ranges persisted. One of the lowest points of the erstwhile basin is the present-day Lake Amadeus, just north of Uluru. It is a salt lake only occasionally filled with water.

The most numerous small particles produced by the cycles of mountain building and erosion are grains of sand. They are also the most resistant to breakdown and therefore much of central Australia is covered in vast quantities of them. Among the minerals, oxidised iron is also abundant, and resistant to change. The red-coloured iron oxide coats the particles of sand and gives the centre its most pervasive characteristic — red sand.

This sand was blown into ridges of dunes in Uluru-Kata Tjuta National Park's last great geological event. On the scale of a 900 million year history this happened a mere fleeting moment before the present, just 30,000 years ago. It occurred during an ice age when the region was cold and forbidding and more arid even than today. There was little vegetation and strong winds roared in from Antarctica. It was during this most inhospitable time that the first humans appeared at Uluru.

The upheavals over the aeons as well as the never-ending action of wind and rain have sculpted the smoothly rounded shapes of Kata Tjuta and Uluru. This roundness is the result of what are called topographic joints. Whenever a body of rock is freed from the pressures of overlying sediments by erosion, topographic joints appear at the exposed angular corners. These are in the form of long curved cracks. Weathering and erosion remove the fragmented material above the fracture. Subsequent topographic joints continue the process, rounding the outcrop's corners. Such fractures are clearly visible at Uluru. One is at the north-west corner, the formation called Ngaltawata. Another runs across the western face (see photograph).

A topographic joint has formed a long fracture on Uluru's western aspect. Over many millions of years these kinds of joints have given Uluru its characteristic rounded shape.

Uluru remained a single monolith, but Kata Tjuta has become a series of domes intersected by passages and canyons. These have their origins about 400 million years ago at the time of the Alice Springs mountain-building period. The formation's conglomerate was then compressed and pushed upwards along a fault line. This movement fractured the rock in long straight cracks. The corrosive action of water and wind widened the cracks to fissures and over time the fissures became canyons and valleys.

From a distance Uluru's and Kata Tjuta's surfaces look much the same, but up close they are very different. Uluru's surface is of a reasonably fine, even texture. The rock is composed of sand containing many feldspar grains in addition to quartz. Under enormous pressure, aided by chemical action, the sand was compressed into a particular kind of sandstone known as arkose. Kata Tjuta's surface, on the other hand, is coarse. Lumps of rocks from tiny pebbles to boulders are set in a sand and mud matrix.

Some of these stones, mostly waterworn and rounded, are exposed during weathering and fall out, leaving a dimpled impression on the rock face. Many such pebbles and boulders have accumulated at the bottom of Kata Tjuta's slopes and in the streams, now usually dry, that run through the larger valleys. The process continues today and in several places quite large boulders are poised to fall. When the rocks do fall many of them shatter or break in half, exposing their original colours — a light pinkish-grey in the case of granite and dark blueish- or greenish-grey if they are basalt. Once these rocks have been exposed to weathering for long periods they take on the rusty red colour of the iron oxide that coats their surfaces. That is why Kata Tjuta's rock faces are of a consistent red-brown colour and not a speckled light and darker grey.

Top left: Uluru is made of a sandstone called arkose, which was laid down in strata of various thicknesses. During mountain-building periods these strata were tilted almost 90° until they were at right angles to the plain. Different rates of erosion make the strata stand out clearly. Top right: A close-up through a piece of basalt. There is some granite in the top right corner. The white calcite and green epidote crystallised in what were originally gas bubbles in the basalt. Epidote, a common mineral in the conglomerate, is formed by heat and pressure out of finely ground minerals. The red veins are iron oxide, probably the result of the movement of oxidising fluids through the rock. Above left: Caverns have been eroded out of Uluru's surface in many places. Above right: Uluru's surface is covered in angular scales, the result of the action of water and atmospheric oxygen.

These rock faces maintain a more or less smooth surface without protuberances because of weathering caused by temperature changes. Whenever a piece of conglomerate or even a single large boulder bulges out from the general surface, great stresses are set up. The rock projecting out expands during the heat of the day when surface temperatures can be very high, and contracts again when the temperature falls at night. Eventually the protuberance cracks through at the point where it meets the rock surface and falls to the ground.

Although Uluru seems smooth by comparison, it has its imperfections; it has a weather-beaten face. Uluru's strata were pushed over 90 degrees, till they were almost at right angles to the plain. Some of these strata are more resistant to weathering and these harder layers now stand out like ribs, the softer ones having been worn down to a greater degree. In some corners, such as at Mutitjulu waterhole and Kantju Gorge, deep valleys have been eroded out. Some descend Uluru in a series of smooth, exquisitely sculptured depressions. When it rains water rushes down these valleys, plunging from pool to pool.

At various places caverns have been eaten out of the Rock. Ikari cave on the southern face is one of these, and more extensive formations can be seen on the northern side. There is no certainty as to how these caves came to be. One theory suggests that the caves were originally formed when that part of Uluru was still below the land surface. Moisture and associated chemical action then ate deeply into the Rock. The resultant caverns were exposed when the land surface was eroded away. In support of this theory is the fact that most of the larger caverns are at almost the same height, about 30 metres, above the current level of the plain. But this does not account for the caverns higher up and the extensive honeycombing on the northern face. It is thought that they are the result of uneven weathering. This would start by softer portions of rock being hollowed out, forming shallow depressions. The flaking away of rock was more rapid in these hollows, which consequently became larger and larger.

Uluru's skin is covered in large, angular, sometimes overlapping scales. These flakes are shaped by weathering, in this case the combined action of rainwater and atmospheric oxygen. This action slowly attacks and alters the Rock's component minerals. Apart from creating the scales it also colours the sandstone. The iron it contains is oxidised, giving the Rock its characteristic rust colour. Scales occasionally flake off as part of the weathering process and when they do, the Rock's true colour lies revealed. It is a muddy grey.

Weathering — the decaying of the rocks by water, other chemical action and cycles of temperature change — and erosion — the removal of loosened fragments by wind and rain — continue today. The processes are so slow that it appears as if time stands still waiting for the next era of mountain building or a drastic change in climate.

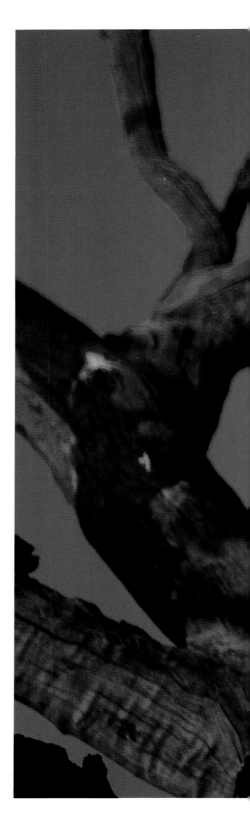

CHAPTER SIX
IN THE ARID ZONE

It is mid-September. The days are balmy and the nights cool but no longer cold. In early winter there was heavy rain and only a few weeks ago drenching storms swept up from the south. Plants are flowering, many extravagantly so. Nomadic birds drawn to this richness are stimulated into song, courtship and nesting. Most mammals produce litters of young, which will grow up quickly and recolonise areas vacated during a recent drought. It is warm enough on most days and nights to coax reptiles from their burrows and other cold-season hiding places, and to loosen the shackles of inertia from the insects. This rush of life, the clear light and the benevolent warmth induce a feeling of great wellbeing. Day in day out I roam the dunes, woodlands and spinifex plains, and immerse myself in all this wonder.

It soon becomes apparent that the Park, away from the monoliths, is not the uniform habitat it at first appears to be; it is not just a featureless stretch of sand and spinifex. In this season of energy and drama I decide to spend thirty-six hours walking from one habitat to another and to see their differences. I exclude Uluru and Kata Tjuta from these explorations.

The sun is not yet up as I arrive at the base of a dune fringing a plain of soft clayey soils. Desert oaks, some old and shaggy with drooping foliage, others mere skeletons with bare black limbs, dot the landscape. A brown falcon sits low in one of the dead trees, tearing at the carcass of a western brown snake. She must have caught the reptile yesterday afternoon before the coolness of the evening. The bird's two half-grown young sit snugly in their stick nest in an old, live desert oak. I sit down beneath the nest tree, but the adult falcon ignores me completely.

Slowly other birds waken and begin to stir. Their songs burst forth from bushes and trees. A common bronzewing pigeon flies by, fast and low. When the sun rises, backlighting Kata Tjuta's domes about 3 kilometres away, the brown falcon drapes her snake over a branch and flies to the very top of another dead desert oak. She sits in the sun, fluffing out her feathers to absorb the day's first warmth. Her move also provokes the mobbing attacks of the smaller birds. Judging by the ferocity and persistence of their onslaughts they probably have nests of their own nearby. Woodswallows and honeyeaters swoop down unrelentingly on the raptor, snapping their beaks in her face. The yellow-throated miners are particularly

pugnacious, striking the falcon several times on her back. She takes this punishment stoically. A pair of pink cockatoos flies in to hurl abuse. The birds land less than a metre from the falcon and scream loudly at her, their crests raised in indignation and apprehension. When a fearless pied butcherbird joins the band of attackers, it is too much. The falcon flies off on strong broad wings, low to the ground to foil the dive-bombers, and disappears over the sandhills, pursued by a swarm of irate small birds.

I walk out onto the plain, which is sparsely covered with emu bushes and wattles of various kinds. Among them are a few mulga trees. Equally sparse is the ground cover of green grass, daisies in flower — pink, pale mauve, yellow, white — and a kind of nightshade. I walk over to a grove of weeping emu bushes studded with freckled pink, tubular flowers. Honeyeaters are busy harvesting their nectar. It seems that in this particular place the birds have rarely, if ever, seen people before and are extremely curious about them. Singing honeyeaters, a plain grey species with touches of yellow, come so close that I can clearly see the pollen dusting their faces. A male black honeyeater lands about a metre away and, tilting his head to one side, looks me in the eye. Two pairs of mulga parrots, which had been feeding quietly on grass seeds, are also overcome with curiosity. They fly towards me and land in a dead emu bush. The males are startling in their brilliance, their rainbow colours enhanced by the early sun — brilliant green with trimmings of yellow, red, blue and orange. Just beyond them a black-faced woodswallow, a brown bird with a black face, lands carrying a moth in its beak. It is on its way to feed its young, either in the nest or just fledged. If the young are nearby I expect to be treated much as the falcon was. After inspecting me closely for a few moments the woodswallow flies straight to a small desert oak, about 5 metres away, and lands on the rim of its nest. As it does three bright-orange gaping mouths are raised on trembling necks. Quickly the moth is pushed down one nestling's throat. The adult closely inspects the young, adjusts some of the grasses that make up the nest and flies off to hunt more insects without so much as a backward glance.

Just as I am about to move on the alarm goes up among the birds around me. The mulga parrots fly to the protection of a dense umbrella bush, and honeyeaters and woodswallows rush off to the attack. The brown falcon has returned, clutching another western brown snake, and lands in a dead tree not far from the nest. Her victim must have come out only minutes ago to warm itself. The wave of alarm spreading among the birds alerts two red kangaroos who sit up suddenly, ears scanning 360 degrees and noses testing the air. I had not noticed them while they were grazing, heads down, about 30 metres away. I freeze. Staring hard at me the two males try to get my scent. They must have got a whiff for suddenly they leap away in great bounds. After only a short distance they stop.

Previous pages: A brown falcon warms itself in the early sun. Above: Mini-daisy flowers.

Leaning back on their thick muscular tails, the sun glowing on their red velvet-like fur, they look around inquisitively. Not unduly alarmed, they bound off and are soon out of view.

Quickly I walk back to the falcon's tree. She flies to the nest where the young rush her. One of them grabs the snake's head and immediately begins to swallow it. Nodding its head back and forth, the chick gradually works the snake down its gullet. Its sibling grabs at the other end of the prey of which about half a metre still protrudes. But it does not try to swallow the tail end. The first youngster seems to be in difficulties. It appears to gag and tries to regurgitate what it has swallowed. The sound brings the parent back to the nest. She inspects the chick closely, nibbles at the snake, but does not intervene. The chick continues its tremendous efforts but is soon exhausted. I leave it, sitting helplessly panting, still with half the snake to be swallowed.

Skirting around sandhills I walk along the plain's edge for several kilometres, moving to the east of Kata Tjuta. Dry wood lies everywhere, branches that blew down or whole trees that died and then toppled. Close-grained and often bleached by many seasons of unrelenting sun and polished by wind-driven sand, the wood has taken on the colour and texture of driftwood. All this arid zone wood is very hard in gnarled and twisted shapes. It seems indestructible and certainly the larger trees would lie about for a century or more if it were not for periodic fires.

Above left: A pair of black-faced woodswallows at the nest. Above: The wood of a dead tree bleached by the sun and polished by the wind.

A nest of mulga ants; the rim is 'decorated' with mulga phyllodes.

The stumps and branches are perfect lookouts for hunting birds — be the prey insects, lizards, snakes or even other birds. One of the great attractions here is the contrast between the hard, weathered wood in grey, straw or dark-brown colours and the soft, brilliantly coloured birds that perch on it. Never have I seen a more striking combination than the one suddenly confronting me as I round a small stand of wattle trees. Sitting immobile on a mulga stump is a rotund small bird with a brilliant red breast and caplike patch on the head. The rest of the head, back and throat are black. The male red-capped robin watches insects coming to a flowering desert heath myrtle. Suddenly it darts after a hover fly, snaps it up and returns to its perch, where once again it sits perfectly still. The female, pale brown with a faint brush of red on her forehead, sits on a fallen branch not far away.

The plain of sparse trees, shrubs and ground plants changes to mature woodland along a sharp demarcation, the result of fire. The sparsely vegetated area was burnt comparatively recently, four or five years ago perhaps. The woodland looks as if no fire has penetrated here for fifty years or even longer. The trees, mostly desert oaks, are tall and grow so closely together that they almost form a forest. Here and there are impenetrable groves of mulga trees with their branches tightly interwoven. In more open places grows hard spinifex, not in clumps but in circles about 5 metres in diameter. Only the thin outer rims are alive; in the centres the plants have died back to expose the red soil. Only very old spinifex looks like this.

The desert oaks too look old. Their bark is thick and fibrous and their branches, weeping to the ground, are covered with knobbly seed cones. The sand is densely carpeted with their fallen needles, which crackle underfoot. Below one leaning oak are the remains of a bower of a western bowerbird, the avenue still visible but the rest buried beneath the dead needles. There is not a sign nor a sound of the bowerbirds — nor of any other bird. It is eerily quiet. All I can hear is the quiet sighing of the desert oaks in the gathering wind. A small collared sparrowhawk flies fast through the forest without being attacked or even eliciting alarm calls. Walking on through the silent forest I eventually see a few birds, a pair of pied butcherbirds at their nest and a pair of magpies. Have these notorious nest robbers discouraged other birds from entering the forest?

Birds may be few, but ants are everywhere. Small black ones scurry and rush about. Under the shrubs are the huge craters forming the entrances to the nests of the mysterious mulga ants. The raised rims are decorated with the fallen leaflike phyllodes of the mulga trees. The nests' cavernous depths seem deserted except for the occasional shadowy movement of a large black ant. Why are the nest rims raised so high, as much as 10 centimetres, and why are they covered so painstakingly with phyllodes? Quite possibly the rims are built to stop the nests from being flooded and phyllodes are buffers against erosion — such elaborate defences against rain in a place where rain is scarce. But then when it comes, it can be very heavy, and drainage in these flat places is slow or non-existent. The ants seem to come out only at night. The ferocious bulldog ants build even higher rims around their nest entrances. They are not particularly fussy about their decorations. I find a nest beneath an umbrella bush whose rim is covered with the fallen yellow puffball flowers. Nor are these ants shy and retiring. When I lightly tap the rim, scores of them come racing out and charge towards me, their long saw-toothed jaws at the ready. The sting of these large ants is painful and I retreat. A little further on a fierce but silent battle rages between two species of ants. Hordes of small ones overwhelm and carry off larger ones.

At first the woodland appears as a monochrome of various shades of grey-green, but as I look more carefully I notice pinpricks and splashes of colour. In an open sunny patch grows a shrub covered in small succulent red fruits — a ruby saltbush. Anangu have told me the fruit are edible. I try some, and they are sweet and juicy. Through the weeping, wind-tossed branches of a desert oak shine larger fruit, the round fire-engine-red quandongs. These taste good as well, both the outer flesh and the kernels inside the hard seeds.

The far side of the woodland also has a sharply defined boundary. Fire here has killed three desert oaks whose hollow skeletons rise out of the heath myrtles, grevilleas and wattles. Some of the fire-blackened trunks are still covered in bark, but it has shrunk away from the dead wood, leaving a narrow gap. This confined but protected space is the home of spiders, beetles and geckoes — mostly nocturnal animals. But one of the inhabitants is a sun-loving lizard, the mulga goanna. I always carefully scan the sunny sides of desert oaks, especially after a cool night, for these small goannas. This morning I finally see one, not on a tree with bark but on a stump reduced to charcoal. The blackness no doubt helps the lizard to gather more warmth. As I go nearer it turns its head and follows my every move with its bright eyes. Only when I try to touch it does it run off.

The limbs and trunks of the dead oaks are full of hollows. These too are homes of animals. From one, only about 2 metres above the ground, peers the yellow head, finely barred with black, of a budgerigar. Budgies are not timid birds and this female is probably not at the nest entrance because she is wary of my approach. I hide behind a small bush and wait. The female looks all around and twitters softly. She is answered by another budgie, which lands near the hollow. After a few seconds the male flutters down to the female and feeds her. With his beak over hers he transfers partly digested grass seeds from his crop to the female's in a rapid pumping action. Once the female has been fed the two birds sit closely side by side and preen each other.

Beyond the dead oaks is another woodland, perhaps a hectare in size, of small

Top: A large species of bulldog ant; its sting is very painful.
Above: A pygmy mulga goanna suns itself on a burnt tree stump.

*A pair of budgerigars at the
entrance to its nesting hollow.*

sturdy trees. It is not a quiet place. Songs and call notes of just about all the species of honeyeaters found in the Park, from the thin songs of the smaller species to the loudly garrulous notes of the spiny-cheeked, blend pleasantly together. The desert grevillea trees are incandescent with clusters of bright-orange flowers full of nectar. Besides the nectar feeders, insect-eating birds such as hooded robins and tiny thornbills are drawn to the flowers and chase after beetles, flies, bees and wasps.

By mid-morning the day's warmth is tempered by a cool blustery wind. I leave the woodlands behind as I set out in a south-easterly direction towards a patch of mallee. To reach it I must cross many kilometres of dunes and swales, the National Park's most extensive habitat. The first dunes are clothed in hummocks of mature, but not old, spinifex — green healthy clumps. Most are hard spinifex, which scratch and puncture the skin around my ankles. Here and there are patches of soft spinifex with thinner, more pliable, but still prickly leaves and stems. Their common name of porcupine grass is most appropriate. For the numerous reptiles spinifex is a boon, providing fortresses where they are safe from the predations of birds. Lizard tracks lead from one clump to another and every so often I see a fast, colourful form racing for its retreat.

Finally a lizard, still some 20 metres ahead, stays out in the open, alert and watchful but apparently not alarmed. Cautiously I creep towards it on hands and knees so as not to look too large and threatening and also so that I will have a closer look should the lizard stand its ground. Several times it catches what I imagine to be small insects. I creep to within 3 metres of the brilliant male military dragon. He is a brick-red, like the sand, except for the yellow and black markings on his head and chest. The sand is getting warm, hot even, and the dragon raises his underside off the ground and lifts his toes, so only his palms and heels touch the ground. His eyes constantly swivel from side to side and every so often he tilts his head to scan the skies for birds of prey. Quite unexpectedly he runs a few steps towards me and grabs a small grasshopper, but when I stand up he streaks for the nearest spinifex.

During the night an orb-weaving spider had stretched a web between a grevillea and a heath myrtle. Something had gone horribly wrong for it, however. It snared an insect, a praying mantis, much larger than itself. The mantis is still alive but trapped in the web. The more it struggles, the more firmly it becomes entangled. The spider was badly injured, or perhaps even killed by the mantis. It lies in a ball below its web and is being carried away, piece by piece, by a swarm of meat ants. I free the mantis from the web.

Other insects criss-cross the sand. Beetles, some black others brown, heavily armoured with thick, hard wingcases and an outer 'skin' called an exoskeleton, plod up and down the dunes. Grasshoppers in mottled shades of red and yellow

hop from bush to bush, or half bury themselves in the sand and so become invisible. Caterpillars of moths and butterflies devour the new growth.

Flowers are all around, but when I descend yet another dune I am confronted by an unusually brilliant kaleidoscope of colours, shapes and textures. Dominant is a dense cluster of colony wattles, closely spaced small trees with pure white trunks. Their branches are so heavily laden with yellow flowers that their phyllodes are obscured. The ground beneath is a carpet of fallen puffballs. The air is saturated with their scent. Large native bees lurch from flower to flower, gathering pollen. Rattlepod grevilleas, dark-green thick bushes with bunches of upright white flowers, also broadcast a pleasant scent, less sweet and more musky. Beside them open bushes of pituri are studded with deep-throated white flowers veined with purple. Anangu used these bushes to catch emus by poisoning waterholes with the plants' toxic leaves.

The swale and lower slopes of the dunes were recently burnt, one or perhaps two years ago, down to bare sand. Spinifex, ephemerals and perennial shrubs, even mulga trees, were consumed. Only the desert oaks, growing very sparsely here, survived. Defiant, tall, shaggy-headed, they dot the landscape as far as I can see. The spinifex has not yet regrown and all the other plants are no more than knee-high. But every regenerating plant, every shrub, every ground creeper, every ephemeral is in flower. I have to wade through them.

Above left: A male military dragon hunts ants and other insects between clumps of spinifex. Above: A male of the horned beetle Blackburnium neocavicolle. *These beetles dig deep vertical burrows in sand where they raise their larvae on leaves and other organic matter.*

Top: The flowers of Latrobe's desert fuchsia are a source of nectar for honeyeaters. Above: Keraudrenia flowers. Right: Courting weevils of the genus Polyphrades. Their larvae are borers in the wood of wattle trees.

It is difficult to absorb it all. Mentally I make a list: yellow flowers on a silver-leafed goodenia; pale mauve and yellow fan flowers; dark-purple running peas; pink-purple swainsonas; glossy-leafed rulingias with small yellow flowers and an unpleasant smell; scrubby desert fuchsias, some with pale-blue flowers, others with satiny dark-purple ones; blue-flowered storkbills; all kinds of daisies, some of them papery everlastings; purple nightshades; intensely yellow cassias; fluffy white and pink silvertails; blue brunonias; and many others. One entire slope is a haze of pale blue-purple, a froth of flowering keraudrenia shrubs. In front of them is a sprawl of low dark-green bushes with racemes of bright-red flowers at their bases, the upside-down bushes. The sand around them is trampled by innumerable honeyeaters that have come to sip their nectar. On the top of the burnt ridge grows a mass of what always seem such outrageous plants for the arid zone — parakeelyas. The flowers open late in the mornings, and are only just unfolding. They are a lurid pink-purple, while the succulent leaves are a deep green. They do not blend with the rest of the plants, but seem a flamboyant, vulgar excess.

Ruby saltbush in fruit.

A list is mere words and can never give more than an impression of the variety and colour of the plants. It says little about the ridge as a whole, the totality of red sand, blue skies, sweet scents, colourful flowers, birds singing, lizards running and benevolent sunshine.

A strip of unburnt land, full of spinifex, and wattle and grevillea bushes, runs through the wildflowers. It is here that several species of honeyeater have built their nests. The nests, made of wisps of bark and grass held together with spiderweb, are well concealed and I only find them by chance or by following the parents as they carry food to their nestlings. I find the singing honeyeaters' nest when I brush against a grevillea bush and the sitting bird flies off the nest practically into my face. The pair brings a steady supply of insects — moths, grasshoppers, mantids, stick insects and others — to the three young. A few times the birds feed them bright fruits of the ruby saltbush. Nectar, it seems, is not a good food for growing chicks.

A pair of white-fronted honeyeaters leads me to its nest through alarm calls of 'truck, truck' and a general agitation. The deep cup nest, slung like a hammock from a forked horizontal branch, is empty but beside it sits a mottled black and white bird with a long tail. It looks nothing like a honeyeater and is much larger. The pallid cuckoo chick has just fledged from the nest and is raised and defended by the honeyeaters as though it were their own.

Only the larger flowers carry enough nectar to attract the birds. But insects can extract enough out of the small flowers to sustain themselves. Walking through a particularly profuse patch of flowers, I flush a cloud of orange and black painted lady butterflies. Almost immediately they settle again on the silvertail bushes to

A white-fronted honeyeater on
honey grevillea flowers.

extract nectar from pink flowers buried in fine white down. As they drink nectar they spread their wings to absorb the sun's warmth.

A bulky, sluggish lizard, boldy marked in pale and dark brown, also lies in the sun. Unlike the long-tailed slender species it does not rush for cover. Hissing and puffing, it distends its body and pushes itself sideways through the sand on incongruously small, stumpy legs. At the same time this centralian blue-tongued lizard waves his fleshy tongue at me. When it reaches a low heath myrtle it scuttles underneath out of sight.

I leave the burnt, flower-covered dunes behind. For hours I walk along a valley between two ridges. It is easier going here and there is some protection from the strong wind. As it is warmer, more and more lizards cross my path. One pauses for a few moments. Its long smooth body is longitudinally striped in black and white, the tail is bright blue and the head copper-coloured. The blue-tailed skink makes short rushes after insects. Every time it stops it swishes its hindquarters to one side, so its tail lies parallel to its body.

A few metres on another skink runs down a burrow to hide, but it miscalculates; the burrow is only a few centimetres deep. It glares at me as I crouch down to have a better look. It is also slender and long-tailed but is spotted in white, circled with black, on a red-brown body. Scientists call it *Ctenotus pantherinus*. 'Panther' or 'leopard skink' would be a fair translation.

Crimson chats are common throughout the dunes and plains. All morning I have seen the intensely coloured males fluttering steeply into the air and then, with their wings held in a V, parachuting vertically down to land among the flowers. At least, that is what was happening earlier when there was little wind. Now they are carried hundreds of metres away during their descent by gusts of wind. Their courtship flights are much like those of larks, except the chats have no song to pour down on prospective mates. All the males utter is a feeble 'teet'. But the larks have little colour and the chats' undersides and heads shine a brilliant red.

I watch a male chat searching for food. He perches on a stick or branch, then flies after an insect or a spider. Other times he walks on the ground and closely inspects the undersides of leaves and flowers. In quick succession he catches a lacewing, a white spider, a brown caterpillar and a grasshopper. He carries a large green caterpillar to a small shrub. I hurry after him, hoping to find his nest, but rather than nestlings it is a female he feeds as part of his courtship. She is mostly brown with a hint of red on her underside.

It is late afternoon when I reach the mallee woodland. It looks a little like a forest except that all the trees are only 4–6 metres tall. Not every trunk forms a single plant; a dozen or more slender stems may grow from a single woody root system. Mallees, as the trees with this growth habit are called, are eucalypts. Two species grow here intermingled. Most are blue mallees, so named because of their blue-green foliage. The others have greener leaves and are named after the caps on the flower buds, the sharp-capped mallees. Both have pale, lustrous, smooth new bark with the older bark hanging in long dark strips from the trunks. The understorey is spinifex. An occasional desert oak towers above them.

Strolling among the trees is a beautifully patterned and coloured sand goanna. As it waddles bowleggedly along, holding its head and body off the ground but dragging the tip of its tail, it tests all irregularities in the sand with its long forked tongue. It stops and digs furiously with its clawed feet. Quickly it grabs something and swallows it. I cannot see what it is. When the goanna finally realises there is someone looking over its shoulder, it flattens its body on the ground, raises its head on its long slender neck and tries to get my 'scent' with its tongue. When I walk closer the goanna runs off at speed.

Several crows, cawing quietly to each other, are worrying at something among the spinifex. They tear and pull at bones among white and soft orange-pink feathers strewn over the sand. Surely they did not kill a pink cockatoo? When I examine the fresh remains more carefully it is quite evident that the cockatoo was dismembered by a bird with a sharper beak than that of the crow, which is really a clumsy pickaxe. More likely the cockatoo was caught and eaten by a peregrine falcon, and the crows are here to see what they can scavenge. The cockatoo's brightly coloured crest feathers lie like small flames on the carpet of white. The crows have not moved far. The late sun glints off their glossy black plumage as they watch me balefully through white eyes.

As everywhere in the arid zone, ants are numerous and busy. Most common is a tiny black species that is never less than frantic. They race along well-worn paths radiating from nests that are no more than small holes in the ground. In each column ants are both coming and going. Are they gathering seeds or hunting minute insects? I squat down low, nose to the ground, for a better look. But the ants are so small that I cannot make out if they are carrying anything at all back to the nest, let alone what it might be.

A slight movement a few metres away draws my attention to someone else closely studying the ant trail. It is not just watching, it is eating the ants, one after the other, in such rapid movements I cannot make out just how the ants are caught. Does the thorny devil use its tongue, or does it snap the ants up in its jaws? This beautiful spiny lizard is brightly patterned in yellow, orange-brown and dark brown, yet on this red earth it is difficult to detect. If I had not sat down so closely beside it, I would probably not have seen it. The lizard ignores me and eats ant after ant after ant. There are records of them eating 2500 at a sitting. This particular little black ant is the lizard's only food.

The crows, much-feared marauders, have moved on and the other birds, which had been silently watching from cover, resume their songs and their foraging. A

Top: Blue mallees. Above: A sand goanna at the entrance to its burrow.

spiny-cheeked honeyeater grabs a large katydid from among the mallee leaves. The birds must have acute eyesight for the insect is the same shape, colour, pattern and texture as the leaves on which it was feeding. A pair of bronze cuckoos flirts in a small tree, chasing each other and calling in soft notes, under the watchful eye of a white-winged triller whose nest the cuckoos may well parasitise. A netted dragon, its feet braced for a quick getaway, turns its large round head and looks back at me. The low sun glints in its eye.

The mallee patch is not very extensive and I have soon crossed it and reached the dunes again. From the top of a ridge I can see Kata Tjuta to the west, now quite a distance away. To the east Uluru is much closer. Thin high clouds streak the sky. After crossing a few more sandridges I am on the edge of a broad flat plain stretching to the north. The spinifex and flowering plants are similar to those on the dunes, but there are differences. The honey grevillea bushes, which grow all over the sandhills, are larger and taller here with denser clusters of flowers. Each bush is like a being with a multitude of long, thin grey-green arms ending in hands, held elegantly palm upwards as if in an oriental dance posture. The 'hands' are racemes of flowers, golden-yellow at their bases, vivid green at their tips. For as far as I can see these 'arms' wave gently in the breeze. Below them is the pink foam of massively flowering fringe myrtles. The long thin canes of the sand hibiscus, adorned with lilac-pink flowers, bend to the wind.

As I lift a honey grevillea flower to my mouth to suck the sweet nectar, I feel I am being watched. Two dingoes with golden-blonde fur stare at me inquisitively from only a few metres away. They too enjoy the nectar, biting and licking the flowers close to the ground and jumping up to grab the higher ones. They are young animals and nothing holds their attention for long. Leaping and running, they chase each other in a small circle around me. One of them, the male, comes right up and then turns and runs away, looking back over his shoulder as if inviting me to play. When I do not he joins the female in the shade of a desert oak where they play with the fallen cones, chewing them, tossing them in the air and wrestling each other for possession. They are completely silent. For about half an hour they stay around me. Many times they come up, almost within touching distance, and invite me to play again.

Pushing my way through the flowers, a male crimson chat tumbles out of a bush not a metre from my feet. He seems to be injured, fluttering pathetically over the sand, dragging his feet as though he barely has the strength to move. But he keeps just ahead of me. Many birds use this 'broken wing act' to lead predators or just large lumbering persons away from their nests.

In the bush from which I originally flushed the chat I find its neatly woven nest. Three young, like shining black pebbles the size of beans, lie huddled together. They must have hatched only a day or so ago.

Flowers of the honey grevillea.

Ants, like the flowers, are also more diverse here. A slightly elevated piece of flat ground, completely bare of sticks, grass or any matter other than minute stones, is a seething mass of meat ants. There are numerous openings into the nests below with hundreds upon hundreds of ants pouring in and out. Like the tiny ants in the mallee but on a larger scale, the meat ants rush out five or six abreast along well-defined highways that radiate from the nests like the spokes of a wheel. Each spoke is well over 100 metres long. An equal number of ants come rushing back carrying prey, mostly other insects or parts of them. One ant carries the clear wing of a grasshopper upright like a banner. A gust of wind catches this 'flag' and carries it, ant and all, off the highway. The ant is not deterred; it struggles back to the road and continues its quick march home.

Not far away shiny black ants carry white fluffy seeds of daisies back to their nest and struggle to squeeze their harvest through its narrow opening. Mounds of sand and pebbles with slit openings are dotted among the spinifex. Their inhabitants, the moneybox ants, are more sedate than most ants. Only a few move slowly about the opening — small dark workers and large soldiers, shiny dark

A pair of dingoes playing.

Above: A pair of crimson chats feeds its nestlings. Right: A male masked woodswallow at the nest.

red-brown, with enormous heads and serrated jaws. They will go out to forage at night. Other ants are shy. When I approach a group of pale-brown ants they rush back down into their nest. Termites, perhaps even more numerous than the ants, too are reticent. Their mounds, raised only 30 or 40 centimetres above the ground, stand closely spaced in all the habitats with the exception of the tops of the dunes, but there is not one of the insects to be seen above ground.

A loosely clumped stand of slender trees with fresh green leaves grows about half a kilometre from the dunes. These desert poplars resemble their European namesakes in the general shape of the trees and the way in which their leaves rustle in the wind. Otherwise the two have nothing in common. The desert poplars belong to a family of plants found only in Australia. They do not grow very large, as their trunks snap off when still only the size of saplings. One fell only recently. It is easy to see why; its entire trunk is riddled with the tunnels of boring insects. The wood crumbles in my hand. When I break a piece open I find larvae still living in some of the passages — small white grubs with black jaws. In another chamber is the pupa of a beetle, a perfectly formed individual but colourless and with the long antannae and wings neatly folded. In another piece of wood I find a mature beetle, a grey species with golden flecks, and ready to sink its jaws into my finger.

Idly I follow a broad slithering track through the sand that must have been made by a sizeable snake. Much to my surprise I soon catch up with it — a python, the woma, the Kuniya of Anangu legend. Unlike other snakes I have come across, the woma is completely indifferent and phlegmatic about humans, even when one squats down beside it. The loosely coiled snake acknowledges my presence by flicking its black tongue and slightly tilting its yellow, shiny enamelled-looking head. Even when I take one of its coils lightly in my hands, it does not move away or strike out at me.

I am well out on the plain. The setting sun colours the streaky clouds, which look like broad brushstrokes on the sky. Larger clouds are building up, pure and white and billowing. Some have dark, rain-heavy undersides. A few big drops of rain splash down and make craters in the sand. Then it is dry again. About a dozen masked woodswallows, dressed in shades of soft grey and with black 'masks', rise twittering high into the sky, chasing each other, a last communal flight before settling down for the night. These birds seem to nest in loose colonies of six to eight pairs. I soon find one of their nests, a rough cup of grasses and dry leaves at the end of a honey grevillea's long arm. The two young, covered in grey down, sway back and forth, up and down all day on the slightest breeze.

This wolf spider hides in a silk-lined burrow by day and hunts around its entrance at night.

The clouds and the few drops of rain ensure a warm night of high humidity. There will be a lot of activity on the dunes. Many reptiles, spiders, insects and nearly all the small mammals come out only at night. By day they live in deep burrows where the humidity remains high, and so avoid the effects of the sun's heat and desiccation. This is essential behaviour for animals living in areas where there is no surface water. Certain reptiles, insects and spiders come out in the day over the cooler months for warmth, as winter nights can be very cold, but then become nocturnal in summer. Most cold-blooded animals, however, spend the entire winter in almost uninterrupted torpor in their underground retreats. Only the small mammals, being warm-blooded, are active all the year round, but even some of them hibernate for short periods. Tonight it is warm enough for nearly all the nocturnal animals to venture out.

Carrying a strong spotlight I walk along the crest of a long sandridge a few hours after sunset. The first thing I notice as I scan the red sand is the myriad green eyes reflecting the light's beam. Nearly all disappear as I come near them. Finally I trace one set of reflections to a spider, the colour of the sand, lying pressed to the ground. It is a wolf spider, a free-ranging huntress. Approaching other reflections with greater care I soon realise they too belong to spiders. They drop down vertical, perfectly cylindrical shafts when I am still several metres away. As these spiders seem to take exception to the strong light, I put it down in such a way that only the periphery of the beam faintly illuminates one such silk-lined lair. After a minute or so the tips of the spider's legs appear on the burrow's rim, then without preamble it pops out and stands astride the opening. When I move to brush an ant from my leg, the spider leaps back down its burrow. A few seconds later it reappears. Sitting perfectly still, just turning my eyes, I inspect the sand closely. There is a lot of movement of minute animal life, most of it too small to identify. These organisms must be the spiders' main prey. One tiny insect meandering over the sand I can recognise, an immature cricket only a few millimetres long. The spider has seen it too and whips around, facing the pale translucent insect. Closer and closer the cricket wanders. When about 25 centimetres away the spider leaps at it and jumps back into the burrow so fast that for a moment I think it vanished, with the cricket, or perhaps I just imagined it had ever been there at all. But the spider's footprints in the sand and a strand of silk drifting in the breeze show it was no hallucination. I sit there a little longer. A large black beetle marches by. With its tail, armed with a poisonous sting, curved over its body, a scorpion scuttles along, also intent on insect prey. A few metres away a blind snake, like a length of polished steel wire, erupts out of the ground. With its body arched in loops, it dives in and out of the sand, then disappears again. These small snakes live almost entirely beneath the sand where they feed on termites.

A species of blind snake that lives mostly beneath the sand where it feeds on termites.

Sweeping the light over the sandridge, which is almost devoid of vegetation, the beam catches something larger than a spider or insect moving about. Quietly I walk over and there, dazzled in the light, is one of Uluru's most enchanting animals. It is so delicate and fragile that I can see some of its veins and even bones and organs through its skin. Its slender fingers and toes are a pale pink. The skin is cool and soft to the touch and on the upperside the colour of red sand. Across it are lines of blue, like tattoos. Its short fat tail is spotted white and has bright pink flashes on the sides. It ends in a knob. This smooth knob-tailed gecko stares at me through huge, dark, lidless eyes. Perhaps to clean them or in a vain effort to wipe away the irritating light, the lizard licks its eyes with its fleshy tongue. A soft-skinned reptile like this could thrive only in the coolness and humidity of the night. It would shrivel and die very quickly in the sun. Geckoes operate at much lower temperatures than lizards of the day such as the dragons and skinks. Knob-tailed geckoes are out when the air temperature is as low as 16 degrees Celsius, whereas dragons and especially goannas are not fully functional until their body temperature reaches the mid-20s. I dim the light and soon the gecko moves on in a hip-swivelling run.

Down in the swale there is more vegetation, spinifex mostly, with a sprinkling of honey grevilleas, heath myrtles and a few tall desert oaks. The spotlight picks up the bright-red reflections of a pair of eyes in one of the trees. These belong to a tawny frogmouth who looks down at me through yellow eyes. A larger animal

The smooth knob-tailed gecko lives among spinifex on the crests of dunes.

The Wongai ningaui is an insect-eating marsupial and one of the tiniest of all mammals. The combined length of its head and body is 5–7 cm and it weighs about 10 g. It will tackle prey larger and heavier than itself.

HAWTHORN SECONDARY COLLEGE
BURGESS STREET
EAST HAWTHORN, 3123

skips away from some spinifex. With a rush of excitement I follow it with the light, but it is only a rabbit.

Here too termite mounds, hard strong structures, bulge out of the ground. There are no tower mounds, so common in other arid regions in Australia. During the day these domes are sealed, and nothing moves in or out. Tonight broad columns of termites swarm out from at least some of the mounds. Those returning carry short lengths of dry spinifex back to the nest, where some will be eaten and the rest stored in chambers. This grass, indigestible to just about all other animals, is these termites' sole food. To digest it they need the assistance of special enzyme-producing protozoa and bacteria that live in the insects' gut. Termite soldiers, with black pincer jaws and enlarged heads to accommodate extra-powerful muscles, guard the nest entrances and parts of the marching columns. They will clamp their jaws on anything and anybody that is perceived as an enemy. Most species of termite, however, build covered tunnels to their food source. Like the gecko, termites cannot survive in the heat and dryness of the day. Unlike the ants, which are protected by hard outer skeletons, they are soft and vulnerable. As I lean over the busy multitudes of termites another snake emerges slowly from the soil. It is not a blind snake, but a larger species, a burrowing snake, boldly marked in black and yellow bands. It is not a termite eater, preferring small lizards. Another kind of knob-tailed gecko, however, is hunting the termites. It snaps up the workers quickly while the soldiers latch onto its legs. This three-lined knob-tailed gecko is much more heavily patterned and looks less fragile, less ghostlike, than its relative of the sandhills.

The last thing I expect to find is an amphibian. Yet there it is, a desert spadefoot toad, almost spherical with large eyes and a wide mouth. It too is probably after termites. Usually these toads are deep underground where they may stay for years, living on moisture and food reserves stored in their bodies. Only during heavy rainfall do they emerge to spawn. Perhaps this cloudy warm night brought it to the surface for one more meal before digging in till the next major rain.

I have spent many nights, torch in hand, stalking the dunes and plains. My only disappointment is that I never have more than the most fleeting glimpses of the small mammals. Yet from their tracks I know they live here in some numbers. Luckily, scientists working on fauna surveys and other studies have shown me some of these exquisite marsupials and rodents. But I can only imagine what they are doing all around me.

Shortly after dark they would have left their burrows, some as individuals, some as families and others as a social group of a dozen or more. The sandy-coloured spinifex hopping mice will be bounding all over the sandhills. With their elongated hindfeet they look like elegant miniature kangaroos, but they are rodents, not marsupials like the kangaroos. They will be digging seeds from the sand and

nibbling green plants. Their huge paper-thin ears pick up any sound, even the stealthy footfalls of predators such as feral cats and the slither of a snake. At the merest hint of danger they bolt down their burrows. One of the smallest marsupials, the Wongai ningaui, weighing only about 10 grams, would have left its grass nest in an underground burrow or spinifex bush and will now be hunting insects. It fearlessly tackles anything, even grasshoppers and crickets nearly as large as itself, biting its prey furiously around the head till it succumbs. The slightly larger hairy-footed dunnarts, also marsupials, will be out on similar missions, listening for the movement of prey beneath the sand with their pointed ears and sniffing out insects and possibly small reptiles with their sensitive noses. Sandy inland mice, true rodents about the size of a house mouse, would have left their communal burrows and will be sifting through the sand for seeds. Their solitary larger cousin, the desert mouse, rotund and shaggy-furred, prefers to nibble green shoots.

A mulgara sniffs out a beetle before eating it. The mulgara, a small marsupial carnivore, is one of Uluru-Kata Tjuta's rarest species.

Giles's desert fuchsia.

The largest of these mammals of the night is the sturdy mulgara, which can weigh as much as 100 grams, with exceptional animals weighing 150 grams. It may have come out of its burrow even before sunset to catch some of the day's warmth. It will be after beetles as its jaws are strong enough to crush their armour. It may even be pursuing lizards and some of the smaller mice. If a female, she will more than likely be carrying tiny pink young, as many as eight, in her pouch.

Of these mammals only the mulgara is rare. Some such as the hopping mouse and the sandy inland mouse are numerous in good seasons. They are all secretive and I have to be content just to see their tracks.

Overnight most of the clouds have blown away, and only a few high feathery ones catch the colours of the sunrise. Birds sing enthusiastically. I am in the last of Uluru-Kata Tjuta's major habitats in a remote part of the Park, just to the east of Kata Tjuta. The plain here is not covered in spinifex and flowers but with a forest of small wattle trees, the mulgas. Their foliage is a smoky grey-green colour. The trees grow mostly in groves, with small clearings between them where spinifex and a few low desert fuchsias have taken root. The mulgas are vigorous and bushy with closely spaced stiff branches. Some are in flower, carrying masses of yellow brushes that contrast with the dark-grey fibrous bark. Fallen dead trees, of which there are a great many, show a hard wood with a tortuous tight grain and a satiny patina. I am soon enveloped by the trees; there are no wide views and I cannot see the monoliths. Little wind penetrates here and it is therefore warmer. It is not a place of flowers, but of birds. There are more species of birds here than in any of the other habitats in the Park.

White-backed swallows skim low over the trees. A male crested bellbird flies up from the ground onto a tall stump and begins his amazing call, 'pan-pan-palala' on and on. While calling, with his black crest raised and his white throat working with the effort, he turns on his perch, so broadcasting his notes through 360 degrees. Only a short distance away I flush his mate from their nest, a deep cup lodged in a fork low in a mulga. It contains three white eggs speckled with brown. About a dozen white-browed babblers, lively dark-brown birds, are busy building their bulky domed nest. Often they interrupt their work to sit closely cuddled together in threes and fours, preening each other with their long curved beaks while nattering away in quiet voices. Deep inside a thick clump of mulgas shines the intense blue of a male splendid wren, where he and his dull-brown mate are inspecting a low shrub as a possible nest site. A zebra finch sits inside its globular grass nest, looking out unperturbed as I peer closely at it. A diamond dove does not show such equanimity and flies off, hoping, perhaps, to draw my attention away from the two young sitting perfectly still on the flimsy nest.

Walking slowly, pausing frequently, I spend some of my most enthralling hours at Uluru-Kata Tjuta. I find more and more nests. A male white-winged triller sits so tightly that I have to lift him gently with my finger to see if he is sitting on eggs or young. There are two blue-green eggs spotted with brown. Willie wagtails scold me noisily as I near their nest where they are feeding three young almost ready to fledge. Spiny-cheeked honeyeaters bring large stick insects, katydids, grasshoppers and the fruit of the ruby saltbush to their three nestlings. Everywhere there are woodswallows — black-faced, masked, white-browed.

Moving around the fallen trunk of a mulga I am suddenly confronted by the whirling movement of a large snake, surprised while sunbathing. Involuntarily I take a few steps back for this is not a placid, harmless python. Head raised and tongue flickering, the mulga, or king brown, snake is ready to strike out. I stand my ground and the snake lowers its head, but distends its neck, almost like a cobra's hood, and slowly sidles away among the trees.

As it does so a small bright bird, another species of wren, comes skipping along the ground, carrying an insect in its beak. He enters a small bush and soon emerges without it. Obviously this variegated wren has a nest with young. I sit on a log watching both parents come and go. A large skink, dark with white spots along its flanks, comes out from beneath the nest. For a moment I think it may climb up and steal the nestlings, but it is more interested in a grasshopper moving slowly over the sandy ground. I am so absorbed by all this that I am quite startled by a booming, drumming sound directly behind me. Looking back quickly I am face to face with two inquisitive emus. Pacing back and forth they look at me closely for a while, then walk off among the trees.

Sitting there I ponder why so many of the animals are so trusting and approachable. Part of the reason is that if you move quietly and inconspicuously and stop frequently, most animals will be curious rather than alarmed. Also, in places where animals are not constantly pursued and harassed they soon ignore a human presence. This inquisitiveness and acceptance never fail to give me a feeling of privilege.

The last thirty-six hours have demonstrated that Uluru-Kata Tjuta is not always a hot, dry inhospitable place as it is so often depicted. Dryness, even drought, however, is the norm. Seasons of heavy widespread rain, such as the one I was fortunate enough to experience, are comparatively rare. What is important to remember is that the bountiful seasons are necessary for life to survive here at all. During seasons of plenty the plants and animals build up in numbers and at least some of them will survive to carry the species through the inevitable times of scarcity. Adaptations to endure the droughts are just as important as the ability to flourish after rain.

The mulga, or king brown, snake is aggressive and always ready to strike.

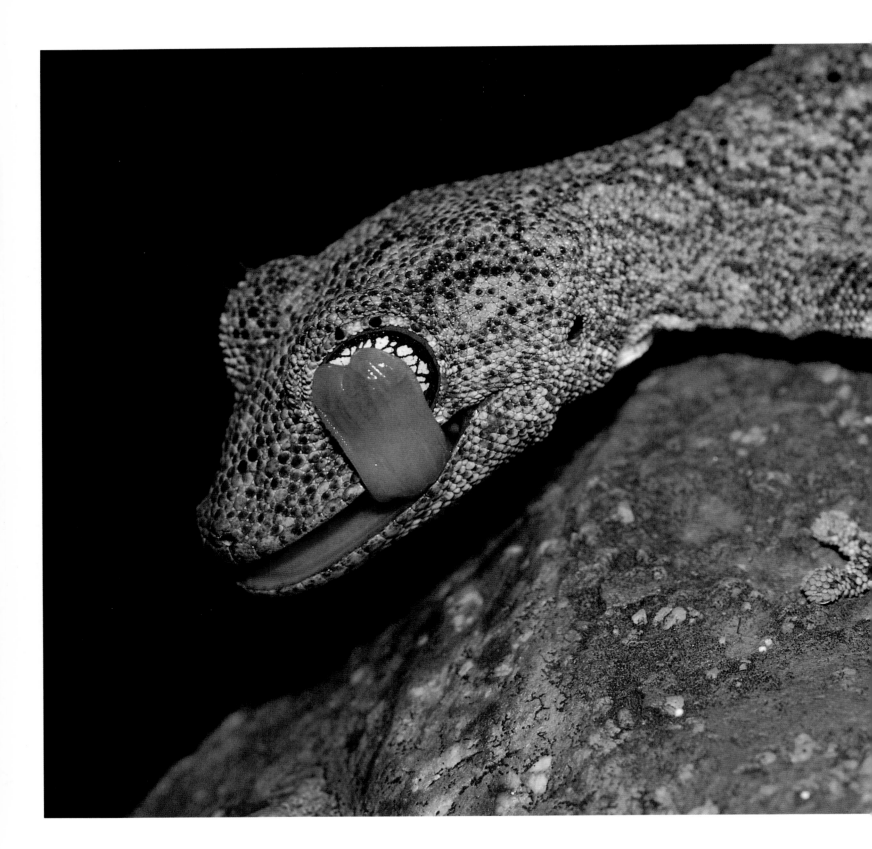

CHAPTER SEVEN

ADAPTED TO FLOOD AND FAMINE

Spring after good rains at Uluru-Kata Tjuta, as elsewhere in arid Australia, is a lively animated season full of energy and growth. But the same country can look desolate and forbidding on a hot day during a long drought. The spinifex is brittle and grey. Trees and shrubs have lost most of their leaves. Many have died. No reptiles dart across the open spaces, few tracks disturb the sand. Water has disappeared from rockpools at Uluru and Kata Tjuta. Only a few birds inhabit the thickets where they glean the few remaining insects. Ants and termites have closed their nests and live on stored reserves. Deep in burrows reptiles aestivate. Many of the small mammals have died but some survive in pockets of slightly better watered country, where they come out to feed on seeds and insects at night. The skies are empty. The bush is silent. The only colour in the grey landscape is the red sand and the blue sky. Hot winds whip the dry stalks. It may be as much as 46 degrees Celsius in the shade.

Severe droughts, when there is not enough rain for sustained plant growth for several years, are rare. There was one in the 1930s, and the worst recorded drought in the area ended in 1965. How the plants and animals have adapted to the extreme conditions, from heavy downpours to years without any significant rain, has only recently been unravelled.

About 70 per cent of Australia is arid or semi-arid — that is, the land, on average, receives less than 375 millimetres of rain per year. Uluru-Kata Tjuta lies at the centre of the arid zone and receives an annual average of 220 millimetres of rain. True deserts are defined as places where the yearly average is less than 120 millimetres. Uluru-Kata Tjuta, therefore, is not a desert.

Australia's arid zone is unique in the world for two reasons: the erratic nature of the rainfall and the ancient soils of low fertility. In the Americas, for example, the arid zones receive no more rain than those of Australia, but it is predictable. Plants such as cacti and succulents can adapt to these conditions by storing water in their stems and replenishing the supply regularly every year. In Africa and parts of central Asia seasonal rains and fertile soils support rich grasslands where vast herds of large mammals graze.

The annual average rainfall of 220 millimetres at Uluru-Kata Tjuta and other huge tracts of the inland is not particularly low. The problem is that the amount is totally unpredictable and the seasons are extremely variable. There may be 900 millimetres one year, falling over just a few days, and 50 millimetres the next. Also there are many tantalising days when the skies darken and rain sprinkles down — but only a few millimetres fall. This will add to the annual rainfall figure but will make no difference whatsoever to plant growth.

The soils are mostly sandy with phosphorus and nitrogen levels about half of those in soils of other arid zones in the world. Sandy soils do not hold moisture, and rainwater rapidly percolates down to the watertable where it is out of reach for most plants. Like other arid zones, however, there are great fluctuations in temperatures at Uluru-Kata Tjuta. On summer days the maximum temperature may soar to over 46 degrees Celsius, although the average maximum for January is 39.2 degrees. In winter there are frequent frosts with the average daily range of temperatures in July being 4.3–20.9 degrees Celsius.

The plants that grow in Australia's arid zone must, therefore, be able to withstand flood and drought, heat and frost, and draw their nourishment from sandy soils low in nutrients and moisture. The animal life, in turn, has had to adapt to harsh, woody plants low in digestible food and to a scarcity of surface water. It is these conditions that have given Australia's inland its unique assemblage of plants and animals, and also a less tangible quality, a special 'feel' and ambience.

The area is vast, covering about three-quarters of the continent, but Uluru-Kata Tjuta National Park, small as it is, is remarkably representative of the arid zone as a whole. The plants and animals you find in south-west Queensland, central Western Australia or in the northern parts of South Australia may vary in detail but in the broad aspect there are great similarities — the same forces shaped them and now maintain them.

Most of the soils have their origins in erosion processes that began many millions of years ago. Since then they have been shifted, sorted, re-sorted and moved again, till they were reduced to grains of sand mixed with varying amounts of clay and with most of the minerals, the food of the plants, leached out of them.

For long, long periods the climate was warm and moist, especially since about 125 million years ago when flowering plants first appeared on earth. These flourished to such a degree that eventually most of the continent was covered in rainforest. There is fossil evidence that the first dry-country-adapted plants appeared in small areas of Australia during the Eocene, about 45 million years ago, but rainforests continued over most areas until the Miocene era, 25 million years ago. The extreme and widespread drying out of Australia did not occur until the last million years or so. During that time there were several periods of hyper-aridity when it was so dry, and cold as well, that all but the hardiest plants perished

Previous pages: A spiny-tailed gecko licks its eye. Eleven species of gecko hunt the plains and dunes at night.

over vast areas. Others survived in refuges, protected pockets of higher rainfall and temperatures, from which they recolonised the land when it became warmer and wetter again. The last such hyper-arid time occurred only 15,000–30,000 years ago, a time when the ground was often virtually bare and sand was blown into long ridges, the dunes of today. So the plants we now see at Uluru-Kata Tjuta, and other places in the centre, are the toughest species, plus those that have recolonised the area over the last 30,000 years at most. Quite possibly they came from refuges at such places at Watarrka, and the Musgrave and MacDonnell ranges. Rainforest persists in only tiny areas along Australia's east coast.

Put simply, the flora of arid Australia is made up of those plants that adapted over the millennia to conditions of highly irregular rainfall and poor soils. Those that could not were eliminated. Some of these plants may have had pre-existing adaptations to cope with the increasingly low soil fertility, for it has been discovered that adaptations to low nutrients are also useful in coping with aridity. The desert oak could well be such a plant. It is closely related to the casuarinas, the she-oaks and bull oaks, which were numerous in the ancient rainforests. Its special foliage and complex root system, which enable it to cope so well with the arid conditions, may originally have evolved to extract maximum nutrients from sandy soils.

The desert oak exemplifies many of the adaptations to arid conditions. To survive, arid zone plants need to have systems that extract maximum moisture from the soil and lose a minimum amount through transpiration, the breathing of the plants through microscopic pores in the leaves. The oak's roots are enormous. The taproot may go down as far as 40 metres for it must reach the ground water. One plant ecologist commented that the root could go down even further but no one had ever taken a shovel to that depth. The taproot keeps growing till it reaches the watertable and a more or less permanent source of water. Desert oaks also have a gigantic, shallow lateral network of roots. This is to absorb as much of the nutrients from the soil as possible whenever it rains because the plant food is concentrated in the top 10 centimetres.

Nearly all the trees and perennial shrubs, including spinifex, have a similar elaborate root system, though none goes down as deeply as the desert oak's. In most species there is four to ten times as much bulk below ground as grows above it. The green growth needs a substantial support system.

Being a large tree, and the only one growing away from the enriched habitats around the monoliths, the desert oak needs to solve the additional problem of how to survive until the taproot reaches the ground water. Young desert oaks are candle-shaped, like pencil pines, and bear little resemblance to the mature trees. The young trees grow slowly, putting on a spurt after rain and being more or less dormant during dry times. When less than a metre high they grow only

Top: Desert oaks have thick fibrous bark that insulates the sap from fire. Above: Seed cones of the desert oak beside the small red female flowers. The needles are leaf stalks that function as leaves. The leaves themselves are minute and virtually functionless.

Top: The flowers of this crimson foxtail are wrapped in fine hairs. Hairs trap a layer of air on the leaves, stems and buds of many arid zone plants, thus minimising water loss to hot dry winds. Above: The white stems of the colony wattles reflect heat and so protect the trees' sap flow during times of excessive heat.

a few centimetres a year. Once their root system is established, when they have grown to about 2 metres, they grow as much as 30 centimetres a year. Really large oaks may be hundreds of years old, some people suggest even 1000 years, but there is no way of knowing for there are no annual growth rings in the tree's wood.

The desert oak's leaves are structured in such a way that water loss through them is reduced to a minimum. The characteristic needles that sigh and whisper in the wind are made up of a number of segments. At each join there are minute scales. These are the leaves and they are virtually functionless. The joins in the leaf stalks are marked by grooves and it is in these grooves that the stomata, the breathing pores, are hidden. Having needles that function as leaves helps to conserve moisture in two ways: being derived from leaf stalks instead of being true leaves, the needles have fewer stomata; and being hidden in grooves, the stomata have protection from the drying winds. In the wattles the leaves have not merely been reduced to tiny scales, they have disappeared altogether. The leaf stalks, called phyllodes, have assumed their shape and their function, and they also help to minimise moisture loss. Only as tiny seedlings do wattles have true leaves.

The desert oak's needles have two other adaptations: they droop or weep down so that the least surface area is exposed to the hot sun and they are a grey-green colour that reflects more heat and light than bright-green leaves do. These characteristics are shared by many of the trees and shrubs including such eucalypts as mallees and bloodwoods.

Fine hairs also help to reduce moisture loss and they cover the leaves of many arid zone species such as the sand hibiscus and the silvertails. The hairs trap a layer of air on the leaf surface so that there is less evaporation from the dry winds. Other plants such as the heath myrtles and fringe myrtles have leaves so reduced in size that they are no more than scales on the branches. Native hop bushes, some wattles and other species have waxy, resinous coverings on their leaves and twigs that also help to reduce moisture loss. Bright white bark, as is found in the colony wattle, and thick fibrous bark, characteristic of desert oaks, corkwoods, some grevilleas and heath myrtles, act as reflectors and insulators respectively to keep the plants' sap cool.

More as a response to low phosphorus levels in the soil than drought, most arid zone perennials have thick hard leaves and woody seed capsules. It is a phenomenon also found in plants growing on sandy soils in higher rainfall areas. A preponderance of shrubs and small trees, plants with thick leaves, woody seed capsules, and white or fibrous bark — that and the all-pervasive endemic spinifex — gives the arid zone its uniquely Australian appearance.

The hummocks of spinifex, or porcupine grass, cover some 22 per cent of the

Hard spinifex (left) and soft spinifex growing side by side. Even soft spinifex has needle-sharp points to its leaves.

arid region and plant communities with spinifex as a component cover as much again.* Collectively the various species of spinifex are believed to be Australia's most numerous plants. They certainly are at Uluru-Kata Tjuta. There are four species in the Park. Most common is the hard spinifex, *Triodia basedowii*, followed by the soft or gummy spinifex, *Triodia pungens*, in reference to the strong scent of its resin. (Only species of soft spinifex have resin.) Another species, the aptly named *Triodia irritans*, has a restricted distribution. The fourth kind is the feathertop spinifex, *Plectrachne schinzii*, named after its profuse growth of feathery flowers and seed stems.

Spinifex is abundant on the sandy soils because it can live on very low levels of nutrients, lower than most plants even in Australia. How it is able to do this is still to be discovered. Spinifex also has the ability to fold its leaves lengthways and so close down photosynthesis and other growth systems when there is no soil moisture. During dry spells the plants just sit there, barely ticking over. When it rains the systems are immediately reactivated.

*Some species of spinifex also grow in more humid climates, but always on poor soils.

Typically a spinifex hummock is a clump of closely packed stems. The leaves, the grass blades, fold over after the first dry season and become hard and brittle. A plant, which takes about ten years to grow to maturity, depending on rainfall, is a hemisphere with the sharp tips of the densely packed blades pointing outwards in all directions. Even the soft kinds of spinifex are like heavily armoured impregnable fortresses; protected places where small animals can find sanctuary.

During times of extreme drought or fire the above-ground stems of many perennial plants will die off.* Only the larger trees — the desert oaks, the bloodwoods, river red gums and corkwoods — can endure these forces as entire plants, and sometimes even some of them will perish. But the underground rootstock of most species will remain alive. As soon as there is sufficient rain these plants will grow again, some of them very rapidly. Fire will kill some of the perennials, including the rootstock, most important of which are the wattles. These plants must regenerate from seed, and here too there are adaptations to the dry conditions.

These begin when the plants' flowers are pollinated. Many plants such as the spinifex, other grasses and desert oaks are wind pollinated. In an open windy habitat this is a very effective means of pollination, and it also conserves moisture because the plants do not have to produce nectar to attract animal pollinators. A large percentage of plants, such as the eucalypts, are self-pollinating — that is, they are fertilised without the aid of wind, insects or birds, often before the flowers have opened. Despite the presence of honeyeaters, butterflies and moths, pollination by birds and lepidoptera is not all that common. Only certain eucalypts, grevilleas, corkwoods, shrubs of the genus *Eremophila*, and a few others produce enough nectar to satisfy their appetite. The flowers of most other plants have small quantities of nectar but often generous supplies of pollen. This is the preferred food combination for solitary bees and their larvae of which there are many species in the arid zone.

Seeds once mature are dropped by the plants. Some such as the desert oaks and corkwoods retain their seeds for several years. When the hard capsules do open the winged seeds are carried away by the wind. Other plants, most of the wattles for example, drop their hard seeds below the trees. These seeds are an important food for many animals, from ants to birds and mammals, but enough remain in the ground to ensure regeneration. Seeds may lie in the soil for centuries to await the right conditions of rainfall and temperature to germinate and grow. Many plants have seeds with hard coats that may incorporate a germination inhibitor. This ensures that the seeds will not all germinate at once but after varying lengths of time. If good rains come, only a proportion will germinate. Should this

*The crucial role of fire in the ecosystems is discussed in Chapter Nine.

Ants harvesting seeds.

crop of seedlings perish because there are no follow-up rains, others will germinate the next time or the time after that and so on.

Another group of plants, the ephemerals, must complete their life cycles within a year or even a few months. These are the plants, mostly members of the daisy and pea families, that bring so much colour to the arid zone after heavy rain, especially if that rain is in winter and spring. (Summer rain encourages the growth of native grasses.) The ephemerals have no need for enormous root systems, phyllodes, thick leaves or woody tissues. They are lush, grow quickly, flower profusely and set their seeds. Many have fluffy seeds that travel on the breeze. Their fleshy, and sometimes bright-green leaves soften the otherwise harsh vegetation.

For both ephemerals and perennials, seed dispersal is of great importance. Apart from the wind, animals — especially ants — fulfil that function. When plants drop their seeds, long columns of ants carry them off to their nests. Some seeds are

Top: The seed pods of this dead finish wattle have split open to reveal the black seeds. Each seed is surrounded by a yellow elaiosome. Above: The elaiosome of the seeds of this wattle are white and wormlike. Ants harvest wattle seeds but only eat the elaiosome.

discarded or forgotten along the way and those are of greatest importance from the plants' point of view. They may be carried 50 or even 100 metres from the parent tree or shrub. But for each seed 'planted' by ants in this way hundreds if not thousands are sacrificed. Sometimes ants, and also hopping mice, store seeds in small temporary caches, as an insurance against hard times. These too are sometimes forgotten.

To prevent this wasteful sacrifice of seeds, some plants, certain wattles and pea flowers for example, offer ants a bribe in exchange for the transport of their seeds. In these species each seed has a small appendage of fatty tissue called an elaiosome. This is an attractive and readily available food for the ants who carry the seeds and their appendages to their underground nests. But most ants eat only the elaiosome. The seed itself remains unharmed and lies underground in the insects' nest or is carried out to their rubbish dump, together with all the other detritus of droppings and inedible parts of their prey, and even dead ants. If the seed is not carried too deeply into the nest, both places are excellent seed beds, the rubbish tip especially as it supplies the germinating seeds with extra nutrients. The 'handling' by the ants may also remove the germinating inhibitor or otherwise weaken the hard seed coat and so hasten germination. At Uluru-Kata Tjuta the nests of meat ants are often covered with discarded wattle seeds.

No matter how destructive the forces that assault the tough and hardened perennials and the soft green ephemerals, they will regrow. They will recolonise most habitats, even when these have been reduced to bare ground. As long as it rains occasionally, the vegetation is indestructible.

The two problems that afflict the plant life — erratic rainfall and low soil fertility — also have repercussions for the animal life. The animals must be able to cope with long periods without surface water and to digest the tough woody plants. How do they do it?

Australia's arid zone produces as much grass, 10–15 tonnes per hectare, as the arid areas of North America and southern Africa. Yet in Australia there are no large mammalian herbivores — no marsupial equivalents of herds of zebra and wildebeest, bison and antelope. The reason is simple: Australia's main grass is spinifex. It characterises the landscape of about two-thirds of Australia. But to mammals, its stiff, brittle, hard, rolled and sometimes resinous leaves are not only physically difficult to cope with, but they also contain little food value. Kangaroos, our only large grazing mammals, do not eat spinifex, only the softer more nutritious grasses. In Uluru-Kata Tjuta these are rare, found only in small patches in mulga shrubland and around the fringes of the monoliths where run-off established slightly richer soils.

But look again. There are herbivores among the spinifex, and they are even

Left: There are many hundreds of termite mounds to the hectare. Because the soil at Uluru-Kata Tjuta is sandy and well drained, the termites do not need to build tall towers to keep their nests dry. Most are less than a metre high.
Above: Winged reproductive termites, called alates, emerge from a small slit in a pavement mound. The opening was made by the white workers.

more numerous than the larger mammals of the African savanna. Dotted throughout the spinifex plains are the mounds of termites. In places where the soil is poorly drained and the termites need to build above-ground mounds and towers, their presence is most obvious — they dominate the flat landscape. In the Tanami Desert, for example, well to the north of Uluru-Kata Tjuta, there are as many as 800 mounds to the hectare. In Uluru's well-drained sands tall mounds need not be built but termites are just as numerous. In some areas mounds only about 30–40 centimetres tall are sparsely scattered about. But as well as these there are numerous roughly circular patches of sand about a metre in diameter cleared of all vegetation and debris, as though they had been swept. Unlike the surrouding soil and sand, from which they are barely distinguishable, these pavements are rockhard. These too are made by termites, their so-called pavement mounds.

From their nests the termites build underground tunnels, about 10 centimetres below the surface, to just about every spinifex hummock. A few species march to the spinifex in above-ground columns on overcast days and at night. These are darker than the usual almost-white translucent termites, a protection against the sun's ultraviolet light. The vast majority of termites never see the light of day. Such an insect on its own, only a few millimetres long, withering in the strong light and dry air within minutes, is less than insignificant. But then termites are never on their own and they are never out in the open when it is hot and dry. It is collectively, in their complex and highly efficient social communities, that they are a force that in a large measure determines what other animals live here. They are the only organisms that can eat and digest the spinifex, and also the hard dry dead wood, in significant quantities. Certain grasshoppers and native cockroaches will also eat spinifex but their numbers are small. The heat, the cold and drought have little effect on the termites because they create their own microclimate of a constant 32–35 degrees Celsius and over 90 per cent humidity in their nests.

The harvesting termites of the genera *Drepanotermes* and *Tumulitermes*, rather than the wood-eaters, are important in the spinifex-covered plains and sandridges. Like the spinifex, these termites are unique to Australia. Each colony harbours thousands, in some cases, hundreds of thousands of individuals. There are species with colonies numbering a million termites. In biomass — that is, the combined weight of all the living members — a large termite colony is close to that of a grazing mammal. Each colony can, therefore, be likened to a herbivorous mammal, for in a way it acts like a single being. Each individual termite can be thought of as the equivalent of a single cell in a mammal. These 'cells' communicate and function by obeying complex systems of chemical signals and the postures and gestures of the body and its appendages. The spinifex is, in fact, grazed by enormous herds of stationary herbivores, the termite colonies.

Harvesting termites gather great quantities of dry spinifex and store much of it in galleries in their nests. Should extreme drought or fire destroy their food source, they shut their nests to the outside world and live on these reserves, just as a large mammal would live on its accumulated fat. Always sufficient food is stored to keep the colony ticking over, waiting for rain and regrowth. Well-established termite colonies are long-lived. There are records of some species living in the same mound for fifty years and even 100 years. Theoretically, the colonies are immortal, as new kings and queens, the reproductives, are recruited to replace the ones that die.

Other termites in other habitats are just as common as the spinifex harvesters, sometimes even more so. There are records of 1000 nests per hectare in mulga shrublands.

Termites are a major force throughout the world's warmer climates, but nowhere are they as overwhelmingly important in the structure of the food webs as in Australia's arid zone. Before considering the far-reaching implications of this, it is necessary to mention the other great group of social insects, the ants. Like the termites, ants are social insects living in climate-controlled nests and are, therefore, also ideally suited to the arid zone's cycles of plenty and scarcity. They seem to have taken even greater advantage of it. Ants are far more diverse and possibly just as numerous as the termites.

At the moment some 8800 species of ants have been described in the world. When all the species have been enumerated by scientists this number may swell to 12,000 species, and some estimates reach 20,000. Unfortunately the ants of Australia's arid zone have been little studied. The number of species can only be guessed at. One investigator thinks that there could be as many as 1000 species, which is approximately the same number as in the rainforests of Central America. By contrast, there are only about 350 species of termites in Australia and about 2300 worldwide.

Ants are mostly scavengers and gatherers of nectar and other plant exudates with only a few harvesters of seeds and fierce predators among them. None live on spinifex or dry wood. Just as termites can be likened to the antelopes and bison, the ants are the equivalent of the grasslands' scavengers, the hyenas and jackals. Although they differ in details of their nest building, the social organisation of ants is very similar to that of termites. Several generations live together and there are different castes — workers, soldiers and reproductives — carrying out different functions. The reproductives in ant colonies are queens only, whereas in termite colonies there are both kings and queens. A queen ant mates just once during her lifetime, when she emerges from her nest as a winged adult. If she survives the predators, she will found a new colony on her own. The male dies soon after mating. Like the termites, all the individuals in an ant colony communicate through complex chemical signals and body language.

Ant numbers are even more impressive than those of termites. In a Brazilian rainforest ants of many species live at a density of 8 million individuals per hectare. They share that space with 1 million termites. In the savanna of west Africa, it was discovered, ant density was 7000 nests and 20 million individuals per hectare. A single super colony of ants in Japan contained 307 million individuals in 45,000 interconnected nests spread over 2.7 square kilometres. No figures have been established for Australia's arid zone but ants seem to be as numerous there as anywhere and termites probably more so. Suffice to say ants are everywhere at Uluru-Kata Tjuta.

As one scientist studying ants has said, ants and termites are the superpowers of the insect world. Like other superpowers they are in constant conflict — the ants being the aggressors and the termites the victims and defenders. This war has gone on for most of the 100 million years that the two groups have coexisted. The scientist adds that over that time they have evolved the most elaborate weapons and battle strategies in the animal world. The battles go on constantly and unrelentingly throughout Australia's arid zone. The termites' greatest defence is their impregnable bastions, the hard fortresses they build out of their saliva and

The cockroach Desmozasteria elongata *lives in spinifex tussocks. Cockroaches are among the few organisms other than termites that eat spinifex.*

droppings mixed with soil, brick by minute brick. Each 'brick' is no larger than can be held in the mouthparts of a worker. Their castle walls are so hard that no ant, no matter how powerful its jaws, can penetrate them. To reach their food source most species of termite build covered or underground tunnels, but these are made of a softer substance and more readily breached, if not by ants, certainly by larger animals such as lizards. Here termites are susceptible to attack. The ants, when they discover such a breach, come rushing in with slashing and cutting jaws and venomous stings. Termite soldiers will hasten to defend the ruptured tunnel while workers behind them will work frantically to seal the opening. Some kinds of termites have soldiers with sharp scimitar-shaped jaws, powered by muscles so large that their heads are enormously distended to accommodate them. With these jaws they can literally cut ants in half. Other termite species have soldiers that rely solely on chemical warfare. Their jaws have been fused to form a squirt gun from which they shoot jets of sticky repellent liquid that entangles their adversaries. Their accuracy is impressive, especially as they are completely blind.

More often than not the ants' attacks are rebuffed. The termite workers seal their galleries, sacrificing the soldiers left on the outside. But when the raiders overcome their opponents and penetrate the termite nests, they will devour parts of or even whole colonies.

The main predators on ants are other ants. However, most of the battles fought between ants are over territory, not so much over booty. There are so many species nesting in the soil that space is at a premium. Some kinds avoid territorial battles by going out to forage only when their neighbours are confined to their nests. A species of seed-harvesting ant of the genus *Melophorus*, for example, will build its nest right beside that of the aggressive meat ants. *Melophorus* will come out only when the soil has become too hot for the meat ants to come out. One species of *Melophorus* only emerges when the soil temperature is between 54 degrees and 60 degrees Celsius.

Most ants are scavengers, raiders that set out from their nests singly or in broad columns and then disperse and scour the soil and plants for any small animals, living or dead. Some species will overwhelm and then carve up larger prey, carrying the pieces back to the nest in procession. Other kinds of ants feed on seeds, though few are entirely dependent on that food source, and supplement them with hunted or scavenged insects. The true seed-harvesting ants digest the actual seed, not just the attached elaiosome. Many arid zone plants have seeds with very hard coats. To deal with these, several kinds of seed harvesters have a caste with huge and powerful jaws with which they crack the seeds. The seed kernels are not eaten directly by the workers and soldiers, as their mouthparts can take in only liquid food. The cracked seeds are fed to the larvae who later regurgitate some of the processed food to the brood-tending workers, who in turn distribute it to the others in the nest.

Ants that live on sweet liquids are perhaps the best known of the arid zone species. These are the honey or honey-pot ants. Their food supply is highly irregular, so in times of plenty they store 'honey', not in galleries but inside the bodies of workers. These in effect become honey jars, with enormously distended bodies that are stacked in passages as deep as 2 metres below the surface. True nectar or honey is only part of their food; mostly they collect a substance called honey-dew, which is not secreted by flowers but by other insects. Small insects called lerps tap into the sap of mulga trees and a few other kinds of wattle. The tiny insects live in clusters and cover themselves with brown-coloured scales. After digesting the plant's sap the lerps exude clear drops of sweet honey-dew that are avidly gathered by the workers of the honey-pot ants. At certain times the production of honey-dew is so profuse that the trees and shrubs are covered with syrupy drops as though it had just been raining. Even when the lerps are not producing their honey-dew, the ants tend and protect them. The mulgas do secrete a little nectar, not from their flowers but from tiny nectaries at the base of the phyllodes. The trees supply nectar to keep the ants on the trees and so protect themselves from the attacks of chewing insects, which are removed by the ants. They can afford to give up some carbohydrates from their sap to the lerps. What

Small sap-sucking insects called lerps live underneath the brown scales. They get their food by processing quantities of their host tree's sap, in this case that of a mulga. A by-product of the process is a clear sweet syrup, which the insects exude. These drops of honey-dew are gathered by ants.

they cannot afford is the loss of the scarce nitrogen and phosphorous that is in their leaf tissues.

Other insects seem to have made few concessions to the arid zone's special circumstances of temperature, food and water. This may simply reflect our lack of knowledge. The tens of thousands of insect species have been little studied, so we just do not know of the many adaptations that could exist. Or perhaps insects do not need them. Being small to tiny organisms, they are able to find small niches that insulate them from the rigours of the environment. However, there are a few species within each group — the grasshoppers, bees, wasps, butterflies, moths, beetles, flies, cockroaches and so on — that are especially adapted to dry conditions. Beetles, heavily armoured, so heavily at times that they cannot fly, with a thick cuticle against water loss and heat, do live here, but beetles are far more numerous in humid climates. Among the moths there is an enormous species with a wingspan of 23 centimetres. Its caterpillars, the witchetty grubs, do not feed on their host's leaves or phyllodes, which may become very hard with low nutritional value during drought, and would also expose them to the dehydrating air. Instead the caterpillars feed on the roots of trees or shrubs. Safe and cool underground inside the host's root they eat the growing tissues, for two or perhaps three years, before emerging as moths. The main host for these caterpillars is the witchetty bush, *Acacia kempeana*, a kind of wattle. The huge, white, silky-textured caterpillars are full of yellow fat. In places where the plant hosts grow the witchetty grubs can be very numerous. Part of the reason is that the female moth lays enormous quantities of eggs, as many as 18,000. The eggs are laid in a single mass. When the newly hatched caterpillars are a day or so old they climb to a vantage point, produce long silken strands and on propitious days are carried away on the wind.

Among the vetebrates there is one group that has adapted to the arid zone's special conditions more than any other. This is the reptiles, especially the lizards, and their success is directly related to the spinifex–termite association. They are the predators of the spinifex plains, the equivalent of the lions and cheetahs of the African savanna. So successful are Australia's arid zone reptiles that they are more diverse than in any other habitat in the world, including tropical rainforest; and of all the areas so far studied Uluru-Kata Tjuta has more species of reptiles than any other place its size on earth. Among the skinks alone, thirty species have been found.

Termites rather than ants are the food base for the reptiles. Ants have heavy, indigestible exoskeletons, they sting and are full of formic acid. They are not very attractive prey. Only the thorny devil among the reptiles eats nothing but ants. The insects are part of the diet of the military dragon, and blind snakes will raid ant nests for their larvae and eggs. Reptiles have diversified so spectacularly because of the presence of termites not because of the ants.

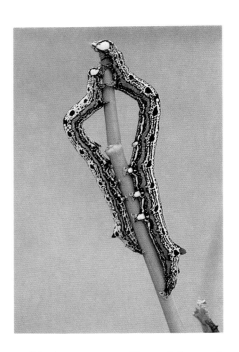

The looper caterpillars of the moth Achaea argilla *feed on a caustic bush, which has a poisonous white sap.*

Top left: A witchetty grub, the caterpillar of a huge moth, inside the root of a witchetty bush, a kind of wattle. The root has been split open to reveal the caterpillar. Top right: Many arid zone grasshoppers show different kinds of camouflage. This katydid lives among eucalypt leaves. Above left: This grasshopper looks like a flake of bark. Above right: This flightless carabid beetle of the genus Euryscaphus *comes out at night to ambush other insects. It seizes its prey with its scissor-like serrated jaws.*

Chlorobalius leucoviridis is a katydid widely distributed throughout the arid zone.

The defenceless soft-bodied termites are easily taken from their feeding tunnels and are at least part of the diet of most of the small lizards — the dragons, geckoes, snake-lizards, smaller goannas, and especially the smooth and shiny skinks. Many lizards, most frequently the skinks that live underground, break into the termites' feeding tunnels. These sand-swimming lizards have very small limbs that in some cases are reduced to mere stumps or flaps pressed against the body. Other reptiles invade above-ground tunnels or burrow under the logs that the insects may be attacking. The spinifex plants themselves also play a role. Each grass hummock is a spiny retreat safe from most predators and gives protection from the sun and the drying winds. Small insects live within them and provide prey in addition to termites. In the mulga shrublands, where the soil is more clayey and difficult to penetrate, reptiles are fewer.

Another adaptation of the reptiles, one similar to that of the social insects, makes them further suited to the arid zone. The reptiles are able to obtain all their moisture needs from the insects they eat. They do not have to drink, though many of them will if water is available. Being cold-blooded they can retreat to

Seventy-two species of reptiles have been recorded at Uluru-Kata Tjuta, making it the most species-rich area for reptiles so far studied in the world. The great diversity is mainly the result of a special association between the lizards, spinifex and termites.
Left: The skink Ctenotus grandis.
Below: The short-tailed pygmy goanna is the smallest of all the goannas. It fits easily on a person's hand.

HAWTHORN SECONDARY COLLEGE
BURGESS STREET
EAST HAWTHORN, 3123

The western scaly foot. The vestigial flaplike hind limb is just visible along the lizard's body, directly beneath the head.

cool, damp burrows when food becomes scarce and there remain torpid, living off their reserves for long periods. Times of hardship are often not as long as might be expected from the desolate appearance of the land in dry times. Termites will continue to feed on dry plant material for many, many months after the last rainfall, and ants and lizards will continue to feed on them.

In the warm arid zones of other continents lizards are diverse, but nothing like what we see in Australia. An additional reason to their association with termites is that the predators on small reptiles in other places are mostly birds and mammals with only a few reptiles among them. In Australia it is the reverse. Only a few birds and fewer mammals hunt down reptiles. In Australia's arid zone the main predators on reptiles are other reptiles — chief among them those voracious, bold marauders, the goannas. They add to the species diversity. There are thirty-five species in the world of which twenty-four exist in Australia and twenty of these are found only on this continent. Most of them occur in the arid zone, six of them at Uluru-Kata Tjuta. These include the giant perentie, the orange and yellow patterned sand goanna and the exquisite pygmy goanna, which is so small it easily fits on a person's hand.

Lizards and snakes are a colourful, abundant and diverse part of the National Park's fauna, but their extent was discovered only over the last decade during intensive fauna surveys. The reptiles are secretive, hiding in spinifex, burrows or the sand itself, and many come out only at night.

Even more rarely seen are the frogs. They have become adapted to the dry conditions by avoiding them altogether. Whenever it is not actually raining, or at least very humid, the frogs burrow vertically down into the ground. Here they live in sealed cells, for many years if necessary, on the water and food reserves stored in their bodies. Their metabolism is slowed down to such a degree that they need miniscule amounts of energy — they seem to be barely alive.

Most birds also disappear when food and water run low. Those living in the arid zone have had to become nomads. But this region is so vast that there will always be places somewhere that are green with growing plants and bursting with all kinds of insects. Among the birds there are no out-and-out termite feeders. Lizards are eaten by many, from kingfishers to eagles, but none is a specialist reptile hunter. There are nectar-feeders, insectivores, seed-eaters, predators and scavengers. All get a rich harvest after substantial rain but most quickly move on again when resources diminish. The influx of birds can be spectacular as described earlier in these pages, and the seasons of 1992–93 were a dramatic example of the birds' movements at Uluru-Kata Tjuta.

After good rains in winter and spring birds were abundant and nesting everywhere. There was no significant rain over the summer months, and by March the country looked brown and dry without flowers. Birds were few. Only the non-nomadic species — the wrens, whitefaces, thornbills, willie wagtails, butcherbirds and a few others — were present in small numbers. The waterholes around the monoliths were drying up rapidly. Many birds, especially such seed-eaters as budgerigars and finches, must drink every day. A number of them perished at the dry waterholes; they had left it too late to move on. In January and March there were flood rains to the west and north. Temporary lakes and marshes were formed, attracting waterbirds from far and wide. Some of these made emergency landings at Uluru-Kata Tjuta on their migrations — a pink-eared duck and grey teal in the swimming pool at the Ayers Rock resort at Yulara, whiskered terns, hoary-headed and little grebes, white-faced herons and two pelicans at the sewage ponds. A white-necked heron died of starvation at Uluru's Mutitjulu waterhole.

Large native mammals are few in the arid zone. There are only kangaroos — the red, the grey, the euro and a few species of wallaby. At Uluru-Kata Tjuta a small number of red kangaroos subsist on the grasses in the mulga shrublands. More palatable grasses grow on the outwash plains surrounding the monoliths

The desert banded snake burrows through sand in pursuit of small lizards.

and here the tough, stocky euro is often to be seen. There are no grey kangaroos or wallabies.

Small to minute native mammals are more numerous and diverse, though there is nothing like the abundance of the reptiles. These exquisitely furred and shaped rodents and marsupials can survive without drinking, like the reptiles and insectivorous birds. They conserve moisture by living in burrows by day and coming out only at night. They can also concentrate their urine. All the water they need they extract from their food, be it seeds, grass or insects. There are eight species of small terrestrial mammals in Uluru-Kata Tjuta: three are rodents that eat seeds and herbage, the others live on insects and are marsupials. Most of the insectivores would eat significant amounts of termites and at least two of them, the marsupial mole and the mulgara, prey on lizards. Both mammals are rare. There are also eight species of insectivorous bats hawking the night sky.

Once eleven species of medium-sized mammals, about the size of a cat, roamed these plains and dunes. They seemed to live on a knife-edge, dying out over large areas during severe droughts and colonising them again from refuges after flood rains. These were the hare-wallabies, bettongs, possums, bandicoots and a species of rock wallaby. All but one of them have disappeared from Uluru-Kata Tjuta, some survive in isolated, remote pockets and some have become extinct. The surviving medium-sized mammal, the echidna, significantly lives exclusively on termites and ants.

Few birds are especially adapted to the arid zone. Many species found at Uluru-Kata Tjuta, like this boobook owl, occur throughout Australia.

To sum up, Australia's arid zone is vast and like no other. The root cause of its uniqueness is the combination of poor soils and totally unpredictable rainfall in both quantity and the time of year it falls. The plants, including the most prolific grasses, the uniquely Australian spinifex, have adapted to these conditions by becoming hard and woody. The diversity of plants is much as it is in the warm-to-hot arid zones in other parts of the world. But the appearance of the land is very different; here there are far more woody shrubs and even trees. These can become established because of sporadic heavy downpours. The hard vegetation and the unpredictable rainfall pattern favour such social insects as ants and especially termites whose way of life is perfectly suited to take advantage of the vagaries of climate and soil. As a consequence, the numbers of these insects in both species and as individuals are as great as they are in the wet tropics. These colonial insects have taken the place of the large herbivores and predators of the grasslands of other continents. Just as termites are so well adapted to the hard vegetation, so reptiles and especially lizards have proliferated to take advantage of the numerous soft-bodied insects as a food source. They have done this so successfully that Australia's arid zone lizard fauna is more diverse than that of any other habitat, arid or humid, in the world. Bird diversity and abundance is much as it is in other dry places around the world but in Australia they are enhanced by the presence of many colourful species of parrots and cockatoos. Unlike in other continents, mammals of any size are few, the small mammals being the most diverse. All these arid zone characteristics of climate, soil and adaptations are clearly represented at Uluru-Kata Tjuta; it is truly Australia's arid zone in microcosm.

A few of the arid zone's broad landforms — salt lakes, gibber plains or stony deserts, bare unvegetated dunes and rocky hill ranges — are not represented at Uluru-Kata Tjuta. But three of them occur very close to its boundaries. Just to the north is Lake Amadeus, a large salt lake surrounded by bare sandhills. To the west are the Petermann Ranges, a typical rocky range of hills. Maybe one day they will be part of Uluru-Kata Tjuta National Park, making it even more representative of the arid zone.

The above is a view of Uluru-Kata Tjuta as it appears to Piranpa naturalists and scientists. It is a view long on theory, the taking of measurements, the intellectual search for patterns and the wide objective view; but short on detailed knowledge of individual species, intuitive affinity with the land, personal attachments, and a religious conviction — based on the land and all its inhabitants — that binds humans, wildlife and landforms together.

For people of another culture, Anangu, it is the reverse. The land, the plants and animals are seen in a direct, finely observed relationship. Knowledge of individual species is detailed and local, and fits into a philosophical framework. It had to, for these people lived entirely on and off the lands of which Uluru-Kata Tjuta was the focus. They did not need or desire anything material or spiritual from outside this area. Their vision of the world went well beyond the monoliths, but worldwide patterns, measurements and intellectual exercises were not their long suit. They lived their entire lives bound up with the land and, before European settlement, lived very well.

There is a middle ground where the two cultures' knowledge and appreciation of the land overlap. This middle ground has only recently been explored by both cultures with mutual goodwill and respect, and it is hoped with benefit to both. This exchange was largely pioneered at Uluru-Kata Tjuta and continues in the Park's joint management.

TRACKS

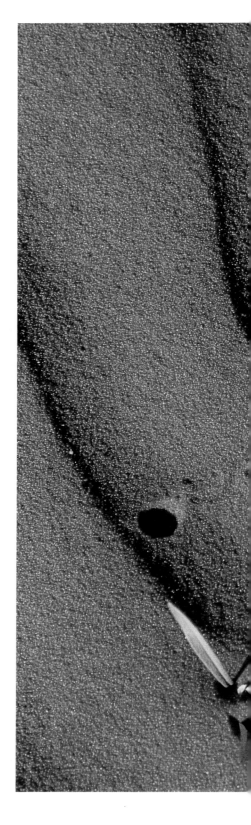

Apart from the red kangaroo, euro, dingo and emu there are no large native animals at Uluru. Only the dingo is common. All but one of the medium-sized mammals, a wide variety of bandicoots, bettongs, hare-wallabies and even some rodents are extinct. So the dense patterns of tracks I see in the sand everywhere are almost entirely made by small to tiny animals, their passages written in a fine handwriting. Luckily the sand is a perfect medium. The smallest toes and the lightest footfalls leave their marks.

For months now I have puzzled over these bewildering scrawls of hieroglyphics. A few I can tentatively identify — the slither of a snake, the unmistakable prints of a bird, the pads of a dingo. Sometimes I see a large beetle struggle through the sand leaving its imprint or a thorny devil lumbering along making its characteristic trail. But most tracks are indecipherable. I need an interpreter. There is none better than Edith Imantura Richards. To her the tracks are a clear text, an open book that she reads in great detail and with a casual ease that comes from long practice. Reading tracks is routine to her but, I suspect, never dull. She enjoys telling interested people about the plants and the animals, to share her knowledge with them.

But like most Anangu at Uluru, Edith is not fluent in English. She can only express her thoughts and her knowledge properly in Pitjantjatjara. I know nothing of the language. This early morning Julian Barry has agreed to interpret for us. He is the Park's training officer and is close to the Anangu. In a way he has been adopted by them. Edith is his aunt in the kinship assigned to him. The two make an interesting contrast. Edith, in her late thirties, is bare-headed and round-faced with a ready laugh. She is of medium height. Julian is tall and has a wiry frame. His face is lean, covered in freckles and with a skin that cannot take the fierce sun. He wears a hat with an enormous brim. Both are dressed in the uniform of Park staff. Edith wears the khaki-coloured version, Julian is in green.

Today is perfect for tracking. It is cool and as yet there is no breeze, though later in this late summer's day it will be hot and inevitably windy. Then the finer tracks left by the night animals will be distorted or even erased. The sun rises over the horizon as we wander across a wide swale between sandhills with commanding views of Uluru. Only when the sun's rays are low are the tracks thrown into clear relief. Later they will be more difficult to read.

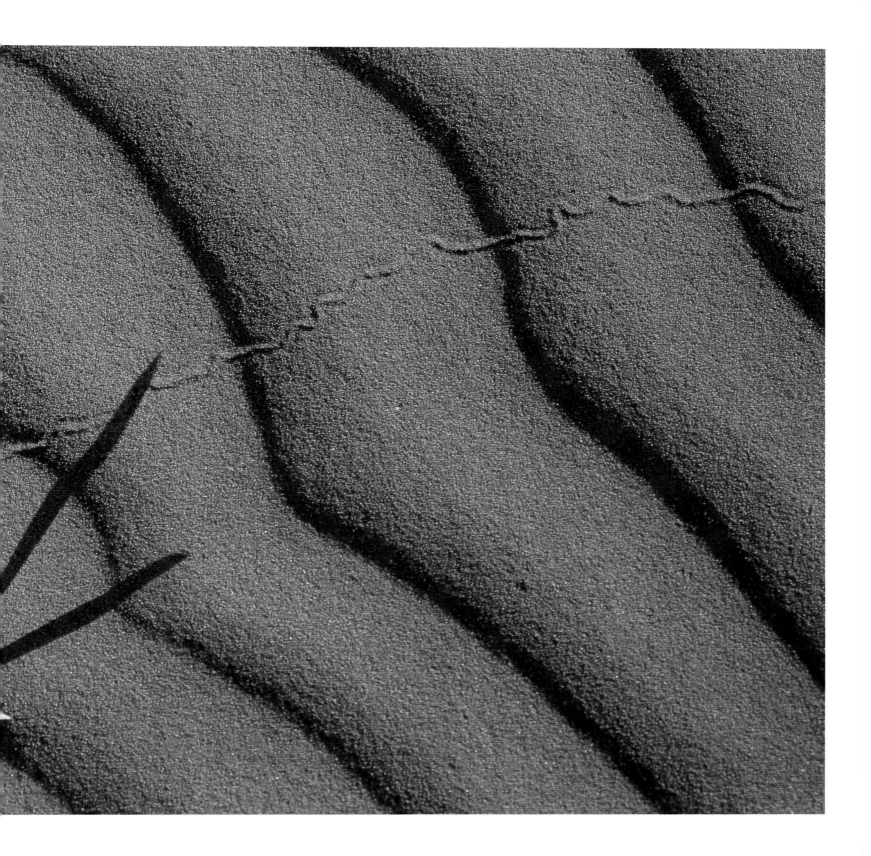

Previous pages: Tracks made by lukupupu, *the ant lion. Above: Edith Imantura Richards, expert tracker and senior ranger.*

Edith hits her stride immediately, pointing out the slightly faded tracks of a sand goanna. Goannas do not come out during the night, so the tracks are yesterday's. Edith points out the sinuous mark left by the lizard's tail, the clear prints of its large feet and how it drags its toes, scoring four parallel lines in the sand. At times Edith is almost as difficult to read as the tracks, and Julian and I have to concentrate hard to follow all that she indicates and says. She talks quietly with great economy of words. Her pointing gestures are subtle — a slight flick of the wrist or a barely raised finger. We follow the goanna tracks for a while. We see where it dug out prey, mostly burrowing spiders, Edith deduces. At one place there is a larger excavation and here the big lizard caught a smaller one, possibly a skink, and ate it. Edith tells us how a female goanna digs a deep burrow to lay her five or six eggs and then fills it in again. Months later, when the eggs have hatched, the goanna will return and dig out her young.

A patch of bare sand between clumps of spinifex is filled with squiggles, lines, dots and foot imprints. We squat down for a better look. Edith, in rapid-fire Pitjantjatjara, speaks about the animal that made a pattern of looping, curving tracks. They were made by a blind snake or legless lizard, *kuyi* she calls it, that moved just beneath the surface. Both kinds of *kuyi* are thin, shiny sand-swimmers that catch insects and spiders. Judging by their tracks they must be very numerous, yet I rarely see one. Diagonally across the sandpatch goes a trail that looks as if it had been made by a miniature caterpillar tractor. It might be a small track but Edith assures us it was made by a very large centipede, one that would be capable of giving a painful bite. She also points out a set of parallel lines of dots and dashes, *niri-niri* she says, a kind of beetle or cricket. 'It makes a lot of noise at night', she adds. A crisp straight line flanked by long-toed footprints leads from one spinifex clump to another. 'That's where *tjati* ran across very fast. They do not live in holes in the ground but shelter in the spinifex. The male has bright yellow and red colours.' I have seen these military dragons, usually dashing at incredible speed between spinifex clumps. Edith also points out the scattered tracks of *tarkawara*, hopping mice, and of *mingkiri*, unspecified 'mice'.

On the far side of the sandpatch Edith spots something of greater interest. She points at what to me look like a series of ill-formed scuff marks. Moving along at normal walking pace, Edith follows these tracks for several hundred metres, picking up the trail without seeming to try. I lose it time and time again and would have needed to backtrack constantly, peering closely at the ground. The tracks, joined by two or three others, disappear down a well-maintained burrow. 'This is the home of *tjakura*', Edith says, the large beautifully coloured great desert skink. She tells us the skinks live in an extensive burrow system that goes deep into the ground. The male and female live down there with their family. As well as the tunnels going down at a low angle, there are smaller, vertical popholes

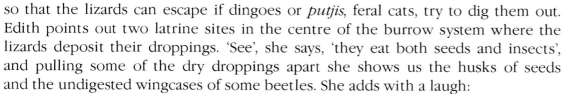

Left: Edith shows Nyinku Jingo, her understudy in tracking, where a poisonous snake caught and ate a small lizard. Above: The great desert skink.

so that the lizards can escape if dingoes or *putjis*, feral cats, try to dig them out. Edith points out two latrine sites in the centre of the burrow system where the lizards deposit their droppings. 'See', she says, 'they eat both seeds and insects', and pulling some of the dry droppings apart she shows us the husks of seeds and the undigested wingcases of some beetles. She adds with a laugh:

> They're also very good tucker, they're large and muscular. But you have to be careful when you catch them because if you grab them by the tail, the tail will come off. It will regrow later.

One of the rangers had told me that when she was on a fauna survey on Pitjantjatjara lands hundreds of kilometres away, she showed the Anangu there a photograph of this great desert skink. The people did not recognise it and could not name it. But when the ranger said its Pitjantjatjara name was *tjakura*, they immediately recognised that and then told her all the things Edith had just told us. The lizard was extinct in the region, but the Anangu's knowledge about it lives on.

This prompts me to ask Edith about some of the animals that are no longer

The tracks of a large beetle crossing those of a lizard.

seen around Uluru. She says she knew the mallee fowl when she was living at Docker River, close to the Western Australian border. She ate some and they were very good. She ate a bandicoot too once and it was also good tucker, as were possums because they live on figs, bloodwood flowers and the fruits of the quandong tree. But as she says:

> That was all long ago, when the old people were young. A lot of these animals are finished up altogether now like the mala [rufous hare-wallaby], *tjungku* [burrowing bettong] and *nyulu* [golden bandicoot]. Even *waru* [rock wallaby] is finished around here. We don't see them but the people still tell the *Tjukurpa* stories about them. Now there are rabbits, foxes and feral cats. Some of them are good tucker.

We have reached the base of a dune. Edith points out the broad track of *kuniya*, a woma python, where it pushed itself over the sand. It made a straight track, so it was moving along unhurriedly. When it needs to move quickly, Edith explains, it throws its muscular coils and leaves a zigzag trail. Patches of sand between spinifex hummocks are dissected by lines of small footprints and tail drag marks. *Mutinka*, Edith calls the animals that made them, which are various kinds of skinks. This is a collective name for many different species. From their tracks it is impossible to tell one from another. Even when you actually see one of these lizards, usually darting for cover, it is difficult to identify precisely. For example, there are thirteen kinds of skinks of the genus *Ctenotus* alone at Uluru. All are smooth, glossy, long-tailed lizards patterned in stripes and spots. Edith's comment sums them up perfectly. 'There's lots of them, all the same but all a little bit different.'

Tacking back and forth up the sandhill is the track a miniature python would make if it were in a hurry. '*Liru*', Edith says. Again this is a general name for a group of species, venomous snakes in this case. This snake 'hopped' along, Edith says — that is, it threw its coils, moving fast. We follow the trail to the edge of a spinifex clump where it becomes a mass of convoluted and intertwining *liru* and *kuyi*, blind snake, tracks. What happened here, Edith points out, was that the venomous snake caught the blind snake under the spinifex, dragged it — struggling — backwards into the open, swallowed it and moved on.

A gravid thorny devil, which Edith calls ngiyari, *leaving its tracks in the sand.*

Even though all venomous snakes are *liru*, several species have their own specific name. In order to find out the names of some I show Edith photographs of them. The western brown snake she calls *walalara*, a burrowing snake is *mulyapurkutitja*, which sounds wonderful if you say it quickly. When I showed her a picture of an obviously large mulga snake, Edith draws in her breath. '*Liru*', she says softly in a way that indicates that this is *the liru*, the ultimate *liru*. 'A dangerous fellow that one', she says. 'He eats rock wallabies.'

Edith is so skilled in detecting tiny and subtle differences in the various tracks that she can tell one *liru* from another just by the marks they leave. She can tell to which exact species it belongs by the shape of the curves and by the way the snake's belly scales made contact with the sand. She explains this to me cursorily in a tone of voice that says 'Must I explain the obvious?', though not unkindly. It is a tracking skill that needs time and a special aptitude to acquire. I cannot tell one *liru* track from another.

Halfway up the sandhill Edith points out two parallel lines of small footprints. These were made by *ngiyari*, a thorny devil, a small, grotesquely shaped spiny lizard. Edith explains these are very common and can be seen everywhere there are ants. They eat only ants. Even in a drought, she says, when most animals are scarce, there are lots of *ngiyari*. We follow the track to the top of the dune. Pointing to where the lizard seemed to have buried itself in the sand or at least wriggled about in it, Edith explains that it had performed *inma*, a ceremonial dance, there and that it was a female. I ask her if she has ever seen such a dance and what

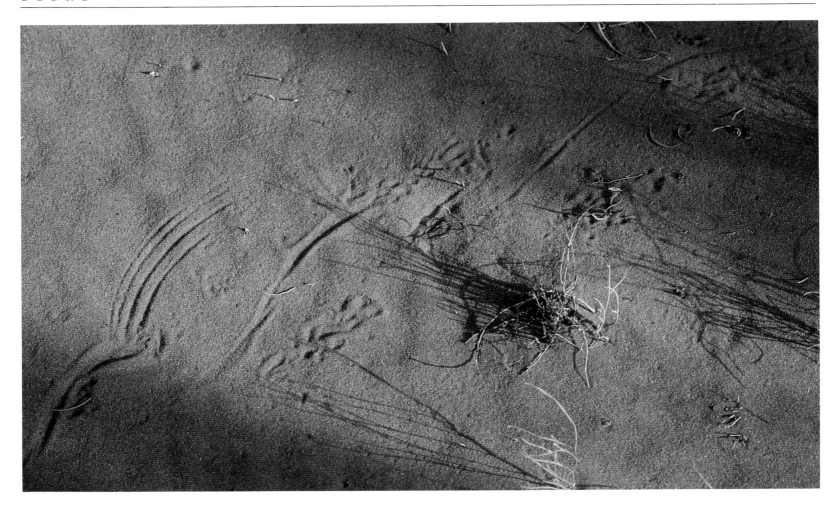

Tracks of a sand goanna.

it looked like. She says it is part of the *Tjukurpa* and changes the subject. It is a clear sign not to press my questions as I am getting close to matters that are *miil-miilpa*, secret-sacred, that cannot be revealed to the uninitiated. I have read in a text on reptile behaviour, however, that the female thorny devil when mounted by an unwanted male will dislodge him by spinning around and so throwing him off, apparently in a lightning-quick movement, uncharacteristic of this slow-moving lizard.

The sun is well above Uluru and the first flies descend on us. A pallid cuckoo calls. 'That is *wititata*', Edith says. 'When it calls, the sun comes out hot.' But not yet.

For some time now we have seen occasional prints like those of a tiny kangaroo. These belong to *tarkawara*, the spinifex hopping mouse. *Tarkawara*, Julian translates, means 'long bone' or 'long shank', and refers to the rodent's elongated

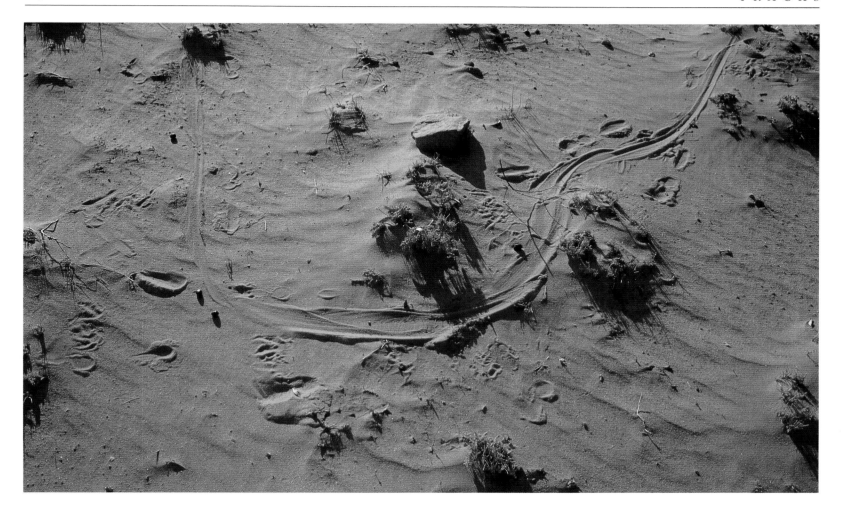

hindfeet. Several of their tracks converge, almost making a pathway. Edith says:

Red kangaroo tracks, showing the drag marks of the tail, and impressions of the front feet (on the left) and the elongated hind feet.

> Those tracks are very fresh. See, they have only just gone, at sunrise. They ran home frightened by the dingo, its tracks are just over here. At daylight the *tarkawara* go down their holes, which go straight down. Here they are. See, there are four holes. Once inside they close the burrow behind them, digging like this.

Edith demonstrates, digging the sand with her fingers pressed closely together.

> Snakes cannot get them now. They live in families in burrows, in nests made out of grass and things. At night they come out again and eat the seeds of plants. Here you can see it has eaten the seeds of this umbrella bush, these

are the husks. Over there they dug the fallen seeds of a honey grevillea out of the sand. They also eat grass, like a kangaroo. In the dry time they gather seeds and other food and store it in a small hole they dig in the ground. In good seasons they have many babies and they run around everywhere with them.

Judging by the tracks, *tarkawara* are very numerous at the moment. There was a good spring.

A whole host of other small mammals — some marsupials that eat mostly insects, others rodents — live at Uluru. Again, Edith tells us, there is a collective name for all of them — *mingkiri*. Another senior Anangu explained the use of a general name as well as particular names of individual species, as follows:

> *Anula* [long-haired rat] is the same as *mingkiri*. There are many animals that are *mingkiri* but have different names, just as there are lots of *liru* that have different names. They live in different places in different countries, not just Uluru and Kata Tjuta. If it has a big tail, a fat tail, not long, it is *murtja* [mulgara]; if it has long legs, it is *tarkawara*; if it has lots of fur, it is *anula*.

Mingkiri tracks are everywhere. Edith points to one set with a slight nod of the head and says, 'This *mingkiri* was tired in the knees', which, Julian says, means it is pregnant. The tracks are perhaps fractionally deeper or further apart, but to me they look like all the other *mingkiri* tracks. But another set looks very different, even to my eyes. The feet are larger and, unlike the others, which were just round depressions in the sand, these tracks show the imprint of footpads and toes. *Murtja*, a special *mingkiri*, Edith says. Indeed it is, for these are the tracks of a mulgara, one of the rarest and largest marsupial carnivores surviving in central Australia.

Suddenly something clicks in my memory. We have seen the burrows of *tjakura*, the great desert skink, the tracks of *kuniya*, the woma python, and now those of *murtja*, the mulgara. Edith has brought us to a very special place. Quickly I ask if she has ever seen *itjaritjari*, the marsupial mole, here. 'Yes', she says, then continues:

> But they don't like coming out when it is hot. That's why we don't see any tracks now. They come out in the early mornings or late afternoons in the cooler seasons, especially when it rains. Then they come out and dig around on top of the sand. When *itjaritjari* sees you, it digs down into the sand and goes down really fast. They just lie in the sand, they don't make a burrow or anything.

The sandplain sweeping towards Uluru and flanked by sandhills not only provides spectacular views of the Rock but is also a vital refuge for many animal species in times of severe drought. Were it not for refuges of this kind, many more species would be extinct. These sandplains seem to be slightly richer in soil nutrients and soil moisture, which maintain the plants longer and in better condition during severe droughts and so in turn support the animal life. The 'enrichment' is so slight that it is barely measurable, yet is sufficient to ensure the survival of key species and a nucleus of most small mammals and reptiles. In times where there is no useful rain at all for years on end it is in these refuges the animals just manage to survive. They perish just about everywhere else. When good seasons return, as they always do, the animal numbers build up quickly and they recolonise the other 'poorer' habitats again.

It is impossible to recognise such a refuge from the topography or the plant species. One theory suggests that these special places overlie buried, ancient drainage lines that beneath the surface still trickle towards Lake Amadeus. The land is too flat for any surface drainage system. So far the only indicator for such vital refuges is the presence of these four special animals together — great desert skink, woma, mulgara and marsupial mole. Unlike the other species that radiate out quickly from the sandplains during good seasons, these four animals only emigrate out of there during long runs of good seasons. For them the sandplains are home rather than a refuge. There are several such places in and around Uluru. Unfortunately, the larger more important one is outside the Park boundary.

It is warm now. Lizards come out to hunt insects. Edith points out fresh tracks and we see scaly bodies dash for cover. We follow the trail of a small *liru*. Even to my eyes it seems exceptionally fresh. As I look up to search for the snake, Edith has already spotted the long tail slowly moving into the spinifex. I make a quick grab for it and pull a Burton's snake-lizard from its hiding place. Luckily, I did not pull too hard or its tail would have come off. This lizard has only rudimentary legs reduced to flaps pressed to the sides of its body. Edith calls it a snake with no legs but small feet, a *liru*, yet not a *liru*. It has its own name, *tiin-tiinpa*. According to the *Tjukurpa* this lizard and the true *liru*, the poisonous snakes, are related, therefore both are *liru*. Edith is not sure if it has a venomous bite for, she says, it is too *tjami*, or timid and faint-hearted, even to bite. She adds that at night these snake-lizards climb to the tops of spinifex bushes where they whistle. This whistling is connected with a ceremony involving this species. Piranpa scientists and naturalists have not recorded this sound so far. But that is of no great significance. Many points of natural history were learnt from Anangu before they were observed by Piranpa, such as goannas digging hatchlings from sealed burrows and hopping mice caching food.

Pointing to a line of tiny footprints, Edith says, 'These are made by *papangaurpa*'. Julian explains that this word actually means 'dog growling'. 'When angry or scared',

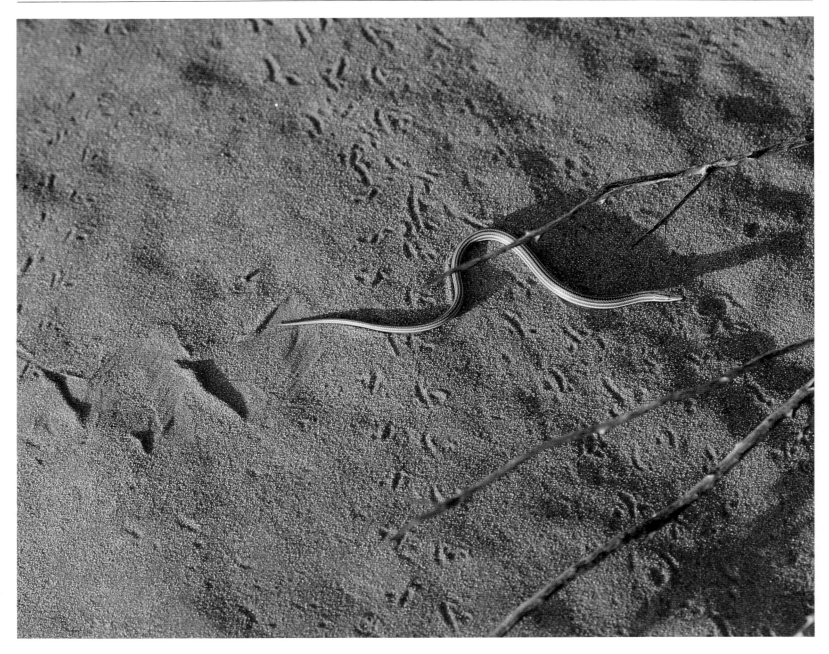

A Burton's snake-lizard, a kind of liru, *hastens for the cover of spinifex.*

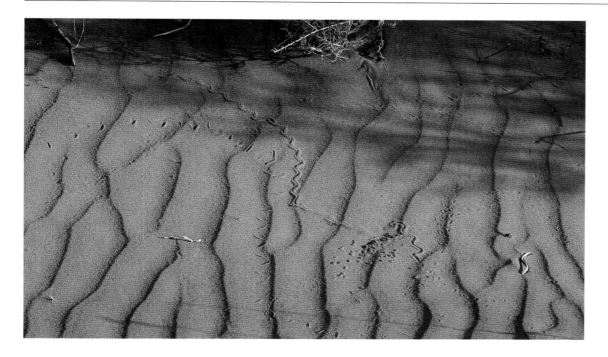

Edith continues, 'it growls like a dog'. Making circles around her eyes with her thumbs and index fingers she says in English 'big eyes'. These knob-tailed geckoes can see in the dark, she says, but have now gone into their burrows to escape the heat and the light.

Crossing this trail of fine and delicate footprints is one of another lizard, a bulldozer by comparison. It is a broad drag mark with impressions of stumpy feet on either side, made by a large, fat *lungkata*, a blue-tongued lizard, pushing its belly over the sand. It reminds me of the story of one of the rangers who had been out working with Edith. They came across large swirling marks and deep gouges in the sand. They were made by *walawuru*'s, the wedge-tailed eagle's, wings and claws as it swooped down to catch a blue-tongued lizard. The tracks, according to Edith, showed the bird had missed. A little further on was a similar set of tracks. Missed again. The eagle had been successful in its third attempt. A few strips of skin and some bones were all that remained of the lizard. Everyone working with Anangu at Uluru has their favourite 'tracking with Edith' story.

The sun is hot now. Four pink cockatoos fly over us as we sit for a while in the shade of an umbrella bush — a well-named species of wattle. A singing honeyeater scolds us briefly then flies to another bush. A *kaanka*, a crow, lands not far from us, eyeing us speculatively. Edith says its Pitjantjatjara name in a way that sounds just like the bird's call. A few crested pigeons pick up seeds, missed

Above left: The zigzag tracks were made by a small liru, *probably a snake-lizard, and the sinuous track is that of a partly buried* kuyi, *or blind snake. Above: A centralian blue-tongued lizard wanders up a sandhill, leaving its characteristic tracks.*

A large flightless beetle of the sandhills.

by the hopping mice, from the sand. A breeze springs up and soon finer tracks will disappear.

I ask Edith when she first came to Uluru. She says:

I came in a motor car with Mr Mike, a Christian minister. He came from Sydney and used to look after us when we were small children. He was old even then. He's dead now, poor man, and in the cemetery.

Swivelling around and pointing to the west, she continues:

I was coming along this bendy, rubbishy bush road in a motor car, not like the flash new ones the rangers drive, but a really old one. That is when I saw Uluru for the first time. It was so big I got scared. That was a long time ago when I could buy a dress for 20 cents at Ernabella.

And how did you learn to track so well, where and when did you learn about the animals?

I was born at a place of Liru *Tjukurpa* not far from Docker River, and grew up all around that place. There was no school there then and I lived outside. My *Tjukurpa* ['totem', or 'dreaming', would be the nearest equivalent] is *mangata*, the quandong tree. I am responsible for looking after the *inma*, the ceremony, and associated objects for that. I learnt tracking while travelling all round the bush and asking, 'What is this track? What is that track? What is this tree and that tree?', and I was told. I'd keep asking and people kept telling me. My grandmother, grandfather, aunt, uncle, mother, father tell me anyway. 'This tree, can I eat this tree?' 'Yes, you can eat that tree.'

Edith takes the various parts in these conversations, a little girl's voice for the questions and a deeper voice for the answers:

Sometimes they'd say this one is a poison tree, don't touch it, but this one here is food. We'd travel around with our feet on the earth to learn. By listening and travelling around and asking lots of questions, I learnt about all these things. During afternoons in the shade in camp I'd really listen hard as people told the stories, and then I'd have a sleep. I also learnt about *Tjukurpa* stories. I learnt from the time when we moved around from rockhole to rockhole, the way people have always learnt. There was lots of water around, you just had to know where to look for it. It was spring water from the rockholes. We pass this information on, it is very important. In the old days we travelled from rockhole to rockhole so we wouldn't die of thirst. 'I'm tired, I want to stop', I might say. But my mother would insist, 'Don't stop now or you might die'. All the older people know that. The country was full of *Tjukurpa* and that is how I learnt it.

In summer when it was very hot we sat in camp in the shade in the afternoon. Sometimes it was so hot and dry that all the grass disappeared. Then there was little tucker. But that was no big worry, we'd always find something to eat. At other times there was plenty of grass and plants for bush tucker. In winter there was food everywhere — honey ants, witchetty grubs, rabbits, emus, kangaroos. We were happy, we didn't mind the cold. In the old days, no worries.

I ask Edith when she moved to Uluru.

I tried working here when the tourists were still staying at Mutitjulu. Then we had the big meeting; that was the Land Rights time and the tourists moved to Yulara [in 1983]. Myself and a lot of others went to Yulara and planted the trees when they were building the resort. We did that to earn money. Then after Handback I became a ranger and now I look after all the wildlife. That is good work. I look after the trees and talk about them. I go out tracking, showing people the tracks of animals and I teach people about the Anangu names for all the animals and plants, and about bush tucker. And we look after the *Tjukurpa* of all this place.

It is okay that the tourists come here but they too have to learn. They might look in books and say, 'Look, this rock fig, this bush tomato and these mulga seeds are all bush tucker', and learn that way. But they should also learn a little bit about *Tjukurpa* because that is really important. There is strong *Tjukurpa* here and it should be talked about strongly. You have to talk strongly for the ground, for the stories, for the hills, for the trees, for all the animals that walk around in this land, and for all of their names. That is why we have to talk strongly about *Tjukurpa*, for the continuity of life. From the *Tjukurpa* the names have become like stone, things have become strong.

To do this we work together, white [National Park staff] and black. Together we look after all the plants and animals. We teach the white rangers how to do this and about the *Tjukurpa* too, for looking after this country is about looking after the *Tjukurpa*. I enjoy telling the stories and talking about the plants and animals. I teach people like Lynn Baker who is a very well known scientist from here. She knows something now.

Before leaving the dune I ask Edith how she can tell the tracks of dingoes

Edith Imantura Richards demonstrates how to make dingo tracks. Top: She makes the dingo's pad, the 'sole' of its foot, with her thumb. Above left: She then uses her index finger to make the toes' impressions. Above right: A set of tracks like those of a female dingo and two pups. Edith explains that fox tracks are narrower and those of feral cats do not show the claws.

from those of foxes and feral cats so easily. To illustrate her point she draws some tracks in the sand. She presses her thumb into the sand to make a dingo track's pad, then her two index fingers a few millimetres apart for the outside toes and the same fingers almost touching for the smaller inside toes. With a twig she draws the nails' impressions. She draws a perfect set of dingo tracks. Those of the fox, she explains, are longer and narrower and usually smaller, although there are also small dingoes. Cat tracks are rounder and do not show any nails.

Some days later I catch up with Edith's niece, Kunbry Pei Pei, who is only a few years younger than her aunt. She too draws dingo tracks in sandhills and she too is preoccupied with *Tjukurpa* stories. But Kunbry is not out among the dunes reading tracks; she creates her own by painting them on canvas.

I am just in time to watch her start a new painting. She sits cross-legged on the ground in front of a large blank canvas. Surrounding her are pots of acrylic paint, which she has just mixed — red ochre, yellow ochre, dark mulga-leaf green, pink and blue-grey as well as white and black. Kunbry sits in the shade of a small clump of trees away from the community and the distractions of small children and dogs. The north-eastern corner of Uluru is close by, visible through the foliage.

Kunbry is a tall woman with long, strong limbs. Her hair is straight and black with the streaks of pale brown so common among Pitjantjatjara people. Ants are swarming over the ground and a cloud of the eternally trying flies hovers around our faces. She quickly builds a small fire over the ants' nest, which keeps them under control. The smoke also keeps a few flies away.

Kunbry finishes covering the entire canvas in black paint with a broad brush. She picks up a smaller brush and for a moment is deep in thought. I ask her what she is going to paint. I do not think she has heard me for she does not answer. Suddenly she dips her brush into the red ochre and quickly draws a series of shapes in the top corners of the canvas. In a swift, assured movement she then paints a snake across the lower half, followed by a meandering path of dingo tracks. She has heard my question and answers it in English, in a quiet, shy voice. 'I paint the story of Uluru', she says. 'The right proper story', she adds with emphasis.

Using white she now paints a number of eggs around the snake. Once more she is completely absorbed. When the eggs are drawn she studies the painting carefully for some minutes. Several times she counts the painted symbols. Finally, satisfied all is correct, she lays her brush aside. It seems the creative process is completed. She tells me these are the stories of the Mala men and women and of Kuniya, the python. 'I'll tell you more about the painting and the stories when it is finished. We can go to Uluru then and I'll show you the places.'

Kunbry picks up a small stick about 10 centimetres long and dips it in the white paint. Using it like a brush, she outlines the red-ochre shapes in white dots. Once these are completed she uses another stick to fill in the entire background with overlapping semicircles of dots of different colours. 'These are sandhills', she volunteers. 'They're different colours because of the different plants that grow on them.' Hour after hour she puts the dots down with the stick 'brush' held in her long workworn fingers. With her other hand she continuously brushes the flies away from her face with slow languid movements.

Life around us goes on as unhurriedly and quietly as Kunbry's painting. A crow 'talks' in low guttural notes, 'arr, arr, arr', above us. A boobook owl watches through slitted eyes from the cover of a dense bush. A few slow notes from a rufous whistler are answered by an equally desultory song of a spiny-cheeked honeyeater. Insects and reptiles, however, are galvanised rather than made sluggish by the mounting heat. A small skink dashes around the leaf litter after tiny insects. I hope it catches a few flies. A flock of twittering budgerigars flies by and a black-breasted kite soars over Uluru. Kunbry says she may take a day or two to complete the painting.

Late in the afternoon three days later Kunbry finishes her painting. She looks it over critically and adds some finishing touches: eyes and nostrils on Kuniya, the python, the nails on the dingo tracks and forgotten dots here and there. With a certain amount of quiet pride, Kunbry says she has not painted these *Tjukurpa* stories like this before, with the Mala and Kuniya stories together. I cannot help but be affected by this painting in patterns of dots in harmonious colours and symbols, expressing the sincere and deep attachment to Uluru of this skilled, soft-spoken woman. And all of it done in Uluru's very shadow.

Kunbry quickly explains the painting's symbols. In the top right corner is a half-circle representing a cavern called Tjukatjapi that is sacred to the women. Within it are horseshoe shapes representing people sitting down. These are the Mala women preparing food.* In front of this are more women sitting down, but Kunbry says she cannot tell me about that because it is secret women's business. From this cavern, she explains, the women could hear and see Kurpany, the evil spirit in the shape of a dingo, coming. They tried to warn the men busy with their ceremony at Malawati a few hundred metres away. Malawati is represented by a three-quarter circle on the top left corner of the painting. Enclosed within it are a number of horizontal bars representing the Mala men asleep. Kurpany's footprints go into the cavern and then re-emerge and lead to a symbol of someone sitting down with a short horizontal bar in front of it. Kunbry explains:

Kurpany, he walk out of the cave after attacking the Mala men. He can hear

*See Chapter Three for the Mala and Kuniya stories.

baby crying and he see woman sitting there with her crying baby. He eat that baby too, then he move on to South Australia.

There is no rock formation representing this tragedy.

Below them lies Kuniya, the python woman, surrounded by her eggs, across abstract shapes and patterns representing dunes, a place where Kuniya used to hunt. She brought her eggs here, Kunbry says, and put them in a rock shelter to hatch. She adds:

When we go out for bush tucker, we sometimes catch *kuniya* [woma python], but I never eat it. When we were out one day I saw a *kuniya* for the first time. We stopped for lunch and cooked it, but I didn't taste it.

It is not long to sunset when we drive the short distance to Uluru's northern face. The sun hovers over Kata Tjuta and bathes us in a soft light, a welcome

Above: The horseshoe shapes represent women sitting down at a ceremony. Following page: Kunbry and the nearly completed painting.

change from the heat and harsh sun earlier in the day. The rock is in shadow, making it an even grey-brown colour. Yellow rays of sun highlight bloodwood and corkwood trees in front of the rock. A small patch of sun illuminates the very top of the monolith, a triangle of deep orange. We stop some hundreds of metres from Uluru. Kunbry explains that she cannot go close to the men's sacred site, called Kuniya Piti, on the rock's north-eastern corner near to Taputji, the small detached outcrop a few hundred metres to the west:

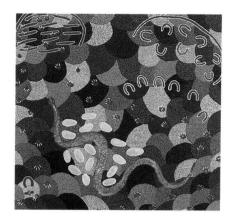

> If we go too close we get sick, we get sores, and if we go into Kuniya Piti we will fall between the rocks and will get great pain. Kuniya herself is still there sometimes.

The completed painting. The symbols across the top represent the Mala men and women. Below them is Kuntya and her eggs. Weaving through them are the tracks of Kurpany, the terrifying giant dog that killed and ate so many Mala men.
© Kunbry Pei Pei, 1993.

Kunbry points out where Kuniya left her imprint on Taputji and tells me that she placed eggs in Kuniya Piti where they still are as a circle of stones: She giggles:

> You see all these stones sitting all together on top of Taputji? They are the Mala women, the widows of the Mala men killed by Kurpany, like group of pensioners.

We move on a little way till we are nearer the women's sacred site, a cavern called Tjukatjapi near the opposite corner of Uluru. It is a large open shelter with grey walls streaked with vertical darker lines like long drips of paint. From the ceiling hang delicate screens of rock, the result of millions of years of erosion, draped like curtains. The floor is littered with boulders and outside lie huge rounded rocks. This is where the Mala women sat and were preparing food when they heard Kurpany coming.

About halfway up Uluru is a honeycombed bas-relief of straight and curved lines sculpted out of the sheer wall, very like those in Kunbry's painting. This is Malawati, where the Mala men were killed by the malevolent spirit dingo. Kunbry points out Kurpany's 'feet', indentations remarkably like those of a huge dog and following a line similar to that in the painting. *Kurpany tjina*, she calls them. In Pitjantjatjara, *tjina* means both 'foot' and 'footprint'. She says:

> You see his tracks going into cave where he catch the sleeping men and eat them all up. He then went further up, see there are his tracks, and come back down again. He can hear baby crying. He find that baby and eat it up too. Then he move on chasing more Mala men.

Briefly, just before it sets, the sun illuminates one of Kurpany's footprints, then it is twilight.

DROUGHTS AND RABBITS, EXTINCTIONS AND FIRE

The sun's first rays stream into Ikari cave's interior. Orange-yellow light blazes on the rocks but does not quite reach the furthest recesses where the barn owl roosts in the darkest, deepest chamber. After less than half an hour the sun has risen high enough for Ikari's overhanging lip to shade the entire cavern. The sun will not enter here again for the rest of the day.

It is one of the coolest places in Uluru, summer or winter, and therefore a favoured daytime roost for the nocturnal hunters. Besides the pellets of indigestible animal parts regurgitated by the owls, I see the scats of dingoes and beneath crevices in the ceiling the telltale droppings of insectivorous bats. Euros and echidnas also come here. I find the droppings of one and the shed quills of the other. I walk carefully to the blocks of stone in the cavern's centre so that I will not crush the tens of thousands, if not millions, of bone fragments that carpet the dusty floor. Most of these bones, now bleached white, have weathered out of the accumulated pellets and scats of many generations of owls, dingoes and other predators. Bats and rodents that have died here have also left their remains. The bones are not fossilised, but in these dry conditions they will persist for several hundred years before disintegrating into dust. In these tiny fragments, especially the countless teeth, is a long history of the vertebrate animals that inhabited the area on and around Uluru.

In 1987 and 1988 the zoologist Alexander Baynes collected 17,000 bones and teeth from Ikari cave and a few other localities, and worked out to what species they belonged. He confirmed graphically a catastrophe of major proportions. Half the native mammal species that once lived at Uluru-Kata Tjuta have disappeared, many not just from this region but from the face of the earth. From the evidence of the bones and teeth and the memories of Anangu elders it has been established that forty-four species of native mammals lived around Uluru sixty to seventy years ago. A two-year search by knowledgeable Anangu and Piranpa scientists of the CSIRO established that only twenty species remained in the late 1980s. Most of the ones that disappeared were medium-sized species, about the size of a domestic cat. Of these the pig-footed and desert bandicoots, the crescent nailtail wallaby, two species of hopping mice and the lesser sticknest rat are extinct; 'finished up altogether', Anangu say. Others, the western native cat, the red-tailed phascogale, the numbat, the burrowing bettong, the rufous hare-wallaby, or mala, the bilby, the Alice Springs mouse and the central rock rat, which were widespread and often abundant throughout the arid zone, have been reduced to tiny isolated and vulnerable populations. None is at Uluru-Kata Tjuta. The process of extinction of arid zone mammals, and one bird, the mallee fowl, began in the 1930s and most species had disappeared in the 1960s. Two hung on a little longer, the black-footed rock wallaby and the brush-tailed possum, but they too disappeared from Uluru-Kata Tjuta over the last decade.

Sitting on a boulder in Ikari cave and looking out over the vast plain, benevolent in the early morning coolness, I realise that half the mammal species that once lived out there, and whose remains lie all around me, no longer exist. It is difficult to take in that life in the superficially unaltered and seemingly unalterable landscape has a large and recent hole in it. The void is partly filled by the Anangu's knowledge and traditions. The people still know the animals' life histories and they are still connected to them through ceremonies embedded in the *Tjukurpa*. But to see the remains of a sticknest rat's home in a cave, the old mound of a mallee fowl or the teeth of a desert bandicoot in dusty ground is to feel a sadness beyond expression.

When animals have disappeared and only their names and a few bones remain, they tend to fade from our consciousness. It is as if they never existed. But I have seen some of these mammals such as the mala, bilby and numbat in other places. Others I know from illustrations and museum specimens. It is no exaggeration to say that collectively the medium-sized mammals now gone from Uluru-Kata Tjuta formed one of the most extraordinary and exquisite assemblages of mammals in the world. The crescent nailtail wallaby and the numbat are among the most beautifully patterned. The bilby with its silky pinkish and blueish shining fur, its long snout and gigantic ears is one of the most delightful. All of them enlivened the arid zone with their elegance as well as their beauty. What we have lost is not a collection of fictitious story-book animals but a vital part of the arid zone's dynamics. We are all the poorer for it.

Neither Anangu nor Piranpa are sure how this devastation came about. Anangu assessments vary. One person, perhaps reflecting his own feelings, said that all these animals moved to the west of Yuendemu, on the edge of the Tanami Desert, because they had too many worries. Most say the disappearance had some connection with an excessively long drought, the coming of such feral animals as rabbits and cats and the relaxation of traditional burning practices. Another person suggested that the sudden disappearance of medium-sized mammals had to do with the advent of Piranpa and the building of towns.

Previous pages: Early morning light streams into Ikari cave. Above: Ikari, in Uluru's southern side. Among the boulders are the bones of many mammals now extinct over vast areas of the continent. Some species have disappeared altogether. More than twenty species of mammals have disappeared from Uluru-Kata Tjuta since the 1930s.

Senior Anangu do not like to be drawn into discussions about these things. It was a great shock to them as many of the species that disappeared, especially the mala, are important in their religious and ceremonial lives, much of them secret as well as sacred. It was as if some essential part of themselves had suddenly been reduced to nothing. A similar feeling of shock would be felt among Christians if one of the gospels suddenly vanished from the New Testament.

During a more than usually severe drought in the mid-1930s some Anangu died of starvation. Most of the survivors moved off their lands to live at missions, cattle stations or in towns. When the rains came again, and Anangu returned to their country, the mala and many other mammals were no longer there. Only the bilby, possum and rock wallaby of the medium-sized mammals remained, but they too gradually dwindled to nothing. The people may well feel responsible for the animals' demise, for they had left their land, and so weakened the cycles of renewal

Bone fragments from Ikari cave. On the right is a pellet of undigested animal parts regurgitated by a barn owl. It contains the skull of a rodent. On the left is a barn owl feather.

as laid down in the *Tjukurpa*. It could be that they feel guilt and responsibility, a feeling of shame they would say.

Piranpa have complex theories that attempt to explain the sudden extinctions. Their theories involve ancient drainage systems, drought refuges, feral animals — especially rabbits, cats and foxes — savage droughts and changing fire patterns.

Before looking more closely at how these patterns may fit together, it is enlightening to listen to Anangu who still remember the days when mammal life was more prolific, and also to the first Piranpa to take note of the animal life.

Anangu say that they used to hunt the medium-sized mammals and that they were good to eat. They say that the mala inhabited the dune country where they made nests in spinifex clumps. They did not live in burrows. Piranpa accounts of areas not far from Uluru describe how Anangu used to hunt the mala by tracking it to its lair. The hunter would then jump on the small wallaby in its nest, ignoring the spinifex spikes piercing his legs. At other times Anangu would use fire in a pincer formation to drive the animals towards hidden spearsmen. A Piranpa narrator, H. H. Finlayson, wrote in his book *The Red Centre*:

[This hunt] is their sport, their spectacle and their meat-getting all in one; and in it they taste an ... intensity of joy which is beyond the range of our feelings.

That was in the early 1930s.

When the old people were young, Anangu say, thirty to fifty years ago, *ninu*, the bilby, was very common. It ate witchetty grubs and honey ants. It sniffed out the grubs with its long sensitive nose and then dug them out from the witchetty bushes' roots. When digging out honey ant nests Anangu sometimes found a bilby already there, devouring the ants. The people then said, 'Let's eat the *ninu* instead for he has already eaten the honey ants'. *Tawalpa*, the beautiful crescent nailtail wallaby, was once very common and Anangu used to ambush it by driving it through a gap between brush fences. One man remembers seeing *walputi*, the numbat, near Kata Tjuta and the nearby Petermann Ranges about sixty years ago. *Waru*, the black-footed rock wallaby, used to live all over Uluru, including in Ikari cave, and even on the very top. It was also common at Kata Tjuta where Anangu say some lived until a few years ago. *Wayuta*, the brushtail possum, was also abundant at both Uluru and Kata Tjuta. Mostly it lived in hollow gum trees but also in caves and even in the burrows of bettongs and rabbits. So many were there that Anangu could catch ten in a day and no possum hunt went unrewarded. Usually the marsupials were caught in trees where they were smoked out of their sleeping hollows. Uncontrolled bushfires killed many possums because the animals' feet were not well suited to walking and running, and so they could not get out of

the way of the fire. Out on the plains lived *wintaru*, the golden bandicoot. It was everywhere and made its home in burrows in the ground. It was like a mouse, only bigger, but not so big that it could not fit in your hand. Its tail was short and the ears and nose small. To catch it Anangu would stamp the ground above the burrow, frightening *wintaru* into flight, and the spears and clubs of waiting hunters.

The first Piranpa to visit Uluru with a specific interest in natural history were members of the Horn Expedition, who briefly visited the area in the winter of 1894. The expedition's zoologist and narrator, Sir Walter Baldwin Spencer, gave some tantalising glimpses of the animal life. He wrote about passing a mallee fowl's mound on approaching Uluru. The burrowing bettongs, now extinct on the mainland, were common. Spencer called them kangaroo rats, and wrote this about them in *Across Australia*:

Riding on all day long we kept mounting one sandhill after another, all covered

The bilby, according to Anangu and judging by the remains found in caves, was once common at Uluru. Now it survives only in small isolated pockets in other parts of the arid zone.

with tussocks of Porcupine grass, amongst which kangaroo rats, *Bettongia lesueuri*, kept dodging in and out with remarkable speed and agility.

He also recorded his excitement at capturing a species of dunnart:

> ... we had an exciting chase after a little, but extremely active, mouse-like creature, which was finally captured as the result of a well-directed shot with a boot, hastily snatched for the purpose from the foot of our energetic leader. It turned out to be a new species of the genus Sminthopsis ... We never had the good fortune to meet with another specimen.
>
> The little animal now captured ... has from its living among sandhills been called *Sminthopsis psammophila* [sandhill dunnart].

Despite intensive searches during the recent Uluru Fauna Survey, this largest of all the dunnarts has not been found again at Uluru-Kata Tjuta. Records from other parts of the arid zone have been sporadic.

The Anangu that Spencer encountered at Kata Tjuta wore decorations and other paraphernalia made from bilby and bettong skins, suggesting these animals were common. Spencer described them as follows:

> The men wore emu-feather 'chignons', frequently seen in this part of the country. These pads are ... made up of emu-feathers matted together ... They are tied on to the back of the head with string made of opossum fur, and into the upper angle on each side is stuck a skewer of wood with a little tuft of the white tips of the rabbit bandicoot [bilby] tails ... or else a tuft of feathers often of the Eagle-hawk [wedge-tailed eagle].
>
> One man was carrying a small bag of skin, probably of the rat-kangaroo, tied round with hair and string and containing, apart from his girdle, shield and womera, his worldly possessions. These odd bits of flint and pieces of kangaroo and emu tendon and also a rather fine tuft of Peragale [bilby] tail tips belonging to his wife and forming her dress and ornament on special occasions ...

The first indicators of the eventual demise of so many kinds of mammals were noted by Anangu not as an ominous sign of devastation to come, but as a welcome addition to their diet. This is how the people at Uluru-Kata Tjuta reacted to the first rabbits to enter their lands:

> Someone was tracking and saw something strange, and it was a rabbit track. Rabbits came after the other things [medium-sized native mammals]. They were

at first considered strange until people began eating them and found them good food. Rabbits then spread out everywhere. Now there are rabbits everywhere and the others have gone.

Some Anangu called the rabbit a kind of *tjungku*, or burrowing bettong, with ears like a donkey and the tail of a goat.

Cattle, sheep and horses never came in great numbers to Uluru-Kata Tjuta; it has never been part of a pastoral lease eaten bare by domestic stock. But there were times when rabbits were just as devastating, when they bred up in such numbers that plants were eaten down to the ground and burrow systems caused erosion.

Before considering the full implication of this and other factors, it must be realised that the medium-sized mammals live on a razor's edge in the arid zone. Unlike the large mammals, they do not have the capacity to move long distances out of drought-stricken land. They cannot shut down their systems during hard times as the social insects and reptiles do, or hibernate like some of the very small mammals. They must eat just about every day, mostly plants, and these must have certain levels of moisture and nutrition to sustain them. As Anangu have known for centuries and Piranpa have recently discovered, the arid zone mammals suffered severe losses during prolonged droughts. They only survived in special refuge areas where there were richer soils with greater reserves of moisture. From these nuclei they would build up their numbers again, for some species very rapidly, and spread out into the surrounding country.

In Uluru-Kata Tjuta such a refuge extends over a sandplain that starts as a narrow band near Uluru and then widens out northwards across the Yulara Reserve, a place outside the National Park and occupied by all the facilities of the Ayers Rock Resort and the Yulara township. It is an area of about 60 square kilometres and the most important habitat in the region. The vital role of this refuge and its preservation were emphasised in the final report of the *Uluru Fauna Survey*. It states:

> The area ... is the faunal habitat containing the greatest range of rare species in the Park district. [These] transitional sandplains and associated land units here provide important habitat for rare species and other animals of limited distribution in the region. The ecological factors which promote this richness are imprecisely known, but buried drainage lines are mapped as underlying the defined area, and the sandplains are likely to receive a greater supply of moisture and nutrients ... than the dunefield spinifex landscapes.

So finely balanced were the refuges' resources during severe droughts and the medium-sized mammals' requirements that it would have taken very little to

The mala, or rufous hare-wallaby, so important in Anangu ceremony, now survives only on a few small islands off the Western Australian coast and in captivity.

tip these mammals over the edge of extinction. It is now believed that a fatal disruption in the age-old pattern of expanding and contracting populations occurred during the mid- to late-1930s. Drought was then so calamitous that even Anangu, the absolute masters of survival in arid environments, did not cope entirely successfully. For the medium-sized mammals a new destructive force — rabbits, and in other places sheep and cattle — entered the equation at about the same time and spelled their doom. These introduced animals ravaged the refuges, tearing the delicate fabric of the native plant–animal relationship. Instead of surviving in small numbers until the end of the drought, entire populations over vast areas were wiped out. The refuges were permanently altered by the alien grazing animals to such a degree that they could no longer give sanctuary to native species during times of stress. This happened not only at Uluru, but throughout the continent's arid zone.

Some mammals, such as the mala, burrowing bettong, crescent nailtail wallaby, numbat and a few others, vanished from Uluru during the droughts of the 1930s. Others, which were less dependent on the refuge areas, such as the bilby, which ate mainly insects, the rock wallabies living in inaccessible places and possums living in trees, managed to hang on. But another severe drought in the 1960s further reduced their numbers. At about the same time, or a little earlier, two new ferocious and efficient predators, the cat and the fox, appeared on the scene. In the end the hardier native species also succumbed.

Some Anangu and Piranpa ecologists say that this catastrophe of extinctions may have, at least in part, been averted if another major force had been properly managed – that is, if fire had been used as Anangu had used it for millennia.

Tommy Wangi, peering through thick-lensed glasses and with a cigarette dangling from the corner of his mouth, and Norman Tjalkalyiri study the country critically. They take in at a glance that this is country ready for burning. The spinifex is mature, in their eyes over-mature. It grows in large rings where the centres have died back to bare sand. The woody shrubs and scattered desert oaks have tinder-dry dead branches, and strips of bark and leaf litter accumulated beneath them. With a quick look at the sky and an exchange of a few cryptic remarks, the two walk off in opposite directions, lighting the spinifex with modern-day firesticks, drip torches trickling a steady stream of burning oil along the base of a sandridge. Skilfully they set a line of fire in an arc around the base of a sandridge, and the slight breeze takes it roaring up the slope where it reaches the crest in a leaping wall of flames. There it slows down as it burns gradually down the other slope. Many fires die out altogether on the dune crests. Earlier, the older men, called *tjilpis* in respect for their grey hair and wisdom, Peter Kanari and Kata Kura, had told me that they never deliberately burn trees. As they too set off with their

Left: This aerial photograph shows over-mature spinifex as rings with dead centres. The eucalypts are marbled gums growing near Lake Amadeus. Above: Rings of over-mature spinifex in desert grevillea–mulga woodland. Spinifex like this needs to be burnt.

drip torches, I notice that they go around several majestic desert oaks and that they burn a firebreak around a mulga woodland. On this cool but sunny winter's day in July with only a little wind, conditions are perfect for burning the country.

David Carter, the Park's assistant manager, also plays a vital role in selecting the areas that need to be burnt. Because Anangu no longer roam over every part of Uluru-Kata Tjuta, another way had to be found to discover the exact places that need a fire through them. David does this by interpreting satellite imagery of the Park. These large photographs clearly show the region's fire history. David and the *tjilpis* then visit likely places on the ground and make decisions about their burning.

The spinifex catches fire explosively, sending up billows of black smoke. The heat is intense; spinifex, no matter what the season, burns at about 950 degrees Celsius. I move back from the fire's front. The slight breeze takes the fire up the dune slope. Dry bushes, crackling and hissing, burst into fireballs, which soon die down again. Desert oaks and their fallen branches and needles produce greater conflagrations with columns of white smoke. Their bark burns for a minute or so in a fierce pillar of flame. But it is so thick that it provides sufficient insulation for the trees' sap. When the fire has passed it leaves a carpet of white ash in which hundreds of smouldering fallen seed cones send up wisps of blue smoke.

Even though the breeze was slight to begin with, the fire sucks in updrafts of air that speed it on, make it roar and send clouds of smoke and ash towering upwards. The sky is darkened. Tommy and Norman and several others are out of view, a line of smoke marking their progress. A few brown falcons drift on the air currents directly behind the advancing gyrating flames, looking for lizards and large insects that may have been hiding in the spinifex and leaf litter. Most of the animals have retreated to burrows deep beneath the sand to escape the winter's cold. The falcons dive down only occasionally to snatch the few casualties from the hot ashes. Because it is cool and the breeze is light, the fires do not race along on a wide all-consuming front. Rather, they stop and start according to gusts of wind or accumulated fuel. As I watch from a tall dune I see long fingers of fire run through the spinifex, creating a mosaic of burnt and unburnt country.

These mosaics make good sense. In a place like Uluru-Kata Tjuta, where burning techniques perfected by Anangu have been practised for ten years or more, their benefits are obvious. Wherever you look, particularly in this season of vigorous plant growth, you can see patches of drab green spinifex interspersed with others where flowers are out in profusion and more succulent grasses grow. Places that were burnt two years ago have different assemblages of flowers than those that were fired four or five years ago. Dune tops of bare sand testify to a recent burn while those with ground-hugging flowering plants, shrubs or trees have been free of fire for long periods. Instead of uniform drab expanses of spinifex there is a dynamic colourful patchwork with a maximum variety of plants, which in turn support the greatest possible diversity of animals.

To the untutored eye the burnt areas are a scene of utter desolation – just ashes, sand and fire-blackened sticks and stumps. Even some of the desert oaks, the bark still smouldering, have scorched foliage, which in a few days will wilt and fall. Yet in time the countryside will return to what it was before the fire. If rains come soon, the ashes will percolate into the soil and act as fertiliser, speeding the growth of short-lived grasses and ephemeral wildflowers. These grow for two or three years if rainfall is average. The shrubs and small trees will resprout from rootstock and the desert oaks will soon replace their crowns. Slowly over a number of years spinifex seeds will germinate and a great many will regrow from their rootstock. The short-lived grasses and wildflowers will gradually fade away as the spinifex reasserts its dominance. With each stage in the re-establishment of the vegetation different animals will be favoured. Over the years there are constant, fluid changes, Eventually all the plants will have put their seeds in the ground and put down strong, deep root systems. How long this process takes depends largely on rainfall. If the run of seasons is average, it will take thirty to thirty-five years; if there is an exceptional run of seasons with high rainfall, it may take only half that time. During years of drought it may take fifty years. Always spinifex is the indicator. When it is over-mature, dying back into rings with dead centres, the country is ready for burning.

The columns of smoke are fewer and fewer as the fires dissipate. By evening they will have run their course. Tommy and Norman reappear, hot and sweaty, the oil supply in their burners exhausted, but their faces show elation rather than fatigue. They have fulfilled an important task in maintaining their country.

David in the meantime has built a small fire beneath a desert oak on the unburnt side of the fire line to boil the billy for lunch. Not far away Edith Imantura Richards looks for tracks. She casually probes some soft ground with her digging stick. Suddenly she digs down quickly and seconds later drags a very cold sand goanna from its burrow and knocks it on the head. It soon joins the billy on the fire. The cooked goanna is given to Kata Kura. He gives portions of it to the other men and with great courtesy offers me a strip of white meat from the goanna's tail.

Sitting in the sand around the small fire, we have a relaxed lunch. Julian Barry is talking and joking with the men in Pitjantjatjara and occasionally translates a few snippets. Kata Kura and Peter Kanari admit to drinking 'a bit' when they were younger. Peter points to a large desert oak and says, 'We sat there once and drank all night till the sun came up'. Billy Wara, a tall man in his early seventies, says he never drank and that is why he is so strong. He certainly is a powerful man with large, stong hands.

Gradually, through Julian, I nudge the conversation towards traditional fire management. It is a subject close to Anangu hearts and soon they have vigorous conversation about it. Julian valiantly tries to keep up with the translation. A fascinating picture emerges.

Fire management, carried out according to guidelines laid down in the *Tjukurpa*, is an essential part of Anangu life. It is a complex system of what can be burnt, when and how. Spinifex country, which comprises the vast majority of Anangu lands, is burnt most often. Mature spinifex is never allowed to remain, for this is considered 'rubbish country' and an indication of gross mismanagement. Mature spinifex plants declining in vigour are burnt to encourage other plants, many, such as the bush tomato, providing vital food for Anangu. Also the removal of such spinifex makes the country easier to travel through.

Mulga shrublands, on the other hand, are never deliberately set alight, perhaps because the trees, which supply a variety of foods and wood for implements, are killed by fire. Lightning-started fires, or ones that accidentally invade the

Andy Daeger, also known as Panpanpalala, burns spinifex country as part of traditional management practices.

shrublands, do burn small portions of mulga country, so even there a mosaic of different stages of recovery is established. Wire-grass plains are burnt when enough dry material has accumulated to carry a fire.

Some sacred places and special trees such as rock figs must be actively protected from fire by burning firebreaks around them. Such firebreaks clearly show Anangu that a place is 'properly looked after'. Areas around springs are burnt to keep water clean and to encourage new green growth. The springs themselves are maintained by clearing away mud and ashes with a scoop made of mulga or bloodwood timber.

In the past fires were also used as signals. A particularly smoky fire was lit or a dry tree set on fire to let others know of the presence of water, a good hunting place, an abundance of plant food or simply the movement of a travelling family or party of hunters. Firesticks, invariably made of dead desert-oak wood, were carried at all times by people on the move. 'Like this', Billy Wara says, showing how they clamped the firesticks under their upper arms. The others nod in agreement. Patting his pockets in dramatic gestures, he adds in English, 'No matches'.

The country is never carelessly or haphazardly set alight. The time of year, the weather conditions, the aspect, the species in the possible fire path, the country's fire history — all have to be taken into consideration. March to April, late summer and autumn are not good times for burning, for the fires would be too hot and travel too fast on the strong winds. Spring, starting in September, is not a good time either, for then the kangaroos are hunted and emus sit on their eggs. Fire would force kangaroos to move away to unburnt places and would destroy the next generation of emus. Summer fires are never lit, for these would be too hot and destructive. Lightning does cause occasional summer fires and these are thought of as a force to the good, sanctioned by the *Tjukurpa*. Anangu would follow these huge conflagrations, hoping for a rainstorm created by the fire's intense heat and roaring winds. They would also pick up any animal life, either killed by the flames and smoke or flushed towards them, deprived of cover. The men say:

A desert oak tree catches alight. The fire burns the tree's foliage but the thick outer bark protects the tender inner bark where the sap flows. Most of these trees survive the fires.

> A fire would burn — sometimes it would go out and sometimes keep going — which we would follow quite fast. Maybe two nights' rest, then the fire would pick up again and keep going far off until the clouds built up and it rained.

The best time to burn is on a cool, windless day in winter:

> When you burn in the winter, you should do it when there is no wind or only a little wind so that the fire moves slowly. If the wind makes the fire burn too quickly, the little animals can't escape, and they get burnt. If fire moves slowly, the animals feel the ground getting hot and move into their burrows and then when the fire is finished they get up and move around in the *nyaru* [recently burnt country].

To Tommy, Norman, Kata Kura, Peter Kanari and other Anangu, well-cared-for country is a patchwork of areas of land at various stages of regeneration after fire, interspersed with pockets of mature spinifex ready for burning. Country like this carries the greatest variety of plant and animal food and, just as importantly prevents wild, lightning-ignited fires from sweeping across vast areas. Always there is enough recently burnt land to act as firebreaks. Wildfires that swept all before them over enormous areas would have been disastrous for traditional Anangu, as such country would then be uninhabitable, devoid of food, for several years. Older

Anangu state categorically that before Piranpa came large-scale fires never occurred. When the country is well looked after, such things are impossible.

To the pastoralists, who invaded Pitjantjatjara lands and the arid zone in general, with their cattle, sheep and horses, fires of any kind were an abhorrence. They thought that fire would wipe out their pastures and kill their stock. By various means, therefore, they discouraged Anangu from carrying out their traditional fire practices. Some were brutal. Kata Kura relates that in one cattle station Anangu were whipped, 'like bullocks', if they lit fires. 'Pitchew, pitchew', he demonstrates with gestures as if cracking a very long stockwhip. 'Yes', the others say, 'it was a very big whip'. Ironically, by preventing Anangu management practices, and never consulting them on such matters, what the pastoralists feared most came to pass. A wildfire that swept through all of Uluru-Kata Tjuta in 1976 burned out more than 20,000 square kilometres to the north-east of Uluru. Fires of a similar magnitude regularly incinerate some part of the arid zone.

For the medium-sized and small mammals these kinds of wildfires, which rage with frightening intensity usually in summer, are yet another major disaster. As wildfires race along at a devastating speed, pushed along by hot dry winds, most mammals cannot get out of the way of them. There is destruction on the grand scale. Refuges are burnt in their entirety and the whole mammal population within them may be wiped out. Then there will be no nuclei left to recolonise the devastated land.

Also, the medium-sized mammals need at least some green food in their diet. Only when the spinifex is burnt will green food be available, but only for a few years. During controlled, limited winter fires, lit according to Anangu Law, only small patches burn. So when green food runs out in one patch, there is always another newly burnt one within easy reach. Moving from one patch to another, the mammals never run out of food. But when huge areas are stripped bare in a single fire, the mammals will perish long before they find their next meal of greens, no matter how good the seasons.

So was it the rabbits that pushed so many mammals over the brink or was it feral predators or large-scale fires or perhaps drought? It is impossible to say. They may have survived any one or even two of these ecological disasters, but all of them at once were impossible to absorb.

Can this trend be reversed? Can the missing mammals be returned? For those that are extinct, the pig-footed bandicoot, the crescent nailtail wallaby and others, it is obviously too late. But for others that just survive in tiny isolated pockets or in captivity, the bilby, mala, burrowing bettong, possum and rock wallaby, it may be possible. Before any thought can be given to actually reintroducing these mammals, two conditions must be met: a proper fire regime and the eradication, or at least the control, of feral animals.

A mosaic of burnt and unburnt country. These patches are necessary to maintain maximum species diversity among both plants and animals. They also prevent wildfires devastating the country.

HAWTHORN SECONDARY COLLEGE
BURGESS STREET
EAST HAWTHORN, 3123

In the 1970s when there were massive wildfires in many parts of the arid zone, Piranpa at last also became concerned about their effects. They were worried about the fodder supply for their stock. Their way of preventing such disasters was to bring scientists in to study the problem and to find solutions. One of the pioneering scientists in this field was Graham Griffin, now working as an ecologist with the CSIRO Division of Wildlife and Ecology in Alice Springs. He is also on the Uluru-Kata Tjuta Board of Management. Graham is a co-author of a book on the management of fire in the National Park.

We talk in a corner of his Alice Springs laboratory. Computers and other apparatus hum quietly. Graham, a slim figure in white shirt and dark trousers, and with a flowing brown beard, gives the impression of being more at ease in the bush than the laboratory. He speaks eloquently, with conviction and authority, without ums and ahs or meandering qualifications. I ask him how he became involved with researching the effects of wildfire in the arid zone and with Uluru. He says:

This goes back to my early times here in 1972–74 when we had terrific rains. As a consequence, we had a great build-up of fuel followed by massive wildfires, and people were becoming concerned about what these fires were doing to the country.

In those days the concern was voiced mainly by non-Aborigines. If there was an Aboriginal opinion, we certainly weren't hearing it at that time. That's not to say they weren't voicing it, it just wasn't getting through.

And so we became interested as to what the role of fire was in these arid ecosystems, and we read what little there was in the literature. One of the most important and interesting aspects was to go back through the early documentations of the explorers and anthropologists. It was almost incidentally that they kept saying that every day they could see fires; the Aboriginal people were lighting fires. They constantly stated that they were travelling across recently burnt country or country that had a green flush because of recent fire and so on. It became obvious to us that there was a very strong connection between Aboriginal people and fire. That sat for a while at the back of our minds.

But being aware that Aborigines were actively involved in fire and that fire was going to happen whether Aborigines were there or not, and observing that the landscapes changed in response to that fire, we needed to work out whether fire was having a detrimental effect, a beneficial effect or didn't make any difference one way or another. If it didn't matter, we asked ourselves, then why were the Aborigines burning? If it did matter, what were we going to do about the wildfires?

During our researches it also became obvious that there was a connection

A Wills's desert fuchsia has come up among the fire-blackened stems of a dead shrub. The most spectacular displays of flowers occur when there is a heavy winter rain after fire.

between fires and the loss of so many of our smaller mammals. These need a regular supply of green food. They can't get that in spinifex country but when you burn it, you do get green feed for a while. In a wildfire you burn tens of thousands of square kilometres of country where you will have green feed for a few years but nothing after that. It all becomes spinifex again. But if you burn the country in small patches, little bits and pieces, you can graze on this bit this year and another nearby patch that has just been burnt next year. If you only have to go a few kilometres to your next patch, you're in business as a small mammal. That's probably how the Aboriginal people worked out their fire strategy. By burning little patches here and there at different times, they created a patchwork in the environment that was of great benefit to the smaller mammals. Whether this was a deliberate, conscious process or something that evolved and just happened to suit everyone along the way — well, who knows? It didn't matter in the end. A strategy had been developed, things were locked into it and it worked.

We started our work with fire at Uluru in 1982. At first Anangu were very, very cautious and non-committal. They very much kept away on the sidelines, worried presumably about what we were doing. We got on with our experimental burns without having much contact with Anangu. That was very much a function of the management regime at the time, which was in the hands of the Conservation Commission of the Northern Territory. Had we known what the Anangu's thoughts and concerns were, we would have done things in a very different way. But we carried on and developed our fire management strategies, and in doing so demonstrated to Anangu, if only from a distance, that we weren't going to burn everything down. When eventually the people came closer they realised that we were trying to manage the country in a way that they themselves had managed it in the past.

So Anangu overcame their reservations, and when the Australian National Parks and Wildlife Service [now the Australian Nature Conservation Agency] took over the Park late in 1985 we had direct consultations with Anangu. People approached us and said, 'Yes, that's how people burnt in the past. We were worried about what you were doing but we now see that it is right'. From then on people like Kanari and Kata Kura joined us. They were just champing at the bit to start burning country. They were amazing, doing it very, very skilfully and with great caution. They were not just burning randomly and mindlessly, but carefully selecting the places and controlling their fires. They were very knowledgeable about what they were doing. To see that change from no burning at all to careful patch burning was most impressive.

That is how Piranpa science 'discovered' what Anangu had known all along.

A proper fire regime is now in place at Uluru-Kata Tjuta. Work is also carried out to rid the place of rabbits, cats and foxes. Contractors and rangers periodically conduct eradication campaigns that keep rabbits down to small numbers. With the cats and foxes much work still needs to be done, and it is not an easy task. Anangu themselves, with their tracking and hunting skills and an appetite to eat them, are the most effective eradicators of cats. But no comprehensive plan is yet in place.

Once the stage is set to reintroduce the mala, the golden bandicoot, the bilby, the possum, the rock wallaby and the burrowing bettong Uluru-Kata Tjuta's wounds will, to a degree, have been healed. Nothing can be done, however, till the cats and foxes have gone. Reintroduction trials with the mala and bilby in other parts of the Northern Territory have so far failed, not because the animals could not live off the country, but because huge and ferocious feral cats killed them as soon as they were released.

CHAPTER TEN
THE COMING OF PIRANPA

Anangu say they have always been at Uluru-Kata Tjuta and that one way or another they always will be. White people, Piranpa, were latecomers not only on the scale by which Anangu reckon time, but even in their own 200-year history on this continent.

Tucked away as it is in the south-west corner of the Northern Territory, Uluru-Kata Tjutu was far away from the routes chosen by the earliest Piranpa explorers. Their epic journeys took them almost exclusively over Australia's eastern half. It was not until the Scot Thomas Mitchell, an impetuous man given to duelling with pistols, travelled from Bathurst to the Minindee Lakes in New South Wales that the arid interior was first penetrated. That was in 1835. The German explorer Ludwig Leichhardt attempted to cross the continent from east to west in 1848 but his entire expedition vanished. No trace of it has ever been found. In 1844–46 Charles Sturt tried to cross the continent from south to north. He was forced to wait out a six-month drought, and even after rain he was thwarted by the Simpson Desert. Burke and Wills tried the same journey in 1860 and 1861 but died in the attempt. John McDouall Stuart, who was a member of Sturt's expedition, made a successful north–south crossing from Adelaide to the top end of the Northern Territory in 1860–62. This was the expedition that came closest to Uluru-Kata Tjuta, passing to within 300 kilometres of it.

The overland telegraph line largely followed Stuart's route. It connected Adelaide to Darwin and Australia to the rest of the world. It was completed on 2 August 1872, although due to some technical problems outside Australia the first cablegram was not received until 21 October. This was the same year that Piranpa first sighted Kata Tjuta and Lake Amadeus, but another year passed before Uluru was given its Piranpa name and the monoliths received their first white visitors.

It seemed that the completion of the telegraph line, which effectively cut the country in half, signalled the Piranpa's readiness to face the interior of the western portion of the continent. At that time they knew absolutely nothing about it, but there were great expectations of mountains and grassy plains, fertile soils and expanses of fresh water.

The first and also the toughest and most persistent man to explore the western regions was Ernest Giles. Giles was an Englishman born in Bristol in 1835. He emigrated to Adelaide at the age of fifteen. Two years later he went to Victoria, first to the goldfields and then to Melbourne, where for a time he worked as a postal clerk. In the 1860s he was a member of several small expeditions into western New South Wales that reported on the possibilities of pastoral settlement. These explorations rasied his ambitions and prepared him for his remarkable feats in finding an overland route to the west coast. In his book *Australia Twice Traversed* he explains what drove him to undertake such journeys:

> For several years previous to my taking the field, I had desired to be the first to penetrate into this unknown region [the western half of Australia], where, for a thousand miles [1600 km] in a straight line, no white man's foot had ever wandered, or, if it had, its owner had never brought it back, nor told the tale.
>
> My object, as indeed had been Leichhardt's, was to force my way across the thousand miles that lay untrodden and unknown, between the South Australian telegraph line and the settlement upon the Swan River [in the south-west corner of Western Australia]. What hopes I formed, what aspirations came of what might be my fortune, for I trust it will be believed that an explorer may be an imaginative as well as a practical creature, to discover in that unknown space.
>
> There was room for snowy mountains, an inland sea, ancient river, and palmy plain, for races of new kinds of men inhabiting a new and odorous land, for fields of gold and golcondas of gems, for a new flora and a new fauna, and, above all the rest combined, there was room for me!

Giles's first expedition was to explore the ranges west and south of Alice Springs, or Stuart as it was then called, and then proceed to the Murchison River on the west coast.

The expedition entered the unknown at Chamber's Pillar, just west of the overland telegraph line, on 22 August 1872, not quite three weeks after the line was completed. Giles had two companions, Samuel Carmichael and Alec Robinson. The latter Giles later referred to as 'a strange, indeed disagreeable and sometimes uncivil sort of man'. The three rode horses and carried their supplies and equipment on packhorses. Neither camels nor wagons were used.

Early in October, after exploring the rocky ranges south-west of Alice Springs, Giles found himself in dry country not far from King's Canyon, looking for a passage that he hoped would eventually take him to the west coast. To reach a small hill from which to survey the surroundings, he crossed a spinifex plain, as he had

Previous pages: The zoologist and anthropologist Baldwin Spencer reached Uluru-Kata Tjuta in June 1894. 'At length we reached the top of the . . . sand dune and saw Ayers Rock not far away.'

done so often. In his book he refers to the grass as 'that abominable vegetable production'. He goes on to say:

> We next ascended a hill to view the surrounding country, and endeavour to discover if there was any feature in any direction to induce us to visit, and where we might find a fresh supply of water. There were several fires raging in various directions upon the southern horizon, and the whole atmosphere was thick with a smoky haze. After a long and anxious scrutiny through the smoke far, very far away ... I descried the outline of a range of hills, and right in the smoke of one fire an exceedingly high and abruptly-ending mountain loomed.

This 'exceedingly high' mountain became the object of Giles's explorations and appeared to him to be the gateway that would lead him to the west.

He and Carmichael left the uncivil Robinson at base camp at a waterhole, departing on 17 October with a week's supply of food. On and on they pushed with great determination but they were unable to find water. Finally they discovered a rocky gully that had some gum trees growing in it. They found water, 'thick and dirty with a nauseous flavour', by digging a hole 6 metres long, 2 metres wide and 2 metres deep in the sand. As the water slowly percolated into the hole 'large and small red hornets' and what Giles called 'diamond birds', probably painted finches, came and drank in 'great numbers'. So slow was the seepage that it took them all night to water their horses. The temperature rose to 37 degrees Celsius in the shade.

After a day's rest, when the temperature reached 38 degrees, they set off again to what Giles called 'my old friend, the high mountain', which now loomed large. Suddenly '... we had a white salt channel right in front of us, with some sheets of water in it; upon approaching I found it a perfect bog, and the water brine itself'. They went around the channel and saw '... stretching away to the west, an enormous salt expanse'. They travelled east for a few kilometres only to find it swept away to the horizon in that direction as well. As far as they could see, east and west, there was salt lake. Giles tried crossing it, but while the salt crust held his weight, the horses sank through it and became bogged in a hot, salty, sticky, slimy blue mud. They nearly lost some of them. Giles noted Anangu fires on the opposite shore. They tried unsuccessfully riding around the salt lake to the west and again to the east. But they had to go too far without water. As he viewed the terrain from a sandhill Giles wrote:

> From where we are, the prospect is wild and weird, with the white bed of the great lake sweeping nearly the whole southern horizon.

Kata Tjuta seen across the salt flats of Lake Amadeus. The explorer Ernest Giles was the first Piranpa to see Kata Tjuta, in October 1872. He named it Mount Olga. He could not cross Lake Amadeus to reach it. Uluru was apparently hidden from his view by smoke from Anangu fires.

The two men and exhausted horses returned to the tank with 'nauseous' water and drank their fill. As they left the salt lake Giles commented:

> I was heartily annoyed at being baffled in my attempt to reach the mountain, which I now thought more than ever would offer a route out of this terrible region; but it seemed impossible to escape from it. I named this eminence Mount Olga, and the great salt feature which obstructed me Lake Amadeus, in honour of two enlightened royal patrons of science.*

Giles made no mention of Uluru. He and Carmichael reached the tank they had dug, 'hungry, thirsty, tired, covered all over with dry salt mud' and 'overrun by

*Queen Olga of Württemberg in what is now Germany and King Amadeo of Spain. Mount Olga and its associated rocky domes are now known by their Anangu name of Kata Tjuta.

ants, and pestered by flies'. That day the temperature rose to 40 degrees Celsius and during the night there was fierce thunder and lightning but no rain.

Giles and Carmichael made their way back to base camp. Giles had already decided to dismiss Robinson but Carmichael had agreed to go on and seek a different route. It was not to be. Carmichael changed his mind and gave up the attempt. He and Robinson rode on ahead and Giles, with five horses, made his way to Adelaide on his own. On the way he learnt that the South Australian Government had sent William Christie Gosse to find a way to western Australia. He also met Edgerton Warburton and his son who were going to attempt the same.

Gosse was also born in England, in 1842, and emigrated to Adelaide with his family in 1850, the same year as Giles. Gosse left Alice Springs on his explorations on 23 April 1873. He was accompanied by five Europeans, including his brother Henry, three Afghans to look after the camels and an Anangu man he called Moses. They travelled with a horse-drawn wagon as well as camels and bullocks. When he reached the western extremity of the MacDonnell Ranges, named Mount Liebig by Giles only a few months before, Gosse turned south. He crossed Giles's tracks several times.

On Friday 11 July Gosse arrived at King's Canyon and the next day noted in his diary, 'I could see what I suppose to be Mount Olga'. He also recorded sharp morning frosts over the ensuing days. Exactly a week later, after having travelled south for some days, part of his diary entry reads:

> ... came upon some clay pans and a large native camp which has not long been deserted. Here I found a small hole of water; the camels seemed very thirsty ... [from the] top of a ridge, saw native fires to the south-east and west; a white lagoon, or part of lake ... seen over a low place in the sandhills ... to the east, Mount Olga, and a hill east of it, also a high flat-topped hill which I have named Mount Conner, after Mr M. L. Conner ... I shall now make an attempt to reach hill east of Olga ... Travelled seven miles [11 km] over the roughest spinifex sandhills I have yet seen ... The camel travelling is very tiring, it is more like riding a knocked-up cart colt, than any animal I have ever mounted.

Gosse, with the Afghan Kamran, went on ahead of the main party. His diary entry for the next two days reveals the identity of 'the hill east of Olga':

> Saturday July 19th ... The hill, as I approached, presented a most peculiar appearance, the upper portion being covered with holes or caves. When I got clear of the sandhills, and was only two miles [3 km] distant, and the hill, for the first time, coming fairly in view, what was my astonishment to find

it was one immense rock rising abruptly from the plain; the holes I had noticed were caused by the water in some places forming immense caves. At 34 miles [55 km] reached foot of rock; only found enough water to replenish our bags, but none for the camels — they seem very thirsty, though only twenty-four hours since they had water. No sign of a creek on this [the north] side ... I have named this Ayers Rock, after Sir Henry Ayers [premier and chief secretary of South Australia].

Sunday, July 20 — Ayers Rock. I rode round the foot of rock in search of a place to ascend; found a waterhole on south side, near which I made an attempt to reach the top, but found it hopeless. Continued along to the west, and discovered a strong spring coming from the centre of the rock, and pouring down some very steep gullies into a large deep hole at the foot of rock. This I have named Maggie's Spring. Seeing a spur less abrupt than the rest of the rock, I left the camels here, and after walking and scrambling two miles [3 km] barefooted, over sharp rocks, succeeded in reaching the summit, and had a view that repaid me for my trouble — Kamran accompanied me. The top is covered with small holes in the rock, varying is size from two to twelve feet [0.6–3.6 m] diameter, all partly filled with water. Mount Olga is about twenty miles [30 km] west ... How I envied Kamran his hard feet: he seemed to enjoy the walking about with bare feet, while mine were all in blisters, and it was as much as I could do to stand ... This seems to be a favourite resort of the natives in the wet season, judging from the numerous camps in every cave. These caves are formed by large pieces breaking off the main rock and falling to the foot. The blacks ... amuse themselves covering [the cave walls] with all sorts of devices — some of snakes, very cleverly done, others of two hearts joined together: and in one I notice a drawing of a creek with an emu track going along the centre ... This rock is certainly the most wonderful natural feature I have ever seen. What a grand sight this must present in the wet season; waterfalls in every direction.

That is how the first Piranpa saw Uluru, a mere hill from the distance.

Ayers Rock is now Uluru again; Maggie's Spring is Mutitjulu waterhole. Gosse and the Afghan Kamran were the first non-Anangu to climb the rock. They followed the same route as Anangu elders do at the commencement of the Mala ceremonies. Since then a million or more visitors have followed in their footsteps.

Gosse, because he made for Uluru rather than Kata Tjuta, avoided Lake Amadeus, skirting around its eastern side. But on his return to King's Canyon to pick up the rest of the party he did find himself on its shores:

Tuesday July 22nd ... struck an arm of Lake Amadeus, bearing east and west, and about one mile [1.6 km] wide where I struck it, but increasing on either side ... While I was taking bearings I sent Kamran to ascertain whether we could cross the lake. He found it much firmer than I supposed, so I decided to try it, as in case of not getting over I should have to ride forty miles [65 km] round. We got over safely.

The barrier that had confounded Giles was easily crossed.

On 28 July Gosse approached Uluru once again and he observed:

This rock appears more wonderful every time I look at it, and I may say it is a sight worth riding over eighty-four miles [135 km] of spinifex sandhills to see.

Gosse and his party camped at and around Uluru for twelve days. For several of them it rained and Gosse was moved to write:

... water rushing in all directions. The rock presented a grand appearance this morning; close to our camp was a waterfall about 200 feet [60 m] high, the water coming down in one sheet of foam.

During a lull in the rain on a 'beautiful day', Gosse met Anangu at Uluru for the first time. His diary entry records:

Walking about the rock on west side I observed native fires quite close to us, and soon after two natives came for water, and after our making signs they came up to us, but seemed terribly frightened. I fancy they must have heard of whites before. They were all fine looking young men, about 5 ft 8 in [1.75 m] high, wearing their hair in the shape of a chignon, a string being tied tight, close to the head ... they seem very peaceable. All I could make out from them was that they call water 'carpee'. I gave them a fire stick, and they walked away.

Rain continued, but on Friday 8 August in boggy conditions Gosse started off for Mount Olga with his brother, ahead of the main party. He did not share Giles's passion for Kata Tjuta and this first Piranpa to reach it was rather dismissive of it:

This range is formed of a number of round-topped masses of solid conglomerate rock (known as pudding stone) ... each hill is a separate rock ... On the south side of the mount I found a spring, which I have named Felix Spring.

Those were his only comments before pushing westward.

Lack of water was the greatest hazard for the first Piranpa travellers. Few knew the locations of Anangu rockholes such as this one, called Yulara Pulka.

But Gosse too was soon forced back because of lack of water, after having penetrated only a short distance into Western Australia. He arrived back at the telegraph line on 13 December 1873.

Giles in the meantime had organised a new expedition and on 4 August 1873, the day Anangu told Gosse at Uluru that water was 'carpee', he departed from Ross's waterhole at the junction of the Alberga and Stevenson rivers.

This time Giles approached from the south, from the Musgrave Ranges, and made straight for Mount Olga. He described his arrival in mid-September 1873, just a few days before Gosse decided to turn back, as follows:

We now pushed on for [Mount Olga] over some stony and some scrubby country ... and by the middle of the next day we arrived at the foot of Mount Olga. Here I perceived the marks of a wagon and horses, and camel tracks; [these] I knew at once to be those of Gosse's expedition ... I had now travelled four hundred miles [650 km] to reach this mount, which when I first saw it was only seventy five or eighty miles [120 or 130 km] distant.

Giles's imagination, unlike that of Gosse, was stirred by Kata Tjuta, perhaps even over-stimulated:

The appearance of this mountain is marvellous in the extreme, and baffles an accurate description. I shall refer to it again, and may remark here that it is formed of several vast and solid, huge, and rounded blocks of bare red conglomerate stones, being composed of untold masses of rounded stones of all kinds and sizes, mixed like plums in a pudding, and set in vast and rounded shapes upon the ground. Water was running from the base, down a stony channel, filling several rocky basins ... I made an attempt to climb a portion of this singular mound, but the sides were too perpendicular; I could only get up about 800 to 900 feet [250–280 m], on the front or lesser mound; but without kites and ropes, or projectiles, or wings, or balloons, the main summit is unscaleable. The quandong fruit here was splendid — we dried a quantity in the sun. Some very beautiful black and gold butterflies, with very large wings, were seen here and collected. The thermometer to-day was 95 degrees F [36°C] in the shade. We enjoyed a most luxurious bath in the rocky basins. We moved the camp to softer ground, where there was a well-grassed flat a mile and a half [2.5 km] away.

The appearance of Mount Olga from this camp is truly wonderful; it displayed to our astonished eyes rounded minarets, giant cupolas, and monstrous domes. There they have stood as huge memorials of the ancient times of earth, for ages, countless eons of ages, since its creation first had birth. The rocks are smoothed with the attrition of the alchemy of years. Time, the old, the dim magician, had ineffectually laboured here, although with all the powers of ocean at his command; Mount Olga has remained as it was born; doubtless by the agency of submarine commotion of former days, beyond even the epoch of far-back history's phantom dream. From this encampment I can only liken Mount Olga to several enormous rotund or rather elliptical shapes of rouge mange, which had been placed beside one another by some extraordinary freak of convulsion of Nature.

Giles did not go to Uluru on that occasion but moved south-west to the Mann Ranges, mostly through spinifex, which he still roundly cursed as '... the porcupine, triodia, spinifex, Festuca irritan, and everything-else-abominable grass'. From there he proceeded due west. He roughly followed Gosse's route and reached about 75 miles [120 km] further west than he had. Then Giles too had to retreat. But when he came into view of Mount Olga once more he wrote:

... [Mount Olga's] appearance from here ... was most wonderful and grotesque. It seemed like five or six enormous pink hay-stacks, leaning for support against one another, with open cracks or fissures between, which came only about half-way down its face. I am sure this is one of the most extraordinary geographical features on the face of the earth, for, as I have said, it is composed of several enormous rounded stone shapes, like the backs of several monstrous kneeling pink elephants. At sixty miles [100 km] to the west its outline is astonishing. The highest point of all, which is 1500 feet [460 m] above the surrounding country, looked at from here, presents the appearance of a gigantic pink damper, or Chinese gong viewed edgeways, and slightly out of the perpendicular.

All that summer and autumn in fearful heat Giles and his men probed and pushed westward. In the end it became a never-ending search for water. One of the men, Alfred Gibson, died — he simply disappeared. Giles named the Gibson Desert after his companion. Giles, in a march that nearly claimed his own life, reached base camp and water. He soon recovered. On 21 May 1874 Giles admitted defeat and began the return journey to the telegraph line. On 5 June he reached his touchstone, Mount Olga, once again, and he wrote:

I rode completely round the mass of this wonderful feature; its extraordinary appearance will never be out of my remembrance. It is no doubt of volcanic origin, belched out of the bowels, and on to the surface, of the earth, by the sulphurous upheavings of subterraneous and subaqueous fires, and cooled and

Apart from the scarcity of water, spinifex, or porcupine grass, growing on seemingly limitless plains was the greatest impediment to the explorers. Giles called it 'that abominable vegetable production'.

solidified into monstrous masses by the gelid currents of the deepmost waves of the most ancient of former oceans ... Could I be buried at Mount Olga, I should certainly borrow Sir Christopher Wren's epitaph, Circumspice si monumentum requiris ['If you seek a monument, gaze around'].

On the 9 June 1874 Giles finally reached Uluru and was enraptured by it as well:

Its appearance and outline is most imposing, for it is simply a mammoth monolith that rises out of the sandy desert soil around, and stands with a perpendicular and totally inaccessible face at all points, except one slope near the north-west end, and that at least is but a precarious climbing ground to a height of more than 1100 feet [350 m]. Down its furrowed and corrugated sides the trickling of water for untold ages has descended in times of rain, and for long periods after, until the drainage ceased, into sandy basins at its feet ... The great difference between it and Mount Olga is in the rock form-ation, for this is one solid granite stone, and is part and parcel of the original rock, which, having been formed after its state of fusion in the beginning, has there remained, while the aged Mount Olga has been thrown up subsequently from below. Mount Olga is the more wonderful and grotesque; Mount Ayers the more ancient and sublime. There is permanent water here, but, unlike the Mount Olga springs, it lies all in standing pools ... It might almost be said of this, as of the Pyramids or the Sphinx, round the decay of that colossal rock, boundless and bare, the lone and level sands stretch far away. This certainly was a fine place for a camp. The water was icy cold; a plunge into its sunless deeps was a frigid tonic that, further west in the summer heats, would have been almost paradisiacal, while now it was almost a penalty ... We are encamped in the roomy cave, for we find it much warmer than in the outer atmosphere, warmth being as great a consideration now, as shade had formerly been.

Giles never found his snowy mountains or palmy plain, his fields of gold or golcondas of gems, but he did find his Mount Olga, Kata Tjuta, which always occupied a special place in his heart. Mount Olga made him grope for words as no other place in all his travels had. To express his feelings and his admiration, he was moved to excesses of purple prose and into the realm of science fiction.

In 1875 he found a way across western Australia — from the telegraph line to the Swan River. In 1876 he journeyed from Geraldton on the west coast, across the Gibson Desert, back to the telegraph line. But John Forrest and Warburton had both crossed before him.

Giles received honours from many European countries for his feats of exploration. In 1880 the Royal Geographical Society of London made him a fellow and awarded him their gold medal. However, unlike most notable explorers, he was denied an official government position. Governor Jervois of South Australia dismissed the idea with the comment, 'I am informed that he gambles and that his habits are not strictly sober'. Giles held various positions in Victoria, South Australia and Western Australia. He died of pneumonia on 13 November 1897, aged sixty-two.

William Gosse, the first Piranpa to climb Uluru, rose to the position of deputy surveyor general of South Australia. He died of a heart attack at the age of thirty-eight.

Twenty years after the discoveries of Giles, Gosse and others, visions of rich grazing country and snowy mountains, though not yet pots of gold, to the west of the telegraph line had been extinguished. Piranpa were now curious about the exact nature of central Australia — its natural history, geology, weather patterns and its original human inhabitants. The next Piranpa travellers of note to reach Uluru-Kata Tjuta were members of a scientific expedition, the Horn Expedition of 1894. As in the earlier journeys the primary objective lay elsewhere; in the case of the Horn Expedition it was the MacDonnell Ranges. But as before, Uluru-Kata Tjuta evoked a sense of wonder and drew the travellers inexorably. Only three members made the journey south from King Creek, the same setting-off place as Giles's first attempt and that of Gosse. The narrator, photographer and zoologist of the expedition was Sir Walter Baldwin Spencer, an Englishman, and the foundation professor of zoology at the University of Melbourne. On 16 June he and two companions, riding horses, left the rest of the expedition with its slow-moving camels and rode south. They trusted 'to luck in the matter of water'. In the afternoon of their second day out they reached the shore of Lake Amadeus and crossed it at a narrow point, leading their horses. Only one other Piranpa was known to have been here since Gosse's crossing. At nightfall they made camp on the lake's southern side. Spencer wrote about that evening:

> There was not a drop of water, only a dead level surface of pure, white salt, standing out sharply and strongly against the rich, ruddy after-glow in the west, the dull, steel-blue sky in the east and the dark purple banks, covered with scrub, which margined it north and south ... The silence was intense — not a bird's note of any kind and no sign of animal life save a gaunt old dingo ... The white sheet of salt, seen through the thin sharp stems of the mulga amongst which we were camped looked strangely weird ...

The next day Spencer and his companions finally approached Uluru:

> For thirty weary miles [50 km] we traversed the sand-hills and the narrow intervening flats covered with small, funereal looking 'desert oaks', where, at least, the ground was hard and the horses, sore and tired with toiling over the heavy sand and amongst the porcupine grass, had a few minutes' respite. At length we reached the top of the last sand-hill and saw Ayers Rock not far away. From where we stood the level scrub stretched away east, west and south to the distant horizon. Above the yellow sand and dull-green mulga, rose the Rock — a huge dome-shaped monolith, brilliant venetian-red in colour ... it stood out in lonely grandeur against the clear sky.

They camped at the oasis of Kantju Gorge where men and horses could finally drink their fill after three days of waterless travel, something that Spencer merely states as being 'no small pleasure'.

That day, or perhaps the next — that is, 19 or 20 June 1894 — Baldwin Spencer did something that visitors ever since have done or aspired to do to such an extent that it has become one of the major activities at Uluru: he photographed the Rock. He was the first person to do so. For his vantage point he chose virtually the same place as where hundreds of thousands of visitors each year watch the sunset change Uluru's colours.

For Spencer, photography was no casual affair with tiny pocket cameras:

We had with us in addition to our riding horses two pack horses carrying our provisions, a small supply of water and not least in importance the camera, the careful packing of which, to prevent its being completely smashed up as the horses jogged or sometimes crashed through the Mulga scrub, was not an easy matter. Photographing in Central Australia when on the march from day to day is not altogether pleasant or easy. The light is intense and extra precautions must be taken to prevent light fogging of the plates ... The jogging of the horses and camels is very liable to smash [glass] plates — I lost nearly two dozen of mine in this way — and fine sand grains penetrate everything and often scratch the film. It is almost impossible to avoid this in Central Australia ...

One hundred years later I can identify with this last sentiment. While cameras have become light and small, lenses are of better quality and greater variety, images are recorded in colour, electronic devices determine exposures and photography is a great pleasure if not always easy, one thing has not changed — grains of sand penetrate everything, scratching the film and occasionally playing havoc with delicate electronics.

Nonetheless, many of Spencer's photographs of central Australian landscapes and later of Aboriginal people are still unsurpassed.

Also like modern-day visitors, Spencer wished to climb Uluru. He observed:

Just at sunset we made an attempt to climb, but were quite content to stop when we had reached a height of about two hundred feet [60 m]. The surface was so smooth and steep that we could only climb by means of clinging on with our fingers to little projecting flakes of rock. Every now and then there was a hump, on the upper surface of which the incline was less steep than elsewhere, and on one of these we came to rest, quite satisfied that the climb to the top was not worth the attendant risks, as the slightest slip would have been fatal ... Our camp fire began to show out clearly in the dark chasm beneath us and ... we saw a family of wild, sand-hill natives making their way ... round the base of the mountain towards our camp.

In a sense Spencer could be regarded as the very first tourist, the first *minga*, or 'ant', as Anangu would say, taking photographs and attempting to climb Uluru. But there was a lot more to Baldwin Spencer. He was a sensitive and observant zoologist and a more sympathetic and acute observer of the ways of Aboriginal people than was usual for his time. He and his companions had come to learn about the land, the people, the plants and animals for their own sakes, with genuine curiosity, open minds and goodwill — great rarities in the early days of the Piranpa invasion.

By Anangu these three Piranpa must have been viewed with initial apprehension and then with amusement and indulgence. Spencer was passionately interested in all aspects of natural history, something that has been mentioned in Chapter Nine. In the spirit of the time he was a collector, preserving the skins of birds and mammals, pinning out insects or putting them in alcohol. He readily admits that without the generous and exuberant assistance of skilled Anangu trackers the collection, especially of small mammals, reptiles and certain insects, would have been very meagre indeed. Spencer realised that by accepting 'specimens' from Anangu he was taking their food and he was eager to repay them somehow. But there was nothing of his, neither clothing nor food, neither artefacts nor weapons, that they desired or could use. All Anangu could do was to laugh and scratch their heads as Spencer and his assistants peeled off the skin of a small mammal and threw away the rest instead of eating it, or put the honey ants given them in a bottle of alcohol instead of enjoying their sweetness. But Spencer's passion for learning about animals new to him would have appealed to Anangu. The expedition 'discovered' a species of honey ant new to science and it was subsequently named *Melophorus cowlei* after E. C. Cowle, an expedition member. Many other species new to science were collected by the expedition.

After a single day at Uluru Spencer set off for Kata Tjuta. He found the 25 kilometre journey uneventful and described the monoliths as follows:

We steered our course for the southern end, where there was apparently the highest dome-shaped mass, and rounding this just at sunset we turned into a magnificent ravine, the sides of which rose precipitously for a height of 1500 feet [460 m].* The rocks were quite bare and of the usual red colour with great streaks of black looking just as if enormous cauldrons of molten tar had been emptied on to their rounded summits and had flowed down the sides.

*Olga Gorge.

In certain respects Mount Olga is almost more impressive than Ayers Rock: it has the form of a number of huge masses like the latter thrown together and separated from one another by deep ravines ...

Approaching Kata Tjuta, Spencer and his two companions surprised a group of Anangu:

These sandhill blacks had never seen a white man before, and in their alarm one or two of the men seized their spears and poised them on their womeras, or spear-throwers, but fortunately Lungkartitukukana's* powerful voice was heard just in time to prevent what would have been an uncomfortable reception for ourselves. They evidently thought that man and beast were one creature, and when the latter came in two and we dismounted they were much alarmed ... However, we reassured them as well as we could and they promised to come to our camp, but as soon as we were out of sight ... they took all their worldly possessions and fled up one of the lower hills flanking the main mass, and there as the darkness came on we saw their camp fires dotted about.

The next day Spencer and company, with three Anangu men following them on foot, returned to Uluru where they found a gathering of Pitjantjatjara people cooking two red kangaroos they had just speared. The day after that the Piranpa set off to rejoin their expedition.

Spencer's parting comment, written some years later, was:

There is nothing to tempt ordinary travellers into this desolate, forsaken part of Australia; in fact no one has been there since our visit, now more than ten years ago, and no one is likely to go there again for years to come.

His prophecy for the short term was quite correct. For more than thirty years Anangu lived undisturbed by Piranpa except for the occasional dogger looking for dingo scalps or prospector looking for gold.

All that changed in the 1930s when a natural disaster and the Piranpa invasion combined to shatter Anangu's age-old traditional life forever.

---

*An Anangu who had accompanied the party on foot from Uluru, easily keeping up with the horses. *Lungkartitukukana* probably means *lungkata Tjukurpa*, or 'blue-tongued lizard Dreaming'. This man is thought to have been Paddy Uluru's father. Paddy himself was very active in the Land Rights movement that eventually resulted in the return of Uluru and Kata Tjuta to Anangu. His sons live there now.

ANANGU AND HANDBACK

Kata Kura, Barbara Tjikatu, Peter Kanari and Elsie Malpangka are among Uluru-Kata Tjuta's traditional owners. They are in their sixties and seventies, Kata Kura perhaps in his eighties. All were born in the bush and during their long and eventful lives kept in constant touch with Uluru-Kata Tjuta. They never lost their bond with it. In that time they experienced all the changes that Piranpa settlement brought: invasion, dispossession, the sway of missionaries, and finally Handback, the return of their traditional lands in the form of inalienable freehold title. From a carefree childhood living as nomads and learning all the traditional ways and attachments, they have lived to see 250,000 strangers come to their lands each year, and have to deal with managing them. These and other elders are ultimately responsible for management policies and practices. It is a responsibility they address with determination and conviction and a wisdom gathered over long lives and from ancient traditions.

Kata Kura is not very tall with a shock of curling grey hair. He is possessed of a cheerful and, in the past, rebellious spirit. Barbara is a little stout but very fit, often spending long hours gathering bush foods. She has a great devotion to the National Park and when she thinks it necessary uses her forceful personality to see that its integrity is maintained. She and Elsie are half-sisters and have been close friends since early childhood. Peter Kanari is of medium height, thin and frail, his face lined. His left eye is missing as the result of an accident. He is soft-spoken with a quiet, sometimes self-deprecating sense of humour.

The five of us together with Julian Barry, who once again has taken the time to translate, are at the base of a bouldery slope that leads to Kata Tjuta's Valley of the Winds. It is a warm morning with the promise of a hot day. Peter Kanari shows me some cassia bushes covered in bright-yellow flowers and comments that when they are out like this it means that *malu*, the red kangaroo, is fat. Pointing to profusely flowering Victoria wattle shrubs, which they call *aliti*, Barbara and Elsie say that these were favoured food of *ninu*, the bilby. We walk over to what look like old diggings, burrows perhaps, although there are no holes in the ground, just loose mounds of gravelly soil. I venture that these may have been the work of *tjungku*, the burrowing bettong, long since extinct from these parts.

The immediate and unanimous response is 'No, of course not. Don't you know that *tjungku* lived in the sandy country, quite different from this rough ground? These were made by *nganamara* [the mallee fowl]'. Which is equally remarkable for it too disappeared from here many years ago. Elsie and Barbara say they have seen mallee fowl right here at this place when they came on camelback as children. Elsie describes how the male bird would heap up the mound's soil and debris or scratch it away, according to whether he wanted to raise or lower its temperature. That way the temperature remained constant and the eggs were incubated. Everyone agrees that the eggs, when cooked in the fire, tasted very good. They never killed the birds but harvested a good few of their eggs. Not any more though, they comment sadly, for *nganamara*, like *tjungku* and so many other animals, has gone. But when they were young these and other animals were here; they hunted and ate them.

Like many deleterious changes, the decline of animals began in the 1930s when there was a bad drought. So bad, Barbara says, that while she and her family walked away from Kata Tjuta to Uluru, her father died of starvation on the way. Many other people also died. Barbara and other members of her family lived for nearly two years around Uluru, mostly on *maku*, witchetty grubs, before moving on to cattle stations and missions where there was enough food.

Peter Kanari takes me gently by the arm to a small rise away from the others. With his few words of English he explains the significance of landmarks to the north and west. A place called Ngapala, and Mount Currie. Pointing to a mulga woodland in the middle distance, he says, 'That is where I speared my first kangaroo'. He points to other places he had told me about when I recorded his story at Jon Willis's house, where Jon, who also speaks Pitjantjatjara, translated.

Kata Kura joins us and tells of how tough it was in the days of drought. To complement their food, or just to eat, they would sometimes spear sheep or cattle. He and other young men would lie in wait at places where the cattle came to drink. The men would spear a bullock through the neck, then smash its head with a big rock. They were big animals, with lots of fat, but Kata Kura preferred kangaroos. The police would come and take the people away in chains, he says, for spearing cattle. Kata Kura shows me scars around his ankle from the time he himself was taken to gaol. He had speared sheep, taken flour and some horses. When he was caught he and the others were chained together and walked to Ernabella. From there they were taken by truck to Finke and then to Alice Springs by train. He says he was the first prisoner in the new gaol there, which would have been in 1938. While in prison he chopped firewood for the warders' households. He was locked up for a very long time. Other people came and went,

Previous pages: Girls painted for Kuniya inma. *Above and right: Anangu elders. Most were born in the bush and spent their early lives as arid zone nomads, travelling a region of which Uluru and Kata Tjuta were important focal points. Above: Kata Kura was taken in chains to the Alice Springs jail in 1938 for stealing horses. He still bears the scars around his ankles.*

but he stayed, he says. Finally one day he was given a blanket and told to be on his way. 'That was it', he says, 'no money, no food'. So he walked 200 kilometres to Erldunda, south of Alice Springs, to join his family.

When the drought was over it was many years before the land was restored to its original state. Where cattle and sheep had been introduced it never fully recovered. Many animal species important to Anangu were gone forever or became increasingly scarce. Food in the bush was harder to get and the necessity of killing cattle and sheep remained.

The others join in. Barbara says:

I want to tell you something. When I was just a small child I saw my uncle and his relations spearing cattle. We all ate some, but we were really scared, we ran away and hid. We were at Tempe Downs then. One day we saw these policemen coming and they picked up the adults, including some women. They shot all the dogs and threw them on the fire and burnt them.

There were only the kids left and the policeman said, 'Go on you mob, off you go to Wallara Ranch'. It was a long way and we had no dogs to help us hunt and keep us warm at night. But my uncle's younger brother's dog was away in the bush when the police were there. It came back and travelled with us. We saw a kangaroo and killed it and eventually we got to Wallara Ranch. There were no roads then, only footpaths. The policemen, they were crazy men, terrible, evil men.

Not long after that we were walking in the bush when we saw this thing on the path, and we said to each other, 'What is this? What kind of animal made this track?' We looked at it and dug around it. As we were looking we saw this car coming, a really old kind of car. It was the first time we had seen a motor car and its tracks. The car was full of missionaries. They said to us, 'Oh, look at these poor Aborigines, we must give them some food'. So they gave us flour, beef, sugar, tea, even a cabbage. The missionaries were driving around handing out food and telling people they were making a place for Anangu to live so that they would not have to kill people's bullocks. That place was Areyonga and I lived there for a while.

Billy Wara is a tall, strong upright man in his seventies who has lived in the bush all his life.

In 1934 another incident of police persecution took place at Uluru and had far-reaching effects on Anangu's lives. It is only in recent years that Anangu have come to terms with it. It concerned Paddy Uluru's brother. Paddy's name, and that of his sons, is the same as that of the monolith. Paddy was a traditional owner deeply involved in reclaiming his lands. He has since died.

Paddy's brother had been taken into custody suspected of killing an Aboriginal man. He escaped, apparently because he did not trust Piranpa law and feared for his life from the police. The police tracked Paddy's brother to Uluru and pursued him to a cave at Mutitjulu waterhole. There a policeman shot and killed him. Anangu now living at Uluru still speak of the incident with bitterness; they are still haunted by it. Paddy's son Cassidy, looking infinitely sad and bemused, says, 'I'm still constantly thinking about this. I still can't get it out of my mind'.

A board was set up to inquire into the shooting and found that the killing, 'though legally justified, was not warranted'. The policeman concerned received no punishment and remained a protector of Aborigines, rising to a high rank in the force. He later boasted that he had never shown any weakness towards Aborigines and said that he had ignored a 1940 order to stop chaining Anangu by the neck. He claimed the method allowed the prisoners to walk more easily, and when tied up to a tree at night, they could still move around.

The killing of Paddy Uluru's brother, and perhaps also the fact that the police tracked, hunted and killed people as if they were kangaroos or dogs, terrified Anangu. They fled to distant places, a very frightened people.

In the 1930s drought and the invasion by cattle, sheep and horses reduced Anangu's bush foods and water supplies to below subsistence levels. Police patrols drove them from their lands in fear. They retreated to the relative safety of cattle stations and missions. Anangu never returned to a full-time life in the bush. Those days were gone forever.

Gold fever sporadically swept through Anangu lands, in the Petermann Ranges. The search for gold brought Anangu a foretaste of Piranpa bustle and machinery. It also created a legend.

In 1900, while travelling alone through the ranges, Harold Bell Lasseter claimed to have found a huge reef of gold. He persuaded a Sydney-based syndicate, called the Central Australia Gold Exploration Co. Ltd, to mount an expedition to find the gold. The expedition, under Lasseter's leadership, arrived in central Australia in 1930 with trucks and even aeroplanes. No reef was found and the disappointed expedition members left. Lasseter was abandoned by them. When he was in the Petermann Ranges his two camels got away. Peter Kanari remembers him living there in a cave. Peter and his family tried to give him food but, he says, Lasseter was like a crazy man, and kept firing his pistol at Anangu. When Lasseter decided to walk to Kata Tjuta, Kanari and his family again tried to help him by guiding him to water and giving him food. Lasseter refused their assistance. Starving, suffering from exposure in the summer heat and possibly demented, he died near Irving Creek, still well short of Kata Tjuta. Anangu buried him there. Maureen Natjuna, Peter Kanari's wife, then a child, helped in the burial. Other expeditions returned to the place again and again, some as late as 1970, looking for gold. None was ever found.

Not all Piranpa came to terrorise or to exploit. A few came with curiosity and goodwill to learn about Anangu and their world. One was Baldwin Spencer who came in 1894. But he stayed only a few days. In 1935 came another, Charles P. Mountford, one of Australia's most highly regarded anthropologists. He was 'so impressed with [Uluru's] strange beauty and vast size that I set myself the task of making a survey of all phases of aboriginal life associated with this natural feature'. This first visit was also brief, but he returned during the winter of 1940. He then came to Uluru and Kata Tjuta in the course of a journey that lasted several months. He travelled by camel through Pitjantjatjara and Yankunytjatjara heartlands in the Musgrave and Mann ranges in South Australia. This must have been a fabulous journey, one of the great anthropological expeditions, for even then the region was little known to and little travelled by observant Piranpa. According to Mountford:

> In 1940 ... the Aborigines of the Pitjandjara tribe of the Mann Ranges were almost untouched by European culture and those of the Musgrave Ranges had been under the influence of a mission station for only a few years.*

Mountford travelled slowly, took photographs and kept notes. He came to have respect and affection for Anangu. He wrote:

> Anyone who has travelled with these people day after day ... will soon develop an esteem and often a considerable affection for them.

He was also impressed by the Anangu way of life:

> ... a culture with tools so simple that the gaining of a livelihood in that desert environment is a remarkable achievement; a culture with a code of laws so well balanced that there is no need for organised warfare to maintain a social balance, and a culture where the people are at peace with each other and the surroundings in which they live.

Anangu confided in Mountford and allowed him free rein with his camera. The result of the photography alone is a perceptive and wide-ranging view into traditional Anangu life.

Four more times during the next twenty years Mountford returned to Uluru-Kata Tjuta, but each journey was too short to satisfy his thirst for knowledge. Finally, in 1960, he returned for an extended visit and documented what he thought were Anangu associations with the rocks. But by then, he says, 'the effects of civilisation

*Ernabella, which was established in 1937.

Maureen Natjuna eats one of the honey ants called tjala, *which she dug from deep in its underground nest.*

and the restrictive practices of the Christian missions have caused rapid changes to take place in the culture of the Pitjandjara tribe'.

Mountford's writings in *Brown Men and Red Sand, Ayers Rock: Its People, Their Beliefs and Their Art* and the mammoth *Nomads of the Australian Desert* stirred Piranpa imaginations. They are a major source of romantic notions about arid zone nomads. In later life Mountford received many honours from universities, learned societies and governments.

While Anangu who knew Mountford in the past no doubt held a certain regard and affection for him, nowadays they are rather dismissive of him. Other Anangu, such as Tjamiwa, take serious issue with some of his writings and many elders were horrified that photographs of secret-sacred places, ceremonies and objects were published. As a result the above books had to be withdrawn from sale.

Tony Tjamiwa has some trenchant comments about the writings of Mountford and also those of Bill Harney, who came later. He told me:

It's really incomprehensible to Anangu that people whose fathers didn't own this place should take possession of it in this way. Their fathers' places were somewhere like Adelaide or Sydney. When they came here they were overcome by the marvellousness of the place; this enormous rock that had no sand or spinifex or bushes on it. They were overcome by their delight in Uluru and they wanted to explain it and to understand where it was from. But they had no chance; their fathers had nothing to teach them about it. They were older men when they came here but as far as this place was concerned they were children. They understood nothing, they knew nothing.

It seems Mountford's ambitions in documenting Pitjantjatjara and Yankunytjatjara culture were not matched by his methodology. Anangu say he got a lot of it wrong. More recent research by Pitjantjatjara-speaking anthropologists reveal Mountford's work to range from the absolutely accurate to pure fiction. The Kuniya and Liru myths of Uluru, for example, are faithfully told, but the creator beings and their deeds that he assigns to Kata Tjuta are entirely wrong. No one is suggesting that Mountford deliberately invented or falsified anything, rather that he did not speak the language and that some of his informants were the wrong people.

Tony Tjamiwa was brought up at Ernabella Mission. He is a member of the National Park Board of Management and a spokesman for the Anangu community.

Nganinytja, a charismatic woman who lives not far south of Uluru and teaches Piranpa about Anangu life, knew Mountford when she was a child. A photograph of her, captioned 'Girl, Nannindja' appears in *Nomads of the Australian Desert*. Her assessment is: 'Mountford didn't know any Pitjantjatjara. You could tell him anything'. The inference being that without speaking Pitjantjatjara you will never fully understand Anangu and their traditions.

The irreversible changes that projected Anangu into a world dominated by Piranpa began in the 1930s. Some of the changes can be charted through the lives of the elders such as Tony Tjamiwa, Barbara Tjikatu and Peter Kanari. I have conversations with all three in the Mutitjulu community where they live. The community is a collection of houses and offices, a clinic, a store, a garage and a church. It is within a kilometre of Uluru. About 100 to 150 Anangu live here. I am fortunate that Jon Willis, the community liaison officer, agrees to translate.

My first conversation is with Tony Tjamiwa. He is a little younger than Barbara and Peter, of medium height, trim and vigorous. He is a consummate orator with a wonderful imagery to his speech. He is also a natural leader, a highly respected and knowledgeable Law man, and often acts as spokesman for the community. The following is some of what he told me:

As a very small child I didn't live in a house, I just lived out in the bush with my mother and father at a place just south of the Mann Ranges. Then my mother and father went to live in a house at the Ernabella Presbyterian Mission and I grew up there. We still hunted and gathered bush foods. The women would collect plant food and also smaller animals that live in burrows, such as goannas. The men would hunt the bigger animals — kangaroos, euros and emus.

Billy Wara's grandson and pet red kangaroo.

I learnt to use a spear from my father and older brother. They made me a spear and gave it to me when I was still a child. My father would make a target on a gum tree, a small skinny tree, so I had to be accurate. I would practise throwing at that. That is how I learnt how to use a spear and spear-thrower. From then on I used them on my own. That was my father's and my grandfather's way. I learnt properly. I'd see a kangaroo going along its trail and I'd think to myself, 'Where am I going to pierce it and how am I going to get near it?'. Many times I went hunting with my father. I would drive a kangaroo towards him, my father would spear it and I would run up and also spear it.

I really liked school and I learnt to read and write. It was my kind of place. It wasn't like in the city where there are lots of things to distract you. It was just one man talking and the only noise was an occasional motor car that made funny sounds. If you argued with the teacher you got hit. So I never did. There was food in the store. It was a good life and I enjoyed it.

When I finished school at twelve or thirteen and was still an uninitiated boy I learnt how to shear sheep. I also learnt to ride a horse for it was important for the work. I was a shearer for many years. It was hard work.

When I was a man I said to Mr Trudinger, who was the boss at Ernabella, 'Let's go to some places in the Petermann Ranges'. We had a buggy, or jinker, with iron wheels that was pulled by a horse. I drove that. We also had five more horses and four camels. We had lots of food and we also shot dingoes on the way for their scalps. Three Anangu men came with us.

We went north through Amata and then we changed our minds about where to go. We decided to go to Uluru where I'd never been. Mr Trudinger kept saying, 'Where is this place?'. We weren't even halfway yet. We would say, 'Well, we don't know. It's over there somewhere'.

When we got to Patji rockhole we could see Uluru clearly. We woke up in the morning and we said to each other, 'My God, that rock is so close, and so clear and smooth without any plants growing on it'. We decided to go over and spend a night or two there. We got close at sunset and the rock was turning red. Everyone was excited, especially Mr Trudinger. He was made very, very happy by the sight. We felt really good about his having this wonderful experience because he had done so much for us and we wanted to repay him in some way. Mr Trudinger helped raise me and taught me at Ernabella, and this was a chance to show him something, to teach him something.

I was very excited myself. I just couldn't believe it, how big it was, how smoothly formed, how beautiful and red. We camped at Taputji and the next day we rode right around the rock. I understood only a little about Uluru at that time.

I stayed and stayed at Ernabella until my hair and beard were beginning to turn grey. I went through the Law there and became a man. I married and had three children. My father had never taken me to his country at Ulkiya, which is near the Mann Ranges, but I knew all about it because I knew the Law. So I finally decided to go to Ulkiya, that's Mala *Tjukurpa* country. I spent two years looking after Ulkiya and learning about it.

I learnt the Law for Ulkiya, like all *Tjukurpa*, from my father and my older brothers. You learn it and keep it in your head and don't talk about it. You learn through constant repetition. People make things clear to you and you visit the country. That helps to clarify things as well. You start off as a *nyiinka*, a boy about to be initiated, and you are taught particular parts of the Law, particular stories and verses of song. You must learn those by rote. As you get older things are repeated and other things added. When you go and visit the country, the special places, things begin to fall into place in your head. Gradually you build up your knowledge, it builds in layers.

In the earlier stages you learn things that in themselves do not make much sense. Then somebody tells you one other thing, or you're taken to a place and shown something, and suddenly a whole lot of things you didn't understand come together into sharp focus. That is how I learnt the Law for Ulkiya but also for this place and especially the Mala line.

So now I am a holder of the Law and a teacher of it. I help young men to understand what they do not understand. I go to initiation ceremonies in many places because I know the Law that trains boys to be men. Because of my place in the Law, my knowledge of it, I went to Canberra to speak for the Law for this place so that we could get this land back. Since Handback I have lived mostly here at Mutitjulu.

Barbara Tjikatu says she was born in the bush at a place whose name she will not mention for it is a powerful *Tjukurpa* place for women, but it lies somewhere between Docker River and the Mann Ranges. There are lots of big rocky mountains there, she says. She continues:

When I was a baby we travelled around in my grandmother's and grandfather's country. There were lots of people, all my family, and they all walked. But I was very small so they carried me. We lived off bush tucker, figs, desert raisins, desert tomatoes, bush beans. We also gathered the seeds of grasses, ground them, mixed them with water and put the dough in the fire to cook. Just like a damper.

My grandmother was always looking for animals that were living in holes. She would catch possums and bilbies and kill them by hitting them with a

Above: Maku, *witchetty grubs, take two or more years to grow to maturity in the roots of wattles or eucalypts. Above right: Barbara Tjikatu was born in the bush to the west of Kata Tjuta. She is a member of the National Park Board of Management. Right: Cooking* maku. *They are a tasty and nutritious food.*

stick. She would say, 'Look, there is a woma python inside this hole'. She would dig it out and kill it. It was lovely meat. The men killed kangaroos with spears and spear-throwers. They had no rifles in those days. There were huge amounts of all kinds of food. There was plenty of water and lots of animals and plants. There were no Piranpa then.

I first came to Uluru with my mother and father when I was a small naked child, still only eating witchetty grubs. I came again when I was a little older. I came with my mother, grandmother, older sister, older brother and Elsie Malpangka. She was a little girl then. My mother and Elsie's mother were sisters and both were married to my father. We moved to Uluru because there was drought. There was no food. My father grew very thin and died of starvation before we got here. The drought was so bad that all the animals finished and many people also died.

We came to Mutitjulu waterhole because there is always water there. There was no one else. Nipper [her future husband] and his family had gone to Hermannsburg. Malya's [another senior man from Uluru] family had gone to Areyonga. We stayed and we stayed, eating mostly witchetty grubs.

There were no roads here then, only Anangu footpaths. While we were living here at that time we saw a white fella. He had one camel and was camped at Ininti waterhole. This same fella used to bring people from Alice Springs — the first tourists — in some kind of motorised buggy. At that time we did not understand what was going on, we did not know who they were.

Eventually some white fellas took us from Uluru to Wallara Ranch and from there to Tempe Downs. They had food with them and a cart drawn by four camels. The cart had a canopy on it. One of the white fellas was a grumpy old man. He was married but his wife had left him. He was always saying, 'Hurry up, go on, keep moving, don't stop'. And we kept saying, 'No, it is too hot, we're too tired'. The old man then got a whip out and cracked it quite close to us. Peter Kanari's brother, who was quite young, picked up a spear and threw it at the man, hitting him on the arm. It was not a bad wound, just a nick on the inside of his arm.

The old man went really wild. He kicked everyone off the cart and swore really badly at them. He left a little food and water and took off fast. A little later on the man came back and picked me up, because I was very little, and my old grandmother. He left everyone else. Eventually we all got to Wallara Ranch. But after a little while we moved to Tempe Downs, which was a cattle station in those days. While we were there some of the men speared a bullock and there was that trouble with the police I told you about.

After some years and when Nipper's brother Lively got married we all moved to Areyonga. By that time the war had come and Nipper went off to Darwin

Gathering fruits and seeds.

to work in the army. I was a young teenager then and I did not yet know Nipper. We stayed there and stayed there and built roads and a whole lot of houses. The boss was Pastor Albrecht. He was living at Hermannsburg but came to oversee what was happening at Areyonga.

Nipper came back to Areyonga. I was working in the kitchen, an outside kitchen where I made dampers and things. Nipper worked building roads, cutting down trees and looking after the vegetable garden. There were lots of people working there. Nipper was married before to an Arrernte woman, but she passed away. Nipper liked me and he came up to me and said, 'My brother is married to your sister. Why don't we get married?'. I thought Nipper was very handsome and I liked him too, but I was really scared. But my mother said, 'Don't be silly, don't be scared. He is a really good man, you can marry him'. When he came back from Darwin Nipper had this big stockman's hat and he was a good worker. So we got married, in the bush not in the church. I started working in the school after that.

Some years later the missionaries gave Areyonga to the government. Instead of giving rations, they gave out tickets. We had to work to get the tickets. It was very hard for some women who were living there; they were widows or single mothers with children to look after and no husbands. The white fellas would not give them any food. They said, 'Well, you're young women. Go out and get some rabbits'. They were bad people at Areyonga then. But we were happy because we didn't know any better. We didn't really care. We had no money. We were happy to get a blanket or a dress.

We had children there and then we travelled, often by camel, to lots of places, some quite far away. We spent some time at Ernabella. Then at Handback we came to live here, to work here in the National Park and to teach Piranpa how to look after it.

Peter Kanari grew up to adulthood living as a nomad in the arid zone. He grew up in the area that is now National Park, especially around Kata Tjuta and at Mount Currie to the north-west. He says there was a big mob of them, including many children, walking about. He remembers catching bandicoots and burrowing bettongs as well as rabbits. At night when there was a bright moon they would go out hunting possums. They might catch as many as nine in a night. He goes on to say:

We would go to a waterhole, camp there till the animals we hunted were finished, then go to the next waterhole. We would come to Uluru from Kata Tjuta, and stay overnight halfway. If it was dry, my mother would carry water in a *piti* on her head. Our whole family would come here and we'd make a little camp at Ininti waterhole. We'd stay two or three days, do some hunting and then go home towards Kata Tjuta.

My father taught me how to use a spear and I practised on rabbits. When I was still a child, but growing up a little bit, I would see the men bringing back things like kangaroos and emus and I'd think I'd really like to do that too. But I was a bit scared and a bit nervous. Not long after that I speared my first kangaroo. The spear went right through his chest. All the men were very happy and proud of me.

In a very good season, before the big drought, people would travel a long way; a whole lot of people would come together from all different countries, and we'd stay together for a while. It was not really for ceremonies, just to see the country, have a holiday. All the time we'd keep moving in a big circle.

Top: Fruit of the quandong tree; both the flesh and the kernel of the hard seed are edible. Above: Honey ant workers store nectar, or honey-dew, in their abdomens, which swell enormously. Different kinds of 'honey' have different colours.

HAWTHORN SECONDARY COLLEGE
BURGESS STREET
EAST HAWTHORN, 3123

Peter Kanari demonstrates how he used to tie up a kangaroo after it had been speared. He grew to adulthood as a nomad in the area around Kata Tjuta for which he has special responsibilities.

Cassidy's father [Paddy Uluru] — he's passed away now — he took me and other boys on a long trip to teach us the Law. We travelled from Kata Tjuta all the way to the Musgrave Ranges. We came to a place where the men gathered together. I got a bit frightened and ran away, me and another boy. We ran all the way back home to my mother and father, catching and eating rabbits on the way.

We did not wear any clothes in those days. We were all naked, both men and women.

A big drought came and a lot of people died. The animals were finished. I was a grown man by then. I had gone through the Law. I went to Wallara Ranch. All the naked people went there so I went to have a look. A white fella gave me some trousers and I did a bit of work with camels and some really hard work building yards. I didn't like that. I thought to myself, 'Stuff this', and I left, leaving the trousers behind.

Just after the war I wanted to get married and I asked Maureen [Natjuna] if she'd marry me. She said yes. So I talked to all her relatives and they were really happy about it. We got married in a church at Angas Downs.

I saw my first white man quite a way south of here. There were a few of them and they had a lot of camels. I don't know where they had come from but they were travelling to Warburton where they had already started to build a mission. I was still a boy and together with the other kids I'd help look after the camels. The missionaries gave us some food. It was curry and had onions in it. We put it in our mouths, it made them burn. Yuk.

They gave us some old flourbags with holes cut in the sides and in the bottom and they made us put them on as shirts. My father had just passed away. After a few days the missionaries moved on. They went and built a school. I stayed in the bush, a naked boy with no father, no trousers and no shirt. Just a flourbag.

Sometimes there were fights, but not very often. We had some fights with Yankunytjatjara but most fights were about young women. Young men would come and grab them and mistreat them. Straight away there'd be spears. Men who mistreated women would be speared in the fleshy part of the thigh. It could be quite serious because there was no medicine. It happened to me once. I don't know why the man got cranky for I hadn't done anything. The spear went right through my leg. I took the barb off the spear and then pulled it out backwards. Sometimes you have to break the spear and push it through. We had no bandages so I took my headband off and wrapped it around tight to stop the bleeding. I dressed the wound with the belly fat of a rabbit and used the skin as a bandage.

One day before the war we were sitting at Puta-Puta west of Kata Tjuta eating some damper made of grass seeds when we heard a terrible noise — 'whirrrr'. Coming low over the hill was this aeroplane.* Men, women and children took off in all directions. We were sitting in the bushes watching this thing fly over.

Now white men and women and black men and women are working together looking after this place. That's good. That's very, very good.

Back in 1920 Uluru, Kata Tjuta and the Petermann Ranges were gazetted as an Aboriginal Reserve for the exclusive use of Anangu. It meant no pastoral leases could be established and as a consequence cattle and sheep never grazed Uluru-Kata Tjuta and areas to the west of it. However, doggers and prospectors seemed to have roamed the region unchallenged by Piranpa law.

Uluru, after World War II, could no longer be kept a secret. Tourists began to arrive. In 1957 Bill Harney was appointed the first ranger. Harney is a legend among Piranpa. Many of their romantic views of central Australia and its Aboriginal people as well as the white settlers are from his writings — *North of 23, Life among the Aborigines, Content to Lie in the Sun* and others. Despite only a few years of formal schooling Harney wrote with imagination and flair. He apparently was a spellbinding story-teller. For five years, until 1962, he was Uluru-Kata Tjuta's Piranpa 'custodian'. Despite the fact that he lived among Aboriginal people for long periods, was married to an Aboriginal woman and had great empathy with them, he was resented rather than admired by Uluru's Anangu. The main reason was that he assumed 'ownership' of something to which he was not entitled. It was not his father's and his grandfather's country. He did not understand the place and he did not keep visitors out of secret–sacred places. In their view he did not look after the place properly. The fact that he ordered senior Anangu about and made them do menial tasks did not endear him to them either.

Tjamiwa compares the coming of tourists to sheep or bullocks being suddenly let out of a yard through a gate. They all come racing out, just anyhow in a silly way. 'Bill Harney opened the gate.' He adds, 'There's not a lot we can do about it. The gate is open'.

In Harney's second year as ranger, tourism was well established; 2296 visitors came that year. Also in 1958 Uluru and Kata Tjuta were excised from the Aboriginal Reserve and became a tourist and wildlife reserve. Anangu lost control of two of their most sacred places. Ten years on, in 1968, 23,000 people came to Uluru.

As years went by an airstrip was built right beside Uluru and Taputji. Camping grounds, motels and other accommodation sprang up higgledy-piggledy, close to

*In 1930 and 1933 the surveyor and map-maker D. Mackay used aeroplanes for surveys and had an airstrip constructed near Docker River.

the Rock. Many aspects of the complex became eyesores, and erosion and waste disposal problems became apparent.

The Commonwealth Department of the Interior, which looked after the Northern Territory, commissioned a report on the problem, which was published in September 1972. It states:

> The unsightly accommodation facilities and associated activities concentrated in the flat plain surrounding Ayers Rock cheapen and diminish its visual impact besides creating problems of water supply, litter accumulation, waste disposal, health hazards, dust pollution, disturbance of the indigenous flora and fauna and soil erosion. Furthermore, the prevention of vandalism, desecration of Aboriginal sites and damage to cave and rock paintings is made more difficult because of the sprawling village and the ease with which people can get to the Rock in the evening or at night. The Park staff are fulfilling a double role and have divided loyalties and responsibilities. Unfortunately their vital interpretative and wardening roles are diminished when tourists are most numerous because of routine domestic chores such as emptying waste bins or inevitable domestic crises such as blocked toilets. Whilst much could be done to improve the village landscape it will always be an artificial intrusion.
>
> The transfer of the village from its present location to elsewhere, preferably outside the Park boundaries, seems highly desirable since it would greatly improve the environmental situation and enable a more rewarding experience to be gained by Park visitors as a whole.

These are two visionary paragraphs in an otherwise dry and technical report. The response was equally visionary and in 1983 Yulara Village, with all the needed facilities for an enormous tourist influx, was opened 20 kilometres from Uluru, outside the National Park. It is a beautifully and cleverly designed complex integrated into a landscape of spinifex and dunes. It is no eyesore. The old airstrip, motels and camping grounds have all but disappeared from around Uluru and the land has been rehabilitated. The year after Yulara was opened more than 109,000 visitors came to see Uluru.

Progress had also been made in the Land Rights movement. In 1973 the federal government, which administered the Northern Territory at the time, recommended that the rights of Anangu associated with Uluru-Kata Tjuta should be recognised and that they should be involved in the area's management. Three years later the *Northern Territory Land Rights Act* was passed, which made it possible for Aboriginal people to claim title to their traditional lands.

In order to advance the Anangu claim over Uluru-Kata Tjuta meeting after meeting was held between senior Anangu and anthropologists, lawyers, commissioners and public servants. Someone involved in the process estimated that more than 200 meetings were held, a great many of them at Mutitjulu. Paddy Uluru, who had been in the forefront of the movement, became so tired of the lengthy, seemingly futile meetings that he refused to go to them anymore. But persistence was rewarded in the end.

In 1983 the newly elected Hawke Government acknowledged the traditional owners' right to Uluru-Kata Tjuta and the surrounding lands. They would be handed back to them. Tragically Paddy Uluru had died some years before. He was buried within sight of the Rock.

But before title was given two more years passed. Those were years of bitterness and acrimony when people opposed to Handback, especially those in the Northern Territory Government, cast aspersions on the bona fides of the traditional owners and the motives and integrity of their white advisers. These same people said that if Uluru-Kata Tjuta were handed back, Anangu would close them down and non-Aborigines could never visit them again.

Justice finally prevailed. On 26 October 1985 Handback took place in a ceremony at Mutitjulu. For Aboriginal people all over the country this was a day of great rejoicing, as ownership of one of Australia's great symbols passed to them. They came in hundreds from all parts of the continent.

Yami Lester, a Yankunytjatjara man involved with the Land Rights movement and chairman of the Uluru-Kata Tjuta Board of Management, opened the ceremony. In welcoming the governor-general, Sir Ninian Stephen, he said:

> Thank you, sir, for coming to this place ... I'm glad to see you here so that you can see the Rock for the last time. I understand that by tomorrow the Rock will be missing. The Aboriginal people are going to take it away.

The governor-general, surrounded by traditional owners in special T-shirts and red headbands, made a speech before the Handback ceremony. He said:

> Today we stand not merely in the centre of our continent, but at its very heart. We stand beside what has become one of our national symbols, what Aboriginal people know was Uluru and which the rest of us think of as Ayers Rock. For many Aboriginal people this place has still deeper meaning and deep spiritual significance. It is a significance whose roots go back to time immemorial and today the Uluru-Kata Tjuta Land Trust acquires inalienable freehold title under Australian law to this place which is so special to its members and at the same time recognises the special significance of Uluru to all Australians. The Trust will today lease it back to the Australian National Parks and Wildlife Service [now the Australian Nature Conservation Agency] as a National Park.

Judy Trigger instructs girls in the Kuniya, or woma python, inma.

It was a day of great emotion, of euphoria but also relief. Phillip Toyne, who had been a lawyer for the Pitjantjatjara Council during the long and arduous process leading up to Handback, said this of the day:

It was utterly chaotic as I remember it. I have a very blurred memory of it. There was an enormous amount of stress involved because there were such high expectations on the part of Aboriginal people around Australia. Also it had been preceded by vitriolic attacks by the Northern Territory Government. So the day was a mixture of relief and happiness.

Yami Lester said:

It was a really emotional and moving day, a happy day. I was nearly crying and for the first time in my life I was stuck for words for a little while.

Mrs Nellie Patterson, one of the traditional owners and a member of the Board of Management, is an exuberant woman. She perhaps expressed Anangu feelings on the day best:

> I've been thinking about this day for a very long time. At last my whole spirit is released for finally we have Uluru back. Uluru and Kata Tjuta are safe at last. The older women and older men are completely happy, the children and the dogs are happy, even the trees are happy because we Anangu have been given our land back. We've been given back our Aboriginal spirit.

In 1987 Uluru-Kata Tjuta was inscribed on the World Heritage List.

The Park was not closed. Anangu did not take Uluru away. Visitors — 278,509 in 1993 — from all over the world came to admire the Rock and perhaps absorbed some of the Aboriginal spirit.

As the governor-general said in his speech, the traditional owners on receipt of their title leased Uluru-Kata Tjuta to what is now the Australian Nature Conservation Agency to be managed as a national park. This is an agency of the Commonwealth Government. Until the day of Handback the Park had been administered by the Conservation Commission of the Northern Territory.

The new management operates under a Board on which Anangu have a majority. Yami Lester has been chairman since its inception. Reggie Uluru, Paddy's son, was on the original Board but has since resigned. His place has been taken by Malya Teamay. The other Anangu Board members are Tony Tjamiwa, Barbara Tjikatu, Nellie Patterson and Johnny Liddle. The Board's guiding principle is the *Tjukurpa*, as effective a set of guidelines for environmental management as has been devised.

Before Park management reached its present level of harmonious and stimulating relations between Anangu and Piranpa there was one more convulsion.

At Handback all Piranpa staff were CCNT officers contracted by ANCA to carry out the day-to-day management of the Park. But the differences of opinion and the acrimony of the pre-Handback days continued to fester. When a new ANCA Park manager was appointed, CCNT officers were unable to reconcile the conflicts involved in working for two bosses: the Northern Territory Government and the Board of Management. In an atmosphere of anger and frustration, their management contract was terminated, leaving only a few ANCA staff to cope with the multitude of visitors. Anangu agreed to temporarily fill the void left by the departure of CCNT for the months it took to recruit a new ANCA ranger staff.

Anangu instituted the Liru walk, where they themselves tell visitors about their culture. They also ensured that the Piranpa guided walk, the Mala walk, explains the Park according to the truths of the *Tjukurpa*.

Working together of black and white became a reality and has been a positive force at Uluru-Kata Tjuta ever since.

WORKING TOGETHER

Now that the Australian Nature Conservation Agency is firmly in control of the day-to-day running of Uluru-Kata Tjuta, the rangers are charged with ensuring the Park's continuing integrity, controlling visitors and looking after their safety. The rangers are joint management's public face.

Early one hot summer's afternoon Senior Ranger Fiona Peek picks me up at the Ranger Station so that I can accompany her on a patrol to Kata Tjuta to get some idea of the routine work of a ranger. She drives a Landcruiser trayback fitted with a two-way radio and its doors emblazoned with the Park's insignia. Our journey to Kata Tjuta, about 50 kilometres, is frequently interrupted by stops to pick up empty drink cans and other rubbish. Fiona mutters that it makes her mad sometimes when the roadsides that have been so laboriously cleaned on one day are littered again the next.

Our first scheduled stop is at a specially constructed platform straddling a fragile sand dune that overlooks Kata Tjuta. We pick up more rubbish — polystyrene cups, someone's abandoned dirty socks, cans and always tissues.

Several coachloads of tourists come down the trail as we walk up. They greet the ranger with a smile, sometimes a nervous smile. Maybe they are used to rangers being glorified police officers, complete with side-arms, in their own countries. But they soon warm to Fiona when they stop to talk. She answers all questions, from 'Will there be a sunset tonight?' to those about Anangu involvement in the Park, politely and in a friendly manner. The rangers do not carry side-arms.

Large and lucid boards on the partly roofed platform explain in words and drawings the plant and animals on the surrounding ridge — the amazing desert oak, the ubiquitous spinifex, the wealth of night animals. Fiona was involved in designing the boards and gathering information for them. She says it is a pity they are not multilingual as a great many visitors come from non-English-speaking backgrounds.

When I am in the bush, no matter where, I am oblivious to tourists, cars, coaches, the babble of guides and roadside rubbish. I tend to shut them out of my mind. I wander off to more isolated places and concentrate on the natural life. Although quite obvious on reflection, it nevertheless came as a surprise to me that these very things are at the forefront of the ranger's mind — visitors and all their paraphernalia, from giant buses to scattered tissues, are the ranger's constant

concern. However, tourists for the most part are well disciplined and the rubbish, while annoying, is not excessive.

We return to the vehicle and drive around Kata Tjuta to the Valley of the Winds walking track. On the way I ask Fiona how she likes working in the Park. She says:

> Living here is the best part of the job. It's always nice to come home at night and to realise where you are, and in the morning to look out at the Rock. It's always changing, its moods are always shifting. I never get tired of that. Working with Anangu is the most interesting. I grew up with Aboriginal people in Taree in New South Wales, we went to the same school and all that. But in those days, unfortunately, things were very separatist. Perhaps they still are. Here, going out with Anangu is the most important thing to me. I feel so satisfied after going out with them for the day. I'll always remember one particular outing in the southern part of the Park. There were Kata Kura, Peter Kanari and a few others. Kata Kura pointed out an old Anangu walking track from here to Amata in South Australia — just going up and down the dunes. He said, 'This is where we used to walk and there's a waterhole just a little further on'. I'm always amazed at that sort of stuff, how people are so well oriented.

For a while we drive along Kata Tjuta's western side. We fall silent as we pass close to the red domes, dissected by steep dark valleys. We walk down the Valley of the Winds, our faces covered with fly nets. No amount of repellent or waving of hands keeps the flies away. Always some try to drill into the corners of your eyes or fly down your throat as you open your mouth to speak. It is warm, in the high 30s, the afternoon light is clear, the air dry. This clarity and dryness combined with the austere rocks all around give an air of purity to Kata Tjuta.

This is the part she likes best, Fiona says, walking among the rocks, especially if tourists are few. She never tires, even after four years as a ranger, of the play of light, the birds, lizards, flowers and the changing seasons. We walk through the valley's green heart and up to the saddle where we sit on a rock overlooking distant domes and gentle slopes sparsely dotted with wattle trees and spinifex. Little woodswallows chase insects on pointed wings. A kestrel lands in a small cave just below us. Fiona recalls how a year or so ago she was on this patrol when the temperature was about 46 degrees or 48 degrees Celsius. She confides:

> Suddenly it felt as if my blood boiled. I felt weak, dizzy and disoriented. Even though I'd been drinking lots of water I recognised the symptoms of heat stress. Luckily, there were some pools. You can't imagine the relief when you douse

Previous pages: Jon Willis, the community liaison officer, discusses Park management with traditional owners Peter Kanari and his wife Maureen Natjuna.

yourself all over with water. It's only then you realise just how hot you were.

She adds:

> Very occasionally cold can be a problem. It can be a hot day like today when a sudden hailstorm comes across. The temperature drops 10 degrees, 15 degrees with howling wind, rain and hail. We had to rescue tourists, bring them down with a rope on a day like that. I went blue with cold and was just starting to feel myself lose it.

No chance of heat stress today, but we do sip some water and eat an orange. A tour group of young people catch up with us and pause at the saddle. With indrawn breath they exclaim about the wonder of views of rock formations and thinly scattered vegetation. From the languages they speak they seem to be from all corners of the globe. A Finn asks a Swede, in English, what conditions are like in his country. Japanese have their photographs taken by friends. We get up to return to the carpark. Fiona cuts quite a romantic figure. Twenty-seven years old, she is slim, just above medium height and strong looking. She wears a dark-green uniform of shirt and shorts with bright shoulder patches and thick green socks in stout walking boots. Her hair is about shoulder length, straight and blond with a fringe over large blue eyes shaded by a broad-brimmed felt hat. She carries a backpack containing a two-way radio and a bottle of water. The young people in the tour group cast glances in her direction that are mostly a mixture of admiration and envy. Some engage her in conversation and inevitably ask the question, 'How do you become a ranger?'.

Senior Ranger Fiona Peek on patrol at Olga Gorge.

On our way back we stop to look at a white-plumed honeyeater singing in a river red gum. Immediately below it another group of tourists is being addressed by a large tour guide with a strong voice. Few pay any attention, being preoccupied with trying to keep cool and shooing the flies. Fiona stops to talk to an elderly woman who has fallen and scuffed her knee. She offers first aid, but the woman and her husband, cheerful and stoic English people, say they have all they need back at the coach.

At sunset we eat our sandwiches at the Kata Tjuta viewing area. A short distance away a young couple pops the cork of a champagne bottle just as the sun touches the horizon. There are no other visitors watching the rocks glow a vivid orange-red. In the distance fifty or sixty people in the shadow of two huge coaches mill around a barbecue and are oblivious to the splendour.

As the sky darkens I ask Fiona what she likes least about being a ranger. Without hesitation she says, 'Rock rescues' — that is, rescuing people who have got into difficulties climbing Uluru. She continues:

I find that highly stressful. You never know what you are going to face. You can be called upon to rescue someone who has had a heart attack or, as recently, is suffering from heat stress. I just don't like that sort of thing. You really have to use all your resources to cope with it. That whole scene of climbing the rock is the worst part here. I'd love to see the chain taken out. It would change the whole character of the place.

One of the other rangers had told me that Fiona once talked a teenage girl out of jumping off Uluru. I ask her about that. Fiona sighs at the recollection:

Ah yes. We got a call about someone in trouble on top of the Rock. When I got to the bottom of the climb a distraught teacher from a school group came up to me and said, 'We've got a young girl up there and she's going to kill herself'. So up I went, staggering at the end, for no matter how fit you are that climb is very strenuous. I finally got to the girl, who was standing there on the top with a totally stricken face. She had jumped once already but had crawled back up, and she was bruised and scratched all over. That was very demanding for I had to convince her somehow that life was worth living. It was a grim and sad story of a depressed fifteen year old with no family and no friends. She kept telling me, 'Everyone told me to jump'. Eventually she came down with me, and then the worst part was a teacher who came rushing over and got stuck right into her, saying, 'You realise this is a criminal offence and you're going to have to go to the police station, now'. That really upset me.

It is nearly dark and time to check the carparks to see that everyone has left. No one is allowed to remain in the Park overnight or to camp there. A euro crosses our path, nearly banging into the vehicle. At the Olga Gorge carpark three young Japanese men emerge from the gorge. Fiona, in a friendly way, asks them to move on as the Park is now closed. The three are very timid, frightened almost, of the ranger. Fiona tells me how once when another ranger was on a similar mission a group of young Japanese hid behind bushes, some even putting up their arms as though expecting a beating. But all rangers are invariably kind and very, very patient.

We move on to the Valley of the Winds carpark. 'Uh-oh', says Fiona, in a tone of voice reflecting a sinking feeling. A single car remains. It can mean a long walk into the valley to rescue people or to tell them they cannot camp there. But as we draw up the people return to their car and drive off. Just a little way along our return journey an old bomb of a car with a battered canoe strapped to its roofrack comes driving towards us. Fiona flags it down. She tells the occupants that the Park is closed and they must return to Yulara. The people argue, saying over and over again, perhaps expecting that the rules will change through endless repetition, that a ranger had told them they could picnic at the Valley of the Winds. 'Not after dark' is Fiona's firm reply. Eventually the middle-aged couple start their car, which seems to explode, and lurch back to Yulara.

All the carparks are clear and we drive back to the Ranger Station. We surprise a few snakes and geckoes that lie on the warm tarmac. An occasional mouselike animal dashes across the road. As we drive through the darkness with stars bright in the sky and Kata Tjuta's rocks barely perceptible, I ask Fiona if she sometimes finds the constant stream of tourists a little irksome. She says:

> It can be, but it is not always so. Sometimes you get interested groups on the Liru or Mala walks and that is very rewarding. But I can also relate to the Anangu description of tourists. They call them *minga*, which is a small species of scurrying ant. It is obviously a very good description. It is just the whole scene. Half the people come here on buses, so they've got tight schedules. They just pour out, run up and down the rock and in and out of the kiosk, and off again. Yeah, quite *minga*. But you can't be too down on them. Most people are here for the first time and have obvious questions. Even if they are all the same questions over and over again. You have to be patient, stay calm and not start an argument if people are rude or racist on the walks. That is not their purpose.

I ask Fiona to give an example of some of the more difficult people she has had to deal with. She thinks a moment and then says:

> One day in mid-afternoon Greenie [another ranger] and I went looking for a young German couple, who had been reported as walking from Kata Tjuta to Uluru across the sandhills. We'd split up and I was just thinking that there would be no hope of finding them. We had this awful feeling that we might be out all night looking for them. They could have been anywhere. Then Greenie came on over the radio to say he'd found them. He was laughing a bit. I walked over to where they were and there was this chap, stark naked. Not only that, but he was in a sensitive area where he should not have been. I got really angry and said, 'I must ask you to get dressed'. He said, 'No, I'm fine. I'm fine'. 'Oh no, you're not', I said, 'I find this offensive. Get dressed'. Which he did. His girlfriend, who had been a little way away, came and joined him. We pointed out that what they were doing was culturally inappropriate. To which they replied that they had never had to consider anyone's culture before in all the places they had been. They said they were free cosmic spirits, naked

Leroy Lester is the first Anangu to graduate from the National Park's ranger training program.

and at one with Mother Earth, and that they could do as they liked. More like cosmic fruit loops.

A barn owl perched close to the roadside reflects the car's headlights. Fiona swerves to avoid a knob-tailed gecko scuttling across the road, and continues:

But you meet good people too, ones who think the place, and especially the Liru and Mala walks, is just fantastic. They can spark off really good conversations where you feel you're getting somewhere. The Liru walk in particular can be very rewarding when Anangu and visitors sometimes strike up some kind of rapport.

Much of the work we do, however, is routine and mundane, even boring at times. As well as going on patrols we maintain the walking tracks and fences, deal with drainage problems, clean the toilets (definitely the low point of being a ranger), collect the never-ending rubbish and so on.

But there are more exciting things too: being involved with the fauna surveys, the interpretation work and land management such as burning and cleaning out rockholes. And always there are the rocks and the sandhills. The whole country still affects me, it's just stunning.

All the carparks are clear and Fiona heaves a sigh of relief. A half-moon has risen and faintly illuminates Uluru. Being a ranger may often be mundane and routine, but there could be a drama around every corner and you must be prepared to deal with it.

Until early 1993 all full-time rangers at Uluru-Kata Tjuta were Piranpa. For some years now a ranger training program for Anangu has been in place. Its first graduate is Leroy Lester. His path to the job was sharply different from that of the Piranpa staff. The non-Aboriginal rangers all come from far away, often from cities, and have had a long formal education, sometimes to the level of a university degree. Most have a scientific bias with an emphasis on management of the natural environment. Leroy was brought up among the Park's traditional owners, and is fluent in their languages. He went to school in Alice Springs and for a few years to an agricultural college in Adelaide. He also worked on cattle stations. His English is like that of any of the Piranpa rangers.

Now a young man of twenty-six, Leroy shows a remarkable self-possession. He is of stocky build, strong looking with broad shoulders. He is clean-shaven except for a small tuft of beard at the point of his chin. He has an easy and friendly manner, if a little shy to begin with. The time of his childhood that he remembers with most pleasure is the part he spent in the bush at Mimili, his father's country in South Australia. He says:

I must have been between eight and eleven then. I learnt to ride a horse and even at that age I camped in the bush a lot and helped with mustering. That was good fun. There also were old people there and I was learning cultural things and that. Some days you would see the old people go up the hill and come back with a whole lot of spear vines. They'd put them on the fire, strip the bark and straighten them. Or they would make *kiti*, a kind of gum or glue made from spinifex resin. That sort of thing happened every day. I didn't take particular notice of it. It was just everyday life. But it went into my head.

One of the old people I remember vividly from that time is Paddy Uluru, he was my grandfather. He was a pretty powerful *ngangkari*, see — an Anangu healer or doctor. He healed my mother's sore hand one day, a very swollen and poisoned hand. I remember he sucked all the shit out of it and the hand just went down, straightaway. My mum was in terrible pain but the next day it was gone. My grandfather was pretty old then. Very wise, you could just tell he was pretty wise. There is something very special about those old folks. They didn't smoke or drink and were healthy and fit. You really want to know what they are thinking, you know. There's something mysterious about them. They were too wise for me and I couldn't ask them about it.

I should have more contact with the old people now, especially Tjamiwa and Cassidy Uluru, Paddy's son. I could learn more of the traditional things then. I'm learning quite a lot of that already as I've gone through the Law. But it's only the first step of initiation. It is the very first into a big area of knowledge. We've learnt that up north, past Alice Springs, people know more about the emu than us. Down here and into South Australia and Western Australia it is all the *malu*, the red kangaroo. And everyone would know the Malu story. Before white men the whole of Australia would have known that story.

Like his father, Yami Lester, Leroy emphasises that he is a Yankunytjatjara man. I ask him about the difference between Yankunytjatjara and Pitjantjatjara:

Our languages are a little bit different, but we can understand each other. There are not so many Yankunytjatjara now. For a while it seemed we were dying out. There are more Pitjapitjas, which is our teasing name for the Pitjantjatjara. They call us Yanki Yankis. But years ago there used to be heaps of us. We shared and lived and communicated together. Dad says we were more 'think before you do it' and the other mob more like 'do it before you think'. We used to have lots of arguments and fights in the past, even a few deaths.

Leroy was a trainee for three years. Part of the time he was out with the regular rangers on work experience and part of the time studying such things as computer skills and the theory of land management, an arrangement I think he was not entirely comfortable with. He says:

Now that I'm a full-time ranger, it is all different. You're not like a robot trainee anymore. Then they were always watching you but also guiding and teaching you things. Now there is a bit of slack on the rope and you can do your own thing more.

I quite like taking the tours, the Mala and Liru walks. People are just dumbfounded and flabbergasted. It keeps me excited as we go from one stop to the next. I prefer doing the Liru walk because you can demonstrate things. On the Mala tour you just talk.

But I'm not too keen on the roster system. There are so many different duties. One day you might almost need a three-piece suit for a meeting or study course and the next day you've got a shovel in your hand and you're repairing a fence. I like to stick to one thing, you know.

And what of the future and joint management, working together? Leroy says:

> Yeah, it'll go good. We just need a few up-and-comings to really think about the future, where we're going; Anangu politicians and people like that, just to back us up.

In late 1993 there are five more Anangu trainees. Their teacher and confidant, their training officer in the official parlance, is Julian Barry whom we have already met.

Twenty-nine years of age, tall and slim, with blue eyes in a freckled face and an unpretentious manner, the first impression of Julian is one of an easygoing, somewhat laconic man. But underneath it all is an intense commitment to making the training program work, to doing the very best possible for Anangu wishing to become rangers. To that end he works relentlessly and is always ready to assist the trainees without restrictions to office hours, a foreign concept to Anangu in any case. He is close to Anangu, who have adopted him almost like one of themselves. They respect, even love him. Julian feels the same way about Anangu but also has a great empathy with them, understands them, their society, their preoccupations and worries. He has gone through the Law like an Anangu young man.

What made it possible for Julian to cross the barrier from mutual but distant respect into an initiated member of Anangu society was his learning of the Pitjantjatjara language. For that alone Anangu have figuratively drawn him into their bosom. He is fluent in Pitjantjatjara to such an extent that he can have philosophical discussions about the *Tjukurpa* as well as pass the time gossiping. Only one other Piranpa has that ability at Uluru-Kata Tjuta. Despite Julian's university degree in anthropology and linguistics, he did not find it easy to learn the language. It took several years of hard work to reach what he calls 'my modest level'.

For a number of years Julian worked for the Central Land Council, assisting Anangu in their dealings with mining companies. He travelled extensively over central Australia and in the process fell in love with the land and its original inhabitants. He says quietly:

> I love it. I think central Australia is fantastically beautiful and the longer you live here the more you appreciate it. Recently I read a newspaper story about Uluru, which described the centre as no-man's land, or no-person's land or something like that, just empty. Such shallowness. It is a really beautiful place

Julian Barry, the Park's training officer, with four of the trainees. From left to right: Nyinku Jingo, Julian Barry, Andy Panpanpalala Daeger, Rupert Goodwin and Akana Campbell.

and the more you get to know what the place means from an Aboriginal perspective the more interesting it becomes.

Even though the Park staff form a small white community living alongside a larger Anangu community, Julian does not feel isolated here. He echoes the thoughts of most of the non-Anangu when he says:

I feel I've tapped into something much richer than living in the city here. And I'm not just talking about being involved with Anangu although that is obviously a large part of it. We're all people from different backgrounds thrown together, whereas in the cities you tend to hang out with people who are the same age and who have the same sorts of political ideas, enjoy the same music and do the same sorts of things. I found that quite boring. You get to meet a great selection of people here from bus drivers and mechanics to doctors of philosophy and Anangu who do not speak a word of English. That I find really exciting.

The five trainees range in age from under twenty to over forty. Their backgrounds vary from some formal education to an education provided by a hard life in the bush balancing between traditional Anangu ways and trying to make a go of it in the Piranpa world. I ask Julian to give me a thumbnail sketch of each of the trainees. Of the ebullient and extroverted Andy Panpanpalala Daeger, a powerful big man, he says:

He was born on 1 January 1956. He is of mixed Pitjantjatjara and Yankunytjatjara descent and has a long history in the cattle industry. He has been chairperson of the Mimili community, which is his grandparents' country. He's also been a police aide. He said he'd had enough of living at Mimili and came here to start a new life. He's very charming and likes to interact with the tourists. Often he does the Liru walk on his own. He's got bundles of energy and a great knowledge of the traditional way of life, so he's great to have on deck. He's really confident and not scared of letting people know when he's unhappy about something. Provided all goes well I think he'll be ready to graduate in the middle of next year. But you never know with Anangu. He might come and see me one morning and say, 'Right, I'm heading off and doing something else with my life'.

Nicola Coull is an extraordinary looking young woman with a very pale complexion and a halo of fine golden hair. She speaks excellent English. Her movements are delicate and elegant. She is of mixed Pitjantjatjara, Arrernte and European descent. Julian says of her:

Nikki will be twenty-one in a couple of weeks and she will have her third child shortly after that. Then she will have four or five months off work. She has lived here and there, but her parents are from this country. Her father lives on his homeland at Yulara Pulka. Kata Kura is her grandfather. She's had schooling up to Grade 8. Originally she came for work experience, about six months ago. She was pretty shy then and not so confident. Since then she's grown in confidence and is doing well in her Diploma of Applied Science in Natural and Cultural Resource Management at Batchelor College near Darwin. She's gone from someone who probably never had more than 100 dollars to

Top: The ebullient Andy Panpanpalala Daeger, one of the trainee rangers. Above: Nicola Coull is a trainee ranger who has become adept in the use of the video camera to record traditional methods of land management.

*Rupert Goodwin is a cheerful
man of solid character.*

her name to someone who realises she has a great future ahead of her working at Uluru.

Rupert Goodwin at forty-one is the oldest of the trainees. He is a calm, charming Yankunytjatjara man who likes to communicate with non-Anangu, even with limited English. Julian finds him to be a solid person who is not fazed by anything. He likes to work and, in his quiet way, Julian says, has charmed all the staff. He lifts people's spirits. He has been in the cattle industry for a long time.

Nyinku Jingo is the youngest trainee but has been in the training program the longest. She is taking a year off to be with her husband. Perhaps she will come back to graduate after that. Julian says she is very mature and strong with a desire to learn from the old people. He says she's going to be the Edith Richards of the twenty-first century. She's very proud of her work.

Akana Campbell is a young woman of twenty-five with a moonlike face that can be very stern, and then break out in an infectious laugh. She is often very funny, Julian says, and once you get her laughing there is no stopping her, 'like someone rolling down a hill'.

Julian has devised a rigorous training program that covers three main needs. The first is for the trainees to develop confidence in many areas that we take for granted such as written literacy in English. The second is to continue to learn from senior Anangu about their conceptions of land management — the Aboriginal perspective on the environment. The third training need is to learn about the many and often difficult tasks that rangers must perform, such as law enforcement, safety patrols, rock rescues, interpretive walks, cleaning toilets, fixing vehicles, putting up fences and so on. Most of the training takes place at Uluru-Kata Tjuta itself. Those trainees such as Nyinku and Nicola who have good English also learn computer skills and are enrolled in the Associate Diploma in Applied Science at Batchelor College. It is a place where Aboriginal people from all over Australia go. Trainees spend six weeks twice a year at the college.

Not all trainees last the distance. Some drop out under circumstances that border on the tragic; others simply prefer to do something else.

I ask Julian if he thinks Anangu will eventually run the Park entirely on their own. He says thoughtfully:

Well, yes. In the current plan of management the stated aim is to have one-third of the full-time staff Anangu. When the current trainees graduate, in one to two years, we will just about have reached it. Further down the track everybody would certainly like to see all staff to be Anangu. It would be great and I'm sure at some stage that will happen, but not in the near future. At this stage I think that there needs to be much more work done about Anangu's

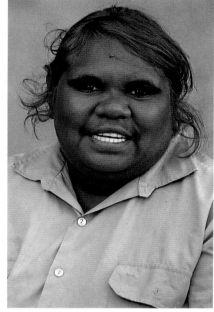

position in the workplace, their interests and aspirations. Personally, I don't think that at the moment Anangu aspire to taking over all or even most of the positions in the Park. Anangu like to employ white fellas because white fellas don't have a whole list of cultural priorities that come before work. Employing white fellas to do the day-to-day tasks frees up Anangu to attend to their cultural commitments and general interests. It still enables them to remain in control of development and policy, and to feel that the day-to-day operations of the Park are in the hands of people whom they have selected — and have since grown to know and trust. At the moment Anangu are not taking up senior management positions. In the future I hope they will. Leroy might.

To that end Julian works very hard for long hours. He is sometimes ribbed about that by his colleagues. His comment is that he feels he has to fill the gap between Anangu ways and Piranpa expectations. It is a difficult, at times trying, balancing act.

Above left: Nyinku Jingo eats a tjala. Nyinku is the youngest trainee ranger. Above: Akana Campbell has a ready laugh but can be very stern.

Elsie Malpangka explains aspects of Anangu life to Assistant Park Manager Caralyn Dean.

One day a week Piranpa staff and senior Anangu go bush as part of the Aboriginal Land Management Program. Anangu are the teachers. They talk about traditional life — the plants they gathered, the animals they hunted, where the rockholes are and how they have to be maintained, how things relate to the *Tjukurpa*, how fire was managed, where special plants and animals are to be found. In short, they impart their knowledge to the new joint managers of their lands. Sometimes only women go on the excursions, sometimes just men and at other times both join forces. Most times the trainees participate and sometimes even for them these trips are true eye-openers. It is also a great opportunity for Piranpa staff to improve their Pitjantjatjara.

After I had been at Uluru-Kata Tjuta for some months, Anangu were used to seeing me around and taking photographs of everything. If I was photographing a lizard or some flowers along a roadside, some would stop for a chat to tell me all about the plant or animal concerned, though communicating was difficult. Eventually I was invited along on the Aboriginal Land Management trips. They were among my most rewarding times in the Park. Anangu were relaxed, at ease in their own country, and always they were teaching, not lecturing, but teaching with patience, humour and a little gentle teasing.

On a warm mid-morning in late summer we reach a small, double peaked outcrop of giant rounded boulders, with a sheet of rock only a few centimetres above the level of the surrounding plain in front of it. The rocks are of the same kind of sandstone as Uluru, about 12 kilometres to the north. Kata Tjuta's domes, purple in the heat haze, are further away to the north-west. I am with three senior Anangu women, Elsie Malpangka, Witjawara Curtis and Marjorie Winty, and Assistant (Park) Manager Caralyn Dean. They have come here to check on the rockhole in the centre of the sheet of sandstone. It is such a small watering point in the vast, flat expanse of the arid zone, such a fugitive and precarious thing for your life to depend on and also such a difficult place to find and memorise.

Elsie says the place is called Tjapia rockhole. It is dry. The hole, which goes a long way down, has filled up with sand, We are here to dig it out. There is dangerous *Tjukurpa* here, they say, and they do not wish to stay too long.

On the return journey we stop on the edge of a sandplain where witchetty bushes, *ilykuwara*, Elsie calls them, grow. Within a few minutes the women have excavated the roots of one of the bushes and extracted half a dozen large *maku*, or witchetty grubs. We light some fires in the meagre shade of another *ilykuwara* bush to cook the *maku*, make some tea and even more importantly disperse the clouds of flies. Over tea and *maku*, Elsie, the ringleader, Witjawara and Majorie talk about traditional times.

Using a stick, Elsie draws a diagram in the sand to show how family groups used to camp in the bush. First, she explained, they built a *yuu*, a windbreak, from the branches of some shrubs. Inside it a number of fires were lit and people lay down to sleep between them in a strict order. In the diagram Elsie indicates the place of each person — father here, mother on the other side, teenage boy here, small boy there and the girls somewhere else. And everywhere among them *papa tjuta*, lots of dogs, she says. Caralyn copies all this in her notebook with Elsie leaning over frequently to ensure she gets it right.

The dogs, the women say, were used to hunt emus and kangaroos. They would run the animals down and bite them. The men had to catch up with the quarry quickly, before the dogs killed it and tore it to pieces. Most of the meat was hunted by the men in the afternoons, except for rabbits, which the women collected by digging them out of their burrows. The women also collected the plant foods — the seeds of grasses and certain wattles, the fruits of bush tomatoes, figs, quandongs and others. Both men and women collected emu eggs.

Elsie is a large woman, not only in physical size, but also in her gestures and dramatisations. She acts out how the men stalked and speared emus. Usually they did so after poisoning the birds at a waterhole. The men would crush the leaves of the emu poison bush and put them in the water, which would turn green. They would put a branch in the water to let people know it had been poisoned. The crows would let the men know when the emus had come to drink. Elsie mimics how the emus staggered about, windmilling her arms and rolling her eyes. They staggered about as if drunk, like people having wine, she says. Elsie being unkempt and at times even a little wild-eyed adds to the effect. Witjawara, a handsome strong-featured woman with a sensible manner, and the shy Marjorie, with neatly combed grey hair and carrying an immaculate white handbag, laugh and interject. Caralyn, whose Pitjantjatjara is pretty good, keeps notes. Elsie is also quite sensible underneath her brashness and very warm-hearted, often putting an affectionate arm around Caralyn's shoulders. As we gather our things together to return home Elsie points out a termite's pavement mound and, with her few words of English and gestures, tells me how they used to pound spinifex on those flat hard surfaces to extract its resin. Everything — rocks, sand, animals, plants, people — is interconnected, sometimes interdependent, in a tightly woven tapestry.

Other joint management excursions have a more direct bearing on the running of the Park. A decision has to be made about the location of a new walking track at Kata Tjuta. Before this can even be planned the senior men, for Kata Tjuta is primarily a men's place, have to ensure that the proposed trail does not go too close to any sensitive places. I have been invited along to check this out. Most of the elders are there, Tony Tjamiwa, Tommy Wangi, Peter Kanari, Norman Tjalkalyiri, and a few others. Senior Ranger Peter Nagel represents the Park, and Community Park Liaison Officer Jon Willis, who represents the Anangu community, translates both ways. Our convoy of three vehicles does not follow the normal

*Community Liaison Officer Jon
Willis (left) discusses the possible
route of a new walking track with
Tony Tjamiwa.*

tourist route to Kata Tjuta. We turn off onto a narrow sandy track that weaves in and out among the mulgas and desert oaks. Eventually it approaches Kata Tjuta from the north-east, a spectacular aspect few people have the opportunity to see.

We drive past Yulara Pulka, another rockhole, this one with a supply of water. The rock is conglomerate like that of Kata Tjuta even though it is much closer to Uluru. Soon we come to another rockhole. Peter Kanari explains that we are really following the old track people used to travel between the two monoliths, going from rockhole to rockhole. We get out of the cars. It is a small outcrop, only a few metres across. The actual hole is filled with sand but green grass grows all around it. Water must be close to the surface. The *tjilpis* talk animatedly among themselves, and sing a few verses of the *inma*, the ceremony, associated with this place. Tjamiwa says that this small outcrop, hidden by wattles and emu bushes is a very, very powerful place. Two *Tjukurpa* lines, song lines, go through it. One is to do with men's initiation ceremonies. The other, he says, is so strong and sacred he cannot even speak of it.

On we zigzag. A red kangaroo bounds across the track. We stop again close to Kata Tjuta and stand silently for a few moments looking at the domes, ones that had been hidden from view at all other places I have been. The *tjilpis'* faces light up. Their eyes shine. In rapid Pitjantjatjara they point out and discuss special places and formations. Tommy Wangi takes Jon Willis by the shoulder and says, still in Pitjantjatjara, this feature means that, the other is this. Jon, like Julian, has gone through the Law and is therefore entitled to know secret–sacred information. Jon, in turn, puts his hand on my shoulder and points to a dome with a prominent pattern and tells me what it means. The meaning is wonderfully apt and imaginative, but secret. Telling me about this one thing in isolation is not breaching any confidence. Anangu, always considerate people, do not wish me to feel excluded. For a few moments we are all swept up by the force of the *Tjukurpa*. Tjamiwa tells me that if anyone who should not, such as children or women, goes near a man's place that is *miil-miilpa*, dangerous and prohibited, he or she must be killed. That is the Law, he says with forceful downward gestures of his hands. But then, he adds, that was in the old days, not now. In the old days people knew the Law and never went near prohibited places. The threat, however, was always there and always real.

Still on the faint track we drive directly towards Kata Tjuta. Peter Kanari and Kata Kura point out all the landmarks and sing the appropriate verses quietly to themselves. We reach the old tourist road, very eroded and bouldery, a few kilometres from the Valley of the Winds. The proposal is that this old road be made into a walking track that loops around the northern end of Kata Tjuta. The *tjilpis* want to see if the track is not too close to a particular sacred place. Eagerly the men climb out of the cars and walk towards the place. Peter Kanari, straight upright but frail, uses a light metal bar as a walking stick, threatening to impale his bare foot at every step. But he never does. He and Tjamiwa beckon me to follow them, but the more conservative Norman feels happier if I do not. It is for initiates only. I stay behind.

Jon Willis is later allowed to tell me what happened when they got to the place. The *tjilpis* approached silently. Then one after the other they spoke to and about the rock in raised voices in the rapid declamatory fashion always used in matters relating to the *Tjukurpa*. They spoke so rapidly that Jon, who knows the language well, could not understand what they were saying. But it was not necessary to understand the words to realise that an important religious event was taking place. There was something uplifting for all of them about being so convincingly and thoroughly at one with the natural environment.

Discussions follow and altogether proceedings take about an hour. The verdict is *wiya!* No. The track cannot go this close to the sacred place. On the way back an alternative, even more interesting walking route is quickly approved — *palya!* OK.

The success of joint management, of working together, to a large extent depends on a special position, the duties of which on the face of it are impossible. The person filling the job must not just reconcile two cultures, he or she must understand both, must live both every day. It is not a balancing act between two cultures, it is a matter of embracing both, of having two cultural selves. This cannot be easily slipped into. An effective community park liaison officer has to be secure in his or her own, in this case Western, culture, yet have the perspicacity and sensitivity to enter Anangu society with empathy. He or she also has to speak English and Pitjantjatjara, look at problems from both points of view, and absorb pressures from two sides. But the person also has the satisfaction of making two cultures mesh together and work towards a common goal. Few people can do it.

After a sometimes difficult and turbulent beginning Jon Willis fills the job perfectly. Because this is such a crucial and extraordinary position, and Jon is such an exceptional person, I talk to him at length.

Jon is thirty-three years of age and of a stocky build. He wears steel-rimmed glasses with a blueish tinge. His brown hair is cropped short and his beard is closely trimmed. Often he wears a stern expression, a mask, I feel, to discourage casual approaches when he is preoccupied — as he nearly always is — by myriad pressing problems. Most people initially approach Jon with some trepidation, but underneath the forbidding exterior is a warm, sympathetic man.

We talk in Jon's house, a new roomy structure, in the Anangu community. One entire wall is covered in bookshelves with titles ranging from Shakespeare's complete works to Nixon's autobiography, and from novels and poems by Vikram Seth to Stephen King mysteries. In one corner stands a collection of musical instruments, harps and a flute. Rows and rows of CDs and vinyl records line other shelves. Opera and Bach are prominent, but so is Abba. It is Sunday. Jon likes to hear Christian religious music on this day and Bach plays softly as we talk. On two sides of the house, only a few paces away, families of Anangu, still desert nomads at heart, are camped with swags and makeshift shelters. Camp dogs bark and growl nearby as they settle some hierarchic argument. All morning Anangu stroll in and out of the house, to ask advice, to watch television or just to chat over a cup of tea, or to ask to borrow Jon's car. Without missing a beat in our conversation Jon responds to the Anangu's requests.

Jon was born and grew up a long way from Uluru, in distance as well as the physical and social environment. He comes from Wollongong on the New South Wales coast, where as a child he ran wild in the nearby bush and was keen on the sea and surfing. He was educated in the local Catholic boys school. Before he left high school his intention was to become a priest, and so he applied to join the order that taught at his school. They told him to come back in a year and then they would think about it. He says, 'They didn't say it very nicely either'. So he left school and began work as a retail cadet in a big department store in Sydney, but it was not challenging and he soon left. He then went to the University of New South Wales and began a degree in clinical psychology. At the end of his second year he had an 'enormous row' with the head of the department about a field project on autistic children he had done. He changed faculties and took up anthropology. He completed his honours degree with a thesis on Eurasians in Singapore. It was an outstanding degree and his professor prevailed upon him to stay at university on a scholarship. Strangely enough, at the time of his anthropology course Aboriginal studies were not taught at that university. But as part of his scholarship he had to tutor students in Aboriginal anthropology and his interest was kindled.

After five years at university Jon thought enough was enough and left without completing his doctorate. He worked for a while for a law firm in Sydney, which gave him the expertise to apply for a job with the Pitjantjatjara Council in Alice Springs. He took up his position in 1985, a few months before Handback. He says of this occasion:

> I was here on the day, sort of helping out, nothing important. I directed traffic, I think. It was very exciting to be here. It was a tremendously emotional moment for everybody, just this huge wash of approval and joy that went through the whole crowd.

When Jon first came to central Australia to take up his position he had not met many Aboriginal people. For his first field trip, which he remembers clearly, he was thrown in at the deep end. He says:

> That first trip with Anangu was really freaky. I came straight from the law office and from wearing a suit. I got off the plane and jumped on to the back of a Toyota, I didn't even go into Alice Springs. I had to ride in the back of the Toyota for two weeks for there was no room in the cabin. Until then I'd never seen a live desert Aborigine before, I'd never been in a four-wheel-drive vehicle, let alone driven off road. I was totally naive.
>
> The old men were teaching me bits and pieces of language the whole way. I wrote everything down in my notebook using classic third-year anthropology techniques. The men kept pointing at things and telling me the words for them. That's the standard way of learning a language. We saw this large bird in the sky, one of the raptors I think, and I asked, 'What do you call that?'. The men said what sounded like 'iggalook' and I duly wrote down 'iggalook', trying to get the phonetics right. But it transpired the man gave the English word — 'eaglehawk'. I felt such a goose.

Even the most experienced Piranpa Pitjantjatjara speakers sometimes have difficulty with Anangu's idiosyncratic pronunciations of English words. Once when I was out with Julian and Anangu, they spoke of how in their younger days they

Uluru's southern side at sunrise.

worked on roads and used dynamite. I picked out the English word in the stream of Pitjantjatjara. Julian began to translate but when he came to the word 'dynamite', he had heard it as 'tin of meat'. He turned to the Anangu and said, 'What on earth did you use a tin of meat in road building for?'. Some Anangu literally fell over with laughter as tears streamed down their faces. For days after Kata Kura would mutter 'tin of meat' and burst out laughing all over again.

In time Jon learnt to speak Pitjantjatjara, but by his own admission is not quite as proficient as Julian. But Julian says that Jon has a better ear for the language and a quicker understanding.

Jon worked with the Pitjantjatjara Council in various capacities for about four years. He took up his current position in 1989. I ask him just exactly what the job involves:

It used to be called park liaison officer but my predecessor didn't like being referred to as the PLO. So she stuck 'community' in front of it and called herself the CLO which is what I'm still called. The job is of the same seniority as the park manager's and is funded by the Australian Nature Conservation Agency.

The traditional owners have certain responsibilities under the lease agreement to provide management advice about how the Park is to be run and my job is to facilitate the giving of that advice.

Jon also deals with applications from film crews, journalists and others who want to film, photograph or write about Uluru-Kata Tjuta and Anangu. The pressures on Anangu from the media are enormous. Applications for filming or writing of one kind or another arrive just about every day. With one or two exceptions requests are all the same. Jon says:

It strikes me that most people want to use Uluru to give their article or their product promotion an Australian flavour or an Aboriginal flavour or both. It conjures up Australia and an ancient solidity, but most of the time it is not used in any way that reflects the natural or cultural values of the place. They just want a location grab.

These kinds of applications are refused by Anangu and it is mostly Jon's job to convey that refusal, and to be abused by many producers and journalists as a consequence.

There are pressures from tourists as well. They wish to have contact with Anangu more and more, but as Anangu are outnumbered several thousand to one by the tourists, who always ask the same questions and always take photographs, they shrink away from this contact. However, they want visitors to understand the Park, the people and the *Tjukurpa*. That is why they instituted and take part in the Liru and Mala walks. But it is a trial to be peered at by hundreds of people, day in day out, as if you were an animal in the zoo. Jon is the buffer against this. As well as that he is involved in all the other things that affect Anangu, the Park and tourism.

Seeing Jon and Anangu interact, I am always struck by the great affection between them. I ask how this came about. He says:

It's a response. If people are affectionate towards you, you're affectionate in return. Anangu are very warm people, they're a very touching and laughing people. They like jokes and they like making fun of people. Also I think I'm very open emotionally, perhaps more so than is necessary. If I'm angry, it's obvious I'm angry. If I'm happy, I'm obviously happy. If I'm upset, I'm crying. I think Anangu appreciate that because I think they find white people a bit hard to read most of the time. I think Anangu warm to me because they've known me a long time, because I express myself as I'm feeling and because I'm scrupulously honest and they know they can trust me.

Billy Wara (seated on left) and Elsie Malpangka explain the traditional way of making resin from spinifex on the Liru walk. The trainee rangers translate.

With Anangu being so close around him and making so many demands on his time, I ask if he ever feels that they are smothering him. Nodding thoughtfully, he says:

> I did feel that. The year before last I was going through a massive change in how I dealt with my material possessions in particular. They are very important to me. You can see I'm a nester.

He gestures at the bookshelves, the musical instruments, paintings on the walls and other ornaments:

> I used to feel that I couldn't maintain my integrity and have all these people

continuously crowding in on me. Then I went away to Brisbane to study for six months. My attitude changed because I left everything behind and went away with a much simpler grab bag of things. When I came back the possessions did not matter that much to me any more. I didn't mind if people put dirty fingerprints on a beautiful book. Also at some stage, there was no particular moment, I slowly realised that I was going to be here a very long time and Anangu were the people I was going to be living with and dealing with. I wasn't just a weekend visitor. If I was going to have friends, they were going to be Anangu.

Like Julian, Jon has gone through the Law, but unlike Julian he has done so right here with the people of Uluru-Kata Tjuta. I ask Jon to tell me about it:

It's a lovely, reverent ceremony. Having been brought up a Catholic and an altar boy and church organist, I've got a feeling for liturgy. It was some of the nicest liturgy I've been involved with, accompanied by lovely music and meaningful and reverent actions, full of references and special activities. The men involved are completely absorbed by it. You get very close to people.

At first I was a little disappointed about what we learned about the *Tjukurpa*. I thought that somebody would drill you until you were familiar with certain aspects, and once you knew them you would be able to move on to the next stage of ceremony and they'd drill you on something else. But it's not like that at all. Like Pitjantjatjara people you learn through repetition, through hearing something again, and again and again. It's not a way of learning I'm particularly good at. Some of the other guys that I went through with were so much better at remembering *inma* verses. But I'm better at remembering strings of place names, which is another important aspect.

You learn by seeing somebody do something. Then you do it yourself with help. After that you do it on your own and the next time you're teaching somebody else — there's always people coming up. The last time I went to a ceremony I really felt a competent practitioner. I was helping people and realised I'd learned what I was supposed to have learnt.

You may not find two guys saying the same thing as to what the ceremonies are about. For me it's about forming relationships between men, relationships that are important throughout their lives. They are very useful, helpful and friendly relationships. The men are people you can borrow money from or lend money to. The formation of those relationships is marked with gift exchanges. It's very meaningful.

After having gone through the ceremonies you also feel an affinity with the land you did not feel before, and a deeper kind of responsibility for protecting it. It also makes me an owner, in a subtle kind of way, though not one that is recognised in court.

Finally I ask how he sees the future of Uluru-Kata Tjuta:

> Well, I don't know. In the back of my mind I think one day it may secede from joint management and become an independent park with its own park service. But I don't imagine that would happen or be realistic for maybe twenty or thirty years. Anangu would also have to be considerably more ambitious about being in charge than they are now.

Leroy Lester, who went through the Law at the same time as Jon, comes in, and Jon cuts his hair while we chat about nothing in particular.

The Piranpa Park staff all come from far-flung places and sharply differing backgrounds. Senior Ranger Fiona Peek was brought up in Newcastle and Taree in eastern New South Wales and trained in resource management; Assistant Manager (Resources) David Carter was raised in Cooma in the Snowy Mountains and did a degree in zoology in Townsville, Queensland; Park Manager Bob Seaborne is from Wales where he trained as an engineer, later joining Victoria's Forest Service; Assistant Manager Operations Caralyn Dean comes from rural south-east Queensland and has a degree from Griffith University in Brisbane; Senior Ranger Peter Nagel is from Sydney and has qualifications in horticulture; Maintenance Officer Lee Webb is a diesel mechanic who grew up on a farm in South Australia; Training Officer Julian Barry grew up in the suburbs of Brisbane; and so on. All are agreed that if it were not for working together, for constant close contact with Anangu, they would not stay as long as they do. Caralyn, in her down-to-earth style, sums it up best: 'This Park is about the size of a pea. Being a ranger here and constantly having to deal with tourists becomes very boring'. She has been here for nearly six years, the longest serving Piranpa staff member. She remarks:

> Staff morale and camaraderie are very good at the moment. Mainly because of Anangu commitment to make the Park work. In the past it was at times faction ridden to the extent that one faction wouldn't talk to the other. One side was pro-Anangu, the other anti joint management.

It has been quite obvious to me over the months I have been coming to Uluru-Kata Tjuta that the right people are here now. It is because of this selection of people that the whole system works. Not that there are no disagreements, frictions, frustrations, disappointments and occasional misdirections, but there is a palpable common purpose among both Piranpa and Anangu that overrides the pettiness that inevitably assails small, isolated communities.

Just how the Anangu connection affects a person, even changes his or her thinking, is different for different people. For Caralyn it is Anangu's detailed knowledge of natural history. She says:

> Even now, after all the years I've been here, I am astounded, even shocked by the amount of information the people have and their willingness to pass it on. Just the other week a scientist came to Aboriginal land. He wanted to kill a goanna Anangu had caught so that he could tell what sex it was back in the lab in Adelaide. I said to him, 'Anangu don't want you to kill it, so you can't take it. Why don't you ask the Anangu what sex it is? They'll know'. 'Don't be stupid', he said. 'I need to dissect it and use a microscope.' So I said, 'There are ten Anangu over there. I'll come over with you and ask them in their language. If you get the same answer from each of the individuals, will you be happy?'. He said, 'Yeah'. So over we went and got the same answer every time — it was a young male. These sorts of things, they have to change you. We might think we're pretty smart because we've done four years at uni, and we've got all these papers and think we're pretty hot-shot scientists. And then you come out here and you realise quite quickly that you are a child when it comes to certain information.

David Carter, the Park's resident scientist, may not agree that Anangu know everything about the plants and animals and Piranpa very little, but he too is impressed with their knowledge. Perhaps more detached than Caralyn, he tries to work out how Anangu can tell so much about an animal from just a glance or, as with Edith and others, its tracks. Anangu themselves do not reflect on and cannot tell you *how* they know these things. They just know and that is the end of the discussion. David has thought about this a lot and has developed some tentative ideas about it. He tells me:

> It has always struck me how much information Anangu can get from even tiny traces of tracks. They'll tell you whether the animal's a male or female, whether it's eaten something, which way — even where — it was going and, if a female, whether it's pregnant or not. I'll tell you a story that helps me to understand a bit more about it. I once read the transcript of the Royal Commission into the Lindy Chamberlain case, where a dingo here took her baby. A lawyer cross-examined Barbara Tjikatu, and he asked her how she knew that the footprints found near the clothing belonged to the same dingo that was near the tent. He kept on quizzing her on that. She said that she recognised the animal from

Assistant Park Manager David Carter (right) and Rupert Goodwin discuss the use of pitfall traps in the Park's fauna survey.

Tony Tjamiwa (in yellow shirt in the centre) explains the purpose and responsibilities of the Mala walk to new seasonal rangers. Jon Willis (in sunglasses) translates.

the footprints and that it was carrying a baby in its mouth. The lawyer was trying to find out how she knew that. His understanding was so unsophisticated and so far removed from Aboriginal knowledge that Barbara was getting quite annoyed with him. The best comparison I can come up with is that if there were just white people in court and a witness was asked, 'Did you recognise your child in a schoolroom?', no one would question the parent's ability to recognise their own child. Parents just know. In this whole concept of recognition there are no simple scientific measurements you can take. You just know. When looking at a track or an animal there are probably thousands of measurements that Anangu subconsciously process in the blink of an eye. The posture of an animal, perhaps its colour, tiny differences in the size and shape of the head and things like that. They recognise all these things and it works the same way as a parent recognising their own child in a room full of other children. No court would ever question or cross-examine a person as to how they recognise their own child.

Bob Seaborne, who is fifty, is the park manager, the most senior Piranpa staff member. He is a soft-spoken, calm, even relaxed man, who likes to run the Park by consensus, as far as that is possible within a public service hierarchy. He explains:

It is not the typical management position because you are working with two distinct cultures that have very different sets of values, and consequently the people that are part of them have different aspirations. The challenge for me is to bring Piranpa and Anangu staff together and make it work.

I ask whether it is working. Bob answers:

It's a great concept, and I think along with Kakadu we're probably the best examples of joint management in Australia.

'In the world, some say', I interject. Bob muses:

I wouldn't be surprised because there are people coming from overseas to find out how it works here on the ground. We've had people from Canada, India, China, New Caledonia and other places.

Bob's admiration for Anangu takes a somewhat different direction from that of the other Piranpa I spoke to. He says he was relaxed with Anangu and identified with them from the beginning. He continues:

It comes from a feelings level, I suppose. I've got great empathy for Anangu. I'm pretty sure that my upbringing had something to do with it. My mother was a very nice and gentle person who was close to nature, and she influenced me. And once I'd learned of the struggle of the Aboriginal people and their lot in life since European contact, I empathised with that very quickly. This might have something to do with being Welsh. The dynamics are not all that different. The business of language, of people being exploited, of almost being wiped out in some cases, of feelings of nationalism — they all exist in Wales.

Among Anangu there is little or no divergence of opinion on the merits of working together. They all say it is good, they are happy with it. Things are straight now, they say, with the *Tjukurpa* up front and in control and Anangu with a majority on the Board of Management. Tjamiwa explains it as follows:

The paintings in a number of caves around Uluru are a legacy of earlier days.

Many of the cave paintings around Uluru are of subjects that had relevance only to the people who painted them and their meaning has been lost. Others are sacred and cannot be discussed with the uninitiated.

Everything at Uluru-Kata Tjuta is properly tight now. All the rangers wear the National Park badge with Uluru on it on their sleeves. The National Park is running properly. Things are not changing in ways Anangu don't like. Since joint management started we've put up all the signs, put them right around the Park. Now the signs stay there, all day and all night, so that visitors always know what they are allowed to do and what is not safe for them to do. Aboriginal land that is a national park run only by Piranpa is like a table with one leg. Push it and it falls over. It has to have the other legs that Anangu Law and ownership provide, that Anangu involvement in running the Park provides, that an Anangu majority on the board of management provides.

Every day at Uluru, park rangers guide visitors along the Mala walk. The mala, the rufous hare-wallaby, is an important animal in the *Tjukurpa*. On the walk from the base of the climb to Kantju Gorge the ranger explains aspects of the Mala ceremony and the *Tjukurpa* in general. Every year a small number of seasonal rangers are recruited to work at Uluru for three to six months.

On my last day at Uluru, I join Tjamiwa, Jon Willis and Rupert Goodwin, one of the trainees, as they 'initiate' three seasonal rangers into the intricacies of the

Mala ceremony, its associated landmarks and the *Tjukurpa*, and also instil in them the principles of working together. Tjamiwa, as the senior man, leads the group and Jon translates, but he and Rupert, both being initiated men, also contribute to the teaching of the seasonals.

At the very beginning of the walk, after inquisitive tourists have been gently shooed away, one after another we squeeze into a small, hidden cavern. 'You see that rock there', Tjamiwa says, 'that *is itjaritjari*, the marsupial mole, the real thing, her essence, that is it'. He emphasises time and again as we go along that what we are shown is real, the truth. He makes us say *itjaritjari* several times.

Just outside the cavern he points to a rock fig and explains that its fruit is an important food; *ili*, he calls it. We all agree that the Pitjantjatjara words have a wonderful sound. *Itjaritjari* is a favourite. Jon loves the word for the dead finish wattle, *wakalpuka. Tjintirtjintirpa* for the willie wagtail and *kiilykiilykari* for the budgerigar are among my favourites. Subtly, by his conviction that the rock *is itjaritjari*, another *is* the mala's pouch and by making us use the language, Tjamiwa stamps the Anangu's authority on all that he tells us. He authenticates it.

Slowly, unhurriedly Tjamiwa takes us from one place to the next. We stop at a huge rock with holes in it leaning against Uluru's sheer wall. Tjamiwa says:

> This is a *yuu*, a windbreak, made by *itjaritjari*. It was used by Anangu also as a shelter during rain and cold weather. We had no clothes so we kept warm here with a fire.

At a rock overhang covered with old paintings in ochre, white and black, Tjamiwa says:

> In the old days paintings were used for teaching, and were related to people's stories; they were particular to them. They are therefore not clear to us now. Others are sacred. Only people who know the Law know what they mean. You know about them.

He nods to Jon. Tjamiwa points to the top of Uluru to a deep depression that was scooped out by *itjaritjari*:

> Tourists climb down in there and then cannot get out, and then you have to rescue them. You must discourage *minga* from doing things like that. We feel very sad when people die or are injured at Uluru. We think of their families and are sad.

At a beautifully sculptured cavern in Uluru's rock Tjamiwa pauses and says:

Tjamiwa tells the new rangers sternly, 'If you do not do your job properly, I will get to hear about it . . .'

This is the visual indication of the truth of the *Tjukurpa*. This is where you can see the mala's pouch, here it is, right here. It is not made up.

Beside it is a large roomy overhang. Tjamiwa tells the new rangers:

People come here and say, 'What a lovely cave, it's so cool and airy'. But you must explain that it is more than just a cave, it is part of the *Tjukurpa*. This is where you must teach people about the Law and Anangu. You must tell the truth, really how it is. A lot has been written in books in the past, nearly all of it is nonsense. A lot of nonsense is still talked by some bus drivers and others.

He uses his fist as a microscope and imitates the drivers. 'You must tell the truth, make your notes and learn it.'

Entering Kantju Gorge we pause, quiet for while, under a tall bloodwood. Dropping his voice and talking more slowly, Tjamiwa says:

This is a different place, there is a change here. There are more trees and shrubs. It is cool. There is serious men's business very close. Women and children when they came here were frightened and moved quietly; this is a religious place. They followed the same path as we do now to get water.

At the waterhole itself Tjamiwa tells the rangers:

When you get to the water, you people with patches on your sleeves, you must talk calmly and slowly and allow no running or shouting, for this is a sacred place. But if people are difficult, don't have an argument about it, don't growl or raise your voices.

You must also tell the Piranpa things, management, history and how we're working together. We're very happy with everything in the National Park now. We can rest easy in our houses knowing that the rangers work hard every day to look after Uluru and Kata Tjuta — to see that *minga* don't go to the wrong places. Our working together is very important in another way too, as you saw a little while ago when a young Japanese boy was lost. Anangu saw the tracks clearly and said, 'He went this way'. The police, they ran the other way. But Anangu together with the Piranpa rangers found the boy.

So think about what I told you this morning and look over your notes. Make sure you tell the true story so that all the visitors who come will not just have climbed the Rock but will have learnt something. If you do not, I will get to hear about it and will give you your marching orders.

He says the last part sternly, grabbing Stephanie's arm. Suddenly bursting into laughter, he says, 'I'm only joking, we all have to learn'.

Tony Tjamiwa, Jon Willis, Edith Imantura Richards, Kata Kura, Fiona Peek, Peter Kanari, Barbara Tjikatu, Bob Seaborne, Andy Panpanpalala Daeger, David Carter, Julian Barry, Caralyn Dean and so many others were the people I came to know during the eight months, spread over a fifteen-month period, that I spent at Uluru-Kata Tjuta. Piranpa will always come and go. In a few years' time many of the people I spoke to will have moved on. Others will take their places and Anangu, who are quick and accurate in sizing up an applicant's character, will recruit the right kind of people. Anangu themselves will never move far away from Uluru-Kata Tjuta, as it is their home, their very lives. May there always be as much dedication and as much affection between the two communities as there is now. It is this harmony and goodwill that make joint management work, that make Uluru-Kata Tjuta the shining example of an indigenous people owning and managing a national park.

People from all over Australia and the rest of the world come to study how it works. But is is not a principle, a concept, that can be transplanted and then guaranteed to work. Tolerance and dedication cannot be imposed, they must grow out of the communities. Also, a large Piranpa staff is only possible in parks that can be lavishly funded because of the huge numbers of visitors they attract. Uluru-Kata Tjuta is unique. It shows what can be done when people come together with mutual goodwill and creative thinking.

CHAPTER THIRTEEN
TO CLIMB
OR NOT TO CLIMB?

At the base of Uluru, where hundreds of people a day begin their assent of the Rock, there is an unassuming sign that states 'Welcome to Aboriginal Land', and goes on to say:

The traditional owners are distressed that many people lose their lives or are injured climbing Uluru. Due to cultural reasons Anangu do not climb Uluru. Although Anangu have given permission to climb Uluru, they prefer that visitors participate in one of the many alternative [activities].

Anangu, being realistic people, bowed to the inevitable and gave permission for visitors to climb Uluru when it was returned to them. Privately, however, they express grave concerns about it. For them it is against their Law, the *Tjukurpa*, to climb Uluru, except by initiated men on very special occasions.

Tjamiwa says this about climbing Uluru:

That's a really important sacred thing that you are climbing ... You shouldn't climb. It's not the real thing about this place. The real thing is listening to everything. Listening and understanding everything. When we say don't climb, maybe that makes you a bit sad. But anyway, that's what we have to say. We are obliged to say. And all the tourists will brighten up and say: 'Oh, I see. This is the right way. This is the thing that's right'. This is the proper way. No climbing.

Barbara Tjikatu adds:

If you worry about Aboriginal Law, then leave it, don't climb it. The chain is still there if you want to climb it. You should think about *Tjukurpa* and stay on the ground. Please don't climb.

Anangu find the compulsion to climb, to conquer, Uluru incomprehensible and

189

Previous pages: Climbing is still the prime objective of most visitors. Above: At the base of the climb to the summit of Uluru is a sign that states that Anangu, who own the National Park, would prefer visitors not to climb the monolith.

also think that it shows disrespect by strangers for another people's land. Equally baffling to them are the rushed short trips of just a day or two, accompanied by the taking of photographs, by most visitors. It shows disrespect of another kind, an unwillingness or an inability to understand the land, the people and the Law that prevails here. It makes Anangu look at the great hordes of visitors with a mixture of disdain, puzzlement and genuine sadness. They feel compelled, therefore, to try to explain their culture and all the intricacies of their attachment to the natural environment; not just for their own pride, but also because they feel concerned for the visitor's ignorance. They want people to understand Anangu and Uluru-Kata Tjuta. Understanding is everything. Once people understand, Anangu are convinced mutual respect will follow.

Tjamiwa expresses it with his usual eloquence and colourful imagery:

The tourists hear a little about this place and a little about that place [at Uluru] and they put it all together in one bucket and shake it up. Everything gets broken and mixed up, and when they pour it out in their own country to try to remember, they don't know what pieces go together. They should take it home in their hearts. Then they'd remember.

The tourists come here with their cameras taking pictures all over. What have they got? Another photo to take home, keep part of Uluru. They should get another lens — see straight inside. Wouldn't see big rock then. They would see that Kuniya living right inside there as from the beginning. They might throw their cameras away then.

We want tourists to learn about our place, to listen to us Anangu, not just look at the sunset and climb the Rock.

That is why visitors are encouraged to come on the Liru walk and why Tjamiwa instructs the rangers on the importance of the Mala walk with such authority. And that is why a new cultural centre is being built. So that people will come to Uluru-Kata Tjuta and *understand* and not only want to climb Uluru.

There is a second reason the rush to climb upsets Anangu. As custodians of the land and of Uluru, they are responsible for the safety of all visitors. Whenever anyone dies or is injured while climbing, Anangu are genuinely distressed. Being people for whom family is the most important thing in their lives, they are concerned about the families of those meeting with an accident. Anangu show great compassion, but also this responsibility is part of *Tjukurpa*, as immutable a part of the Law as looking after the country.

Climbing Uluru is all too often undertaken lightly, but it is neither easy nor straightforward. Accidents do happen. Since 1965 twenty-five people have died climbing Uluru. Each year between twenty and thirty people have to be rescued,

with injuries and conditions ranging from broken bones, being trapped in places they could climb into but not out of, vertigo, asthma attacks to heat stress and others.

On my first visit to Uluru, in 1991, friends there encouraged me to climb Uluru. But I suffer badly from vertigo and I thought I would climb it, perhaps, towards the end of my last visit. I was then unaware of the Anangu's feelings about climbing Uluru. After walking and climbing in different places that are permitted areas, I felt confident I would make it to the summit. But by then I had come to know and respect Tjamiwa, Barbara Tjikatu, Peter Kanari, Maureen Natjuna, Kata Kura and many others. I never climbed Uluru. I stayed on the ground.

Had I decided to climb the Rock my confidence would have been strengthened

Viewing Uluru's changing colours at sunset is the other great attraction of the Park.

Anangu wish that people stayed longer and looked deeper into Uluru's significance.

by the knowledge that the Piranpa Park staff are highly competent and skilled in rock rescues and that in nearby Yulara, the resort town, there is a helicopter used in rescues, an ambulance and the Royal Flying Doctor Service.

Perhaps most reassuring of all is Lee Webb, a young man of only twenty-five and a fully trained senior ambulance officer. His position in the Park service is that of maintenance officer for the small village where the Piranpa rangers live, the Mutitjulu community and all other installations. He is responsible for electricity and water supply, sewerage, looking after the houses and running the workshop where the Park's more than twenty vehicles are maintained. He also takes care of tractors, trucks, chainsaws, small generators and other items. He does not do all the work himself, but is responsible for getting contractors in for the really big and specialised jobs. He does it with good cheer.

Lee is tall and broad-shouldered, the very embodiment of the gentle giant.

Lee Webb, the Park's maintenance officer, is also a senior ambulance officer and is frequently involved in rescuing visitors. He points to a ravine at Mutitjulu where a particularly difficult rescue took place.

His eyes, set in a fresh face, are a clear blue and his blond hair curls over his collar. He has a somewhat shy manner. But in an emergency, such as a serious accident on Uluru, he quickly has everything organised and under control.

We talk about rescues sitting in Lee's office at the workshop. Wearing glasses while doing some paperwork, he seems even more mild-mannered, but some of the rescues he tells me about are not for the faint-hearted.

News of a person in distress on Uluru is usually relayed down the Rock and then to the Ranger Station. By the time the report reaches the rangers it may have undergone several changes. Lee says:

Stories sometimes get twisted as they come down the Rock. For example, someone could be having a heart attack at the top and by the time the story gets to the bottom it has become an ingrown toenail, so to speak. Other times the alarm is raised but there is no problem at all. One time I got a report of a Japanese fellow with heat stress. He was vomiting and apparently had other serious symptoms. I climbed up as fast as I could with all the gear on my back — puff, puff, wheeze, wheeze — but there was no one there who was visibly ill or injured. I asked some Japanese people who were there, but they couldn't understand me and I couldn't understand them. Obviously he felt better, headed down and went off.

Many rescues are of people who, once on top of Uluru, try to descend a different way and then become trapped and unable to go either up or down. Along the chain is really the only way. Lee recalls one such case, exacerbated by injury:

A young American exchange student tried to go down the wrong side of the Rock. He'd made his way down a washout above Mutitjulu waterhole. It is very steep and ends in a pool of water just under halfway down the Rock. He came down fast apparently and put his foot out to stop himself as he got near the pool, but he didn't see the rock just below the surface. He hit it hard and badly injured his ankle so he couldn't walk. The problem was that he was in a place where no one could see him, either from above or from Mutitjulu below. Slowly, sliding along on his backside, he 'bummed' his way to the other end of the pool from where he could just make out the visitors to Mutitjulu. He managed to attract the attention of a bus driver there who then reported it to us.

We got there quickly and through a loudhailer told him to stay where he was. That was about ten in the morning. He could not come down to Mutitjulu and we could not get up that way. So Peter Nagle and I went around to the base of the climb, up Uluru and then down to him. We carried a safety harness, rope, basic first-aid equipment, some water and stuff. Eventually we reached the patient. He was heat-stressed, very distraught from his injury and very embarrassed at causing all this trouble. I stayed with him and treated him for heatstroke while Peter went back up again to organise getting him out of there. I made sure he sipped water slowly; if he drank too quickly he would vomit it up again and be in even worse trouble. I put a sheet over him to stop him from getting more sunburnt than he was already, and dressed the worst of his cuts and abrasions. I sat with him for hours. It takes time to co-ordinate everything for such a difficult place. You can't just jump in and throw the stretcher down and hope for the best. Also the chopper is not there only for rescues so we had to wait for it to return from its tour. It was very hot, about 40 degrees Celsius.

It took us about thirty or forty-five minutes to get him up to the top again.

Several rangers pulled on ropes at the top and two of us pushed from underneath. It was very tiring. When we got to the top a couple of showers of rain came down and it was really windy. Up till then it had been a beautiful day. Some of us had to sit on the skids of the chopper to stop it from blowing over. We loaded the patient onto the helicopter. The ambulance people and one of our staff went with him. Then the chopper came back and picked the rest of us up. Some people walked down. By then it was nearly six in the evening.

It all sounds very matter of fact but these rescues, up and down very steep slopes, often when it is very windy as well as hot, are physically and mentally taxing and not without their dangers.

There is added stress for the rescuers when, despite their very best efforts, the person dies. Lee says:

That's the most stressful, to work on someone and then he or she dies on you. You go home sort of grumpy. You're always thinking, well, what else could I have done? But there is only so much you can do. If it doesn't work, it is very, very unfortunate. You always feel sorry because there is family involved.

He recounts how once he had to work on a fifty-five year old man who had collapsed on a very steep part of the climb. Other visitors had placed him with his legs on either side of one of the chain's supports so that he would not slide down. When Lee got there, together with a paramedic and a ranger, he worked on the man for two hours, trying everything — heart massage, drugs administered by the paramedic and resuscitation. All on a very steep incline and all to no avail.

Lee expresses the sentiments of all Park staff when he says:

My advice to people who come here is to heed the warning signs. We don't put them up for the fun of it — they're there to save lives.

Some of the rangers who have been involved in rescues would put that more forcefully. Lee emphasises that he is not the only one involved in rescues. He is a member of a team and all rangers are trained and competent in rescues.

For the last few years the climb up Uluru has been closed between 10.00 am and 4.00 pm on days when the forecast temperature is 38 degrees Celsius or more. Since then rock rescues have declined sharply and there have been no fatalities.

CHAPTER FOURTEEN
THE NATURE OF ULURU-KATA TJUTA

Ayear has passed since I began this narrative. It was spring then and rain enveloped the rocks. Frogs came to breed in transient pools, birds were stimulated to nest and plants to flower. During last winter more heavy rain fell and soon the sandhills and plains were covered in the green of plants awaiting the end of the cold to put out flowers. Yesterday there were a few showers, brief fresheners, that washed the slight haze from the sky. It is spring again and once more I am fortunate to experience a good season. Much is as it was last year but some things are very different.

At first light, on this day in late August, there is a chill in the air. A small trickle still runs off Uluru into Mutitjulu's dark and shaded waterhole. I tap on the dead bloodwood where the pink cockatoo nested last year. A few seconds later the bird appears at the entrance to a hollow limb and, head tilted to one side, regards me steadily. After her calm inspection she briefly looks all around, a soft breeze ruffling her flamelike crest, and descends inside the hollow tree again to brood her eggs. It is still too cold for the black-faced goanna to be out among the rocks and not enough water has accumulated to lure the frogs from deep underground.

Small ground plants splash the sandy ground surrounding Uluru with white, yellow, pink and the occasional deep purple. Small shrubs of cassia and the taller bunched umbrella bushes densely covered in flowers give bursts of intense yellow against the dark rock. A pipit runs across the sand and snatches up insects attracted to the sun's first warmth and feeds them to its fledgling hiding under a small bush. The strong voices of song birds resonate in the canyons. A male red-capped robin's colours glow as he perches motionless on a stump watching for the movements of insects.

I walk up the sandhill where I began this story. Fresh kangaroo tracks lead on ahead of me. I sit down in exactly the same place as I did last year. This morning it is a little cooler, fresher. Kata Tjuta is vibrant in the early sun to the west, Uluru a deep purple with the light coming from behind it. Last year my feelings were ones of elation and excitement at new impressions and of delight in the plants and animals just for what they were in themselves. They were ones of uncomplicated

Previous pages: A netted dragon uses a small termite mound as a vantage point in a field of saltspoon daisies. Right: A male red-capped robin at his nest. A butcherbird stole one of the young.

joy. These same feelings assail me now, they are no less spellbinding, but they have also deepened, enhanced by my greater understanding of how everything fits together. I look across the stretch of country in front of Kata Tjuta and notice the sturdy yet elegant desert oaks; I now know that they survive here because of their enormous root systems. I scan the stretch of spinifex, now aware of their association with termites and lizards. I can even tell the tracks of *mingkiri* and *tarkawara* in the sand around me. Fingers of delicate wildflowers run through the rough spinifex on country burnt a few years ago, and I watch a large red kangaroo bound slowly, head down, out of the mulga woodland beyond and begin to graze. His fur is bright in the early sun. I know he is there because he prefers to live in mulga shrublands and feeds on the plants that grow after fire, as Anangu told me. *Malu*, as they call him, is also important in the *Tjukurpa* associated with the domes and walls of rock that loom beyond. I am grateful that I have been able to experience the spontaneous intoxication of first discoveries and the quieter, deeper feelings of understanding, if only a little, of the natural forces that shaped this land and everything that lives in it.

Out on the sandplain a black-shouldered kite keeps watch from the skeletal branches of a dead desert oak over a wide expanse of spinifex. Directly below it honey grevillea bushes are just coming into flower. Pied, black, white-fronted, singing and spiny-cheeked honeyeaters dip into the gold and green brushes dripping with nectar. A spiny-cheeked, glancing my way with suspicion through pale-blue eyes, occasionally pounces on an insect and surreptitiously takes it to the interior of an umbrella bush. It is feeding a pair of fledglings sitting snugly side by side. A white-fronted honeyeater sits on two pinkish eggs, spotted with dark purple, in a nest lined with plant down. The pied honeyeaters pause only briefly at the flowers before going off into wild aerobatics. They seem to be too energetic and erratic ever to sit still long enough to incubate eggs.

I climb one of the tall dunes on the plain's eastern edge and there spread out before me are fields and fields of brilliant flowers, nodding and swaying on long stems in the faint breeze, right to the horizon. These fields are not made up of small patches of daisies here, purple peas there or a yellow shrub perhaps — but stretches of solid colour, so dense that no green of leaves or red of sand is visible in this broad view. The swales are filled with flowers that lap up towards the dunes' crests of bare red sand crowned with the occasional clump of tangled burr-daisy. The fields are overwhelmingly yellow, the yellow of saltspoon daisies (so named because of the shape of the petal-like bracts) and orange immortelles. On this canvas are occasional daubs of garish purple parakeelyas and bursts of pale mauve or white mini-daisies. Here and there the expanse of yellow is interrupted by stands of mulga. Beneath them grow low shrubs of desert fuchsias whose profuse flowers are of such delicate purple that they seem to float on the air. Among them are less subtle sheets of pink everlastings. Last year the flowers were tapped for their nectar by waves of painted lady butterflies. This year I have seen only two of them. Instead there are millions of tiny moths, out during the day, the colour of the sand.

I take all this in very slowly, savouring every new discovery, every nuance of combinations of colours. Only gradually do I become aware that the canes with pale-grey leaves standing beside me also carry bunches of large flowers, green-yellow veined with dark green: parrot peas. Some of these flowers, pierced by birds and robbed of their nectar, lie splashed on the red sand. Looking at the wide landscape rather than individual plants, I am reminded of my conversation with Graham Griffin about spinifex and fire. The fields of flowers are in places where a wildfire, started by lightning, swept through two and a half years ago, killing most of the mulga and consuming the spinifex. Fire had prepared an ideal seedbed for daisies, immortelles, parakeelyas, rulingias and others, and the winter rains, followed by lighter falls, had created this spectacle. Among the fire-blackened skeletons of mulga grow the densest clusters of flowers. New honey grevillea stems with a few flowers on them already sprout from among the charred remains of the old bushes. Looking closely among the flowers I pick out a few mulga seedlings and incipient spinifex clumps. In small pockets in the maze of dunes the vegetation

Orange immortelle flowers in bud. The mature flowers are upright when the orange undersides of the bracts are hidden.

escaped the fire. Large tussocks of mature spinifex and copses of mulga, both drab grey-green, survived there. Only a few flowers have sprouted, leaving large patches of bare sand. All the splendour is born of fire.

It is a splendour the likes of which has not been seen at Uluru-Kata Tjuta for twenty-five years or more according to long-time residents. Associating the flowers solely with the amount of rainfall, I looked up the records and found to my complete amazement, bordering on disbelief, that both last year and so far this year rainfall has been *below* average. What is more important than the amount of rainfall over a year, I discovered, is how much falls in a single rain period and at what time of the year it falls. In May and June of this year some 100 millimetres fell in a few weeks, saturating the ground. Because it was cool the moisture did not dissipate and allowed the plants to establish their root systems over some months. Follow-up rain in spring, more showers of 10–15 millimetres, then brought on the explosion of flowers among both the ephemerals, such as the daisies, and the established perennials. Summer rain does not have the same effect; it dries up quickly and flowers come out in profusion only in spring. In the last twenty-five years there have been rain periods that brought up to 800 millimetres in a few days. But they were in the wrong season for flowers.

Stepping as carefully as I can so as to crush as few as possible, I wade into the sea of flowers. While the soil and green leaves are revealed at these close quarters, I am truly dazzled by the intensity of colour. Soon my boots and trouser cuffs are coated in yellow pollen. It is warmer now and lizards dart about. A netted dragon, a similar colour to the sand, sits at the entrance to its burrow. A yellow and brick-red military dragon sprints after insects. Smooth shiny skinks, striped and spotted, red brown and blue, look at me briefly before they race off. A blue-tongued lizard, by contrast, notes my passing by no more than a few brief flicks of its brightly coloured tongue before bulldozing stolidly on through a patch of parakeelyas. A little button quail has a dust bath in a camel footprint, fluffing its feathers and flailing its wings. Crimson chats walk among the flowers and pick insects from their undersides. A pallid cuckoo calls loudly, insistently from the stems of a dead shrub. Woodswallows, twittering and scolding, chivvy a brown falcon. A much larger raptor on broad wings drifts towards me, so low it almost brushes the flowers. When about 30 metres away it lazily turns, revealing first its blue-grey upper side and then as it banks away its rufous underside dotted with white. It is so close I can clearly see the spotted harrier's long yellow legs folded under its even longer barred tail as it sails the fields of flowers.

Just beside Kata Tjuta's northernmost dome, not far from the Valley of the Winds, is one of my favourite places. By mid-afternoon the sun slants in low, emphasising the gravelly plain's special character. The only way I can describe it is 'parklike' in the best sense of the word, but with a balance and symmetry more often achieved

Saltspoon daisies.

Left: During the second spring flowers were even more prolific, in response to heavy winter rain. Above: Pink everlastings.

by natural forces than by humans. Kata Tjuta's many domes, already a warm colour, march in a receding procession to the south. The plain slopes gently, slightly towards the rock wall, its soil made up of reddish gravel of an even size. The pebbles can only be seen up close. In the broad view they are hidden by a carpet of short herbs and forbs. This rubble of soil is even less fertile than the sand and subjects its plants to even greater moisture and heat stress. They respond by having leaves of pale colours to reflect heat and by being covered in fine hairs to minimise moisture loss. The result is a lawn of silver and pearl-grey. Here too there are flowers but on a more modest, muted scale — yellow button daisies, purple nightshades, pink mulla mullas, blue storkbills.

Small trees are few, but classically placed and elegantly shaped — mulgas with multitudes of gently upswept branches dense with fine twigs and blue-green foliage, black gidgees with smoky-grey smooth bark and newly unfolding straplike phyllodes, which turn their spreading crowns a fresh green, the upright brushes of tall witchetty bushes, the sprawling deep-green dead finish dappled with yellow flowers, the gnarled and furrowed dark trunks of corkwoods topped with needle-like leaves and cascades of pale creamy-green flowers. Lower down are the ground-hugging impenetrable clumps of silvertails covered in flower heads where small purple blossoms lie wrapped in fine silvery hairs. Also placed with seemingly

Above: Parakeelya (purple) and saltspoon daisies grow profusely in the swales between dunes. Above right: Waxy wattles in flower at Uluru.

exquisite taste are the sculptures, the polished wood skeletons of bloodwoods and wattles, silky to the touch, and the termite mounds, which echo Kata Tjuta's domes in colour and shape. A large greenish dragonfly with golden eyes zips among the trees, catching small flying insects.

This natural park in times of drought, especially during the heat of summer, will seem totally devoid of life; it is one of the harshest and most unforgiving of habitats. But now, softened by rain and the coolness of spring, it harbours an uncommonly rich array of birds. Scores of male crimson chats chase each other in defence of their territories. Several hundred budgerigars have found a small expanse of grass and are feeding on seeds. Accidentally I flush them. They fly up and land in a whirring flurry of wings on one of the small dead trees, instantly turning it green as if it had come alive again. A pair of red-backed kingfishers, their feathers fluffed, sunbathe in a corkwood. Mulga parrots, a flash of green, yellow and orange, streak by. A ring-necked parrot, its exotic green plumage so

at variance with the muted foliage, lands in a small bloodwood directly above me and begins to feed on the gumnuts. At every step I seem to disturb a little button quail, rising fast in a flurry of noisy wingbeats. So well are they camouflaged that only rarely do I see one before it takes off. From the exposed branch of a black gidgee flash brilliant iridescent bronze-green and purple reflections as if from a mirror. They resolve themselves into the wing feathers of a bronzewing pigeon, a magnificent male sitting motionless on his nest of twigs. He never flinches and never takes his huge dark-brown eyes off me as I pass close by.

It is not just the variety of birds that is so striking, but also their numbers. This impression is created by what I can hear as well as by what I can see. Brown songlarks fly steeply up into the air then descend, half gliding, half fluttering, as they sing their grinding, tinkling metallic songs. With legs dangling as they parachute down, their oversize feet look like boots. Rufous songlarks have clearer voices and prefer to sing from a perch. The shyer birds, the chiming wedgebill,

Dawn over Kata Tjuta. In the foreground are the shrubs and other plants of a vegetated sandhill. Beyond is a spinifex plain studded with desert oaks that merges into mulga woodland.

Female bronzewing pigeon with
young on the nest.

crested bellbird and western bowerbird, call in ringing and hissing ventriloquial voices from deep within prickly bushes. An extraordinary chorus, to which the honeyeaters add their sweeter songs.

Late afternoon and I enter Olga Gorge. Last summer only one or two tiny pools of water remained and these were drying rapidly. Yesterday's rain filled all the waterholes, large and small, the full length of the watercourse that babbling and whispering over the rocks still runs strongly. A small waterfall spouts from between boulders. The vegetation along this stream is deep green with many plants in flower. Halfway up the gorge some soil has accumulated on the scree between the northern wall and the creek. Trees and tall shrubs line the banks. Several river red gums have taken hold and wrapped their root boles, clothed in folds of smooth silvery bark, around dark, rough boulders of conglomerate. Mount Olga wattles, named after the gorge, form dense thickets where pungent hopbushes and deep-green striped mint bushes carrying white flowers hide. Along a narrow elongated pool free of trees and shrubs crowd lush clusters of early nancy covered in spikes of pink flowers. Clinging to a huge boulder is a flowering purple mint bush whose fleshy leaves have a spicy rather than minty scent. Among the scree's boulders stand more lush green shrubs and bushes. Between these are tall yellowtops luxuriant with heads of large flowers and succulent leaves. A butterfly, red, brown and yellow in colour, siphons off their nectar. A spearbush, a scrambler with long and twisted stems, which are made into straight, true spears by Anangu, lies in

Left: Immediately after rain a stream, complete with a small waterfall, tinkles through Olga Gorge. Below left: Flowers of the small bush Isotropis centralis. Below: Flowers and fruit of Sturt's nightshade. Unlike nightshades such as bush currents and bush tomatoes, which are important Anangu foods, this species is poisonous.

a tangle over a rock face, draping it with clusters of cream-coloured flowers striped in deep purple.

With the sun on my face I walk back out of the narrow gorge. The floor and the sheer high walls are ablaze in the setting sun — I seem to be walking through an incandescent valley. Slowly I climb up to the base of the northernmost dome. Hopping from rock to rock I manage not to walk on too many of the less lush, more arid-zone-adapted plants that flower here. At the dome's foot there is a tumble of rock where a single desert fuchsia flowers, purple surrounded by tall yellowtops. I am high above the gorge, the huge blocks of stone at the floor look no more than pebbles. To the west I can see the purple outlines of the Petermann Ranges, homeland of the Anangu. To the north, beyond a flat expanse of spinifex and mulga and uncounted sandhills, lie the salt flats of Lake Amadeus, which the first Piranpa visitors crossed with such difficulty. The sun sets. The clear sky is awash with fiery colours. A pair of kestrels, with wild cries that echo down the canyon, flies along the rock face then lands in a small high cave. A pied butcherbird sings and a flock of budgerigars speeds in for a quick drink. Frogs gather around the larger pools and begin to call. As always I am overwhelmed by the immensity of the rocks.

It has been one of the most stirring days I have spent in the wild, arousing a swirl of conflicting feelings and a kind of rapture. I also have a great sense of privilege, for this day would not have been possible without the insights and perspective of all the months I spent here wandering around and talking to people. The deepest impression I have is of a world of colour — vivid, unrestrained colours on the grand scale of flowers, birds, rocks, sand and sky. But also subtle ones — rocks in fading light, of silver-greys, muted greens, shifting shadows and all the finer details.

I feel a tinge of sadness too for I do miss the medium-sized mammals — the numbat, the mala, the burrowing bettong, the bilby, the quoll, the crescent nail-tail wallaby and so many others. They may never have been here in great numbers but I like to think that during a run of good seasons, as now, I would have seen their elegant shapes, exquisitely patterned in stripes and spots, skipping among the spinifex, sitting at burrow entrances or coming out of caves at this hour of sunset.

What a day like today means to me is difficult to express in words. Words can describe what I see, hear, smell and touch. To a degree I can speculate how all the parts fit together. But that is not the whole of it. Perhaps it has to do with feelings for which there are no words. It is during these inexpressible, even mysterious moments that I have no doubt, that I feel the very spirit of Australia I came looking for.

Anangu when they experience these things in the bedrock of their own country

simply laugh out loud with great joy at the symmetry of their physical and spiritual worlds.

It has become dark and I shiver in the cold. Down at the entrance to the gorge a spotted nightjar, most likely the same one I saw last summer and perched on the same rock, gives its eerie, gobbling call, 'wakka, wakka, chokka, chokka, chokka ...'

Kata Tjuta, with Uluru in the background, glows in the sunset.

HAWTHORN SECONDARY COLLEGE
BURGESS STREET
EAST HAWTHORN, 3123

FURTHER READING

Duguid, C. *No Dying Race*, Rigby, Adelaide, 1963.

Duguid, C. *Doctor and the Aborigines*, Rigby, Adelaide, 1972.

Finlayson, H. H. *The Red Centre*, Angus & Robertson, Sydney, 1935.

Giles, W. E. P. *Australia Twice Traversed*, vols 1 & 2, Sampson Low, London, 1889.

Goddard, C. (comp.) *Pitjantjatjara/Yankunytjatjara to English Dictionary*, Institute for Aboriginal Development, Alice Springs, 1992.

Gosse, W. C. *Report and Diary of Mr W. C. Gosse's Central and Western Exploring Expedition, 1873,* South Australian Government Printer, Adelaide, 1874.

Idriess, I. *Lasseter's Last Ride*, Angus & Robertson, Sydney, 1931.

Institute for Aboriginal Development, *Punu, Yankunytjatjara Plant Use*, Angus & Robertson, Sydney, 1985.

Layton, R. *Uluru, An Aboriginal History of Ayers Rock*, Aboriginal Studies Press, Canberra, 1989.

Lester, Y. *Yami, The Autobiography of Yami Lester,* Institute of Aboriginal Development, Alice Springs, 1993.

Reid, J. R. W., Kerle, J. A. & Morton, S.R. *Uluru Fauna*, ANPWS, Canberra, 1993.

Saxon, E. C. (ed.) *Anticipating the Inevitable: A Patch-burn Strategy for Fire Management at Uluru National Park,* CSIRO, Melbourne, 1984.

Spencer, W. B. and Gillen, F. J. *Across Australia,* Macmillan, London, 1912.

Sweet, I. P. & Crick, I. H. *Uluru and Kata Tjuta, A Geological History,* Australian Geological Survey Organisation, Canberra, 1992.

INDEX